J. K. LASSER'S
MANAGING YOUR FAMILY FINANCES

J. K. LASSER'S
MANAGING YOUR
FAMILY FINANCES

By

J. K. LASSER LASSER (TAX) INSTITUTE, New York.

Garden City, New York

DOUBLEDAY & COMPANY, INC.

PREFACE

J. K. Lasser's MANAGING YOUR FAMILY FINANCES has been planned as a guide for those who want to develop and follow a conscious and intelligent approach to family finances.

Whether you are a young person on your own, newly married, or already established with a family and beset by financial difficulties, you will find methods, advice, and suggestions for dealing with all aspects of money management.

We outline a definite program for the skillful management of income, large or small. Perhaps for you the problem is not lack of money; it is misdirected spending, confusion regarding responsibility, the failure to provide for the future and for emergencies. Or perhaps you, like many others, are caught in the squeeze between inflation and an income that never seems adequate. Whatever your situation may be, the techniques here detailed can be applied to the particular circumstances of every family to promote financial stability and freedom from the constant anxiety that money trouble creates.

MANAGING YOUR FAMILY FINANCES thoroughly explores—

The control of expenses: how realistic plans may be devised to handle present and future commitments, including the spiraling costs of everyday living, of education, of health protection.

Increasing income: how to cut costs, and how people of all ages can embark on personal money-making enterprises; what aspects of the Federal income tax law can be used for your benefit; how and where to save, and how to initiate a sound investment program.

The financial hazards and legal commitments to be faced in buying or selling a home: how to finance purchase of a residence.

The desirability and danger of credit; how to enjoy a state of indebtedness while maintaining complete control.

Protection for the future, for self, dependents, survivors: what you can expect from Social Security and from private insurance; the importance of wills and the effects of joint ownership; the steps to be taken for a secure and healthy retirement.

Your application of the ideas presented in this book can enable you to resolve present financial difficulties and to avoid the many pitfalls faced each day in the use of money.

We gratefully acknowledge here the contribution and editorial supervision of Joyce Clarke, and the sections provided by Helen G. Meyers and Miriam Gelband.

BERNARD GREISMAN, *Director*
J. K. Lasser Tax Institute

CONTENTS

1 Programming Your Financial Future   1

2 An Agenda for Your Financial Program   21

3 Family Cooperation in Financial Planning   33

4 Raising Cash Through Cutting Costs   49

5 How to Increase the Family Income   65

6 Buy Now—and Be Ready to Pay Later   79

7 When You Rent, Buy, or Sell Your Residence   105

8 Financing Your Home   121

9 How and Where to Save Your Money   135

10 Your Life Insurance Program; Annuities   151

11 Investing in Securities   177

12 Investing in Mutual Funds—Letting the Experts
    Manage Your Investments   189

13 Your Health Insurance   201

14 What You Should Know About Social Security   209

Contents

15 Tax Planning Aids to Increase Your After-Tax
      Income   215

16 Decide the Future of Your Estate Now   243

17 Planning Ahead for Retirement   261

      Index   271

J. K. LASSER'S
MANAGING YOUR FAMILY FINANCES

Chapter 1

PROGRAMMING YOUR FINANCIAL FUTURE

FIRST STEPS   2
DEVELOPING A FINANCIAL PROGRAM   2
WHAT YOUR MONEY MUST DO—AND WHAT YOU WANT
    IT TO DO   3
DEFINING YOUR SPENDING GOALS   4
THE BUDGET   5
    Programming the Family Income   6
STEP I—THE PATTERN OF YOUR INCOME   6
STEP II—PROGRAMMING YOUR COMMITMENTS   8
SUMMARIZING STEPS I AND II. ADJUSTMENTS   9
    Here Are Ways to Make an Adjustment   9
STEP III—THE KEY TO YOUR BUDGET   11
    The Categories of Everyday Expenditure   11
    Methods of Keeping Track   12
    Weighing Up Your Spending   13
YOUR STEP III BUDGET FORM   14
UPCOMING VARIABLE BILLS   15
THE DEDUCTION METHOD OF KEEPING TRACK   16
STEP IV—PROGRAMMING YOUR SAVINGS   17
    Savings Bank Interest   18
HANDLING A DEBT PROBLEM   18
LOOKING TOWARD EXPANDED LIVING   19

Today, man can circle the planet in a few hours; he can land vehicles on the moon; he has invented computers to give instant answers to questions that people take hours or days to work out. This is a miracle world, but the average person in it continues to worry about a problem as old as civilization—*Money*.

Money should help to answer problems, not to be a worry in itself. Yet quarrels about money continue to be a major cause of divorce, of dissension between parent and child, and of breakdown in family relationships. Managing money wisely may not save every marriage, but it can go a long way toward it.

FIRST STEPS

This is a work book from which you will draw the information and suggestions most suited to your situation. You will add to it your own facts and figures, according to your circumstances. We suggest you first read the whole book through, noting the points of particular interest and the ideas it gives you. Then talk over problems and discuss *goals* frankly with the family. The program you will develop is your own—not one for the Joneses with whom you may, or may not want to keep up. Your goals will change as one after the other is fulfilled. The steps you take now make each one possible.

When husband and wife sit down together to discuss their financial program, their first step should be to make a pact—to keep emotions in low key. A cool businesslike attitude is absolutely necessary. Let wrangling over past mistakes go. Make a decision to work together to overcome difficulties and to build a more satisfying life through the wiser use of money.

Children should not be left out of financial planning. Their future is involved too. Seek their interest and cooperation early; you will find it a sound investment. The children's part in the family program is discussed more fully in Chapter 3.

DEVELOPING A FINANCIAL PROGRAM

If, like many other Americans, you are earning more money today than ever before, you probably recognize that you are as much in need of a disciplined financial program as the person with a very limited income. Unless he directs spending wisely, the $60,000-a-year executive can land in relatively as tight a money squeeze as the large family who have to get by on $6000. Many men and women who are trained to do professional or technical jobs with the utmost efficiency fail dismally as managers of the money they earn. In to-day's society with its opportunities for travel and entertainment, its tempting advertising and merchandise, money can disappear all too easily without fulfilling any of a family's true objectives.

In Chapter 2, we outline a method for assessing net worth, achiev-ing goals, and establishing financial security. In this chapter, we are concerned with basic planning which can be adapted by young career people, those newly married, and people of all ages who con-stantly run into financial problems.

When young marrieds set up a plan, they will, of course, change their pattern if a working wife stops working; when they start a family; and if they move from an apartment to a house. They will budget afresh with each change, enlarging their system, and redirect-ing saving toward new goals. Through frank discussion and planning together, they can build an invaluable bulwark against future in-harmony.

WHAT YOUR MONEY MUST DO—
AND WHAT YOU WANT IT TO DO

Some of the money the employed person receives is spent before he gets it. A pay check may be accompanied by a slip showing de-ductions for Federal, state, perhaps city taxes; Social Security; un-employment; hospitalization; pension fund; and the like. These deductions cover both *liabilities,* such as taxes which you must pay in any event, and *assets,* such as Social Security benefits and com-pany pension, which you will eventually receive. The protection you receive from a group health insurance plan also counts among your assets.

Your money, then, is at work before you receive your pay; this part of your financial planning is already handled for you. You are responsible for the rest. Therefore, *take-home pay* is what we shall discuss here. (The self-employed person will, of course, make the necessary adjustments for his particular case.)

From your check, you now have to cover certain inescapable expenses which we describe as "fixed." Some, such as rent or mortgage, and insurance premiums are set amounts you can forecast easily; some, your additional taxes, for instance, are still uncertain in amount. To get some idea of what you owe, you have to estimate or use last year's figures.

In addition, you have to pay out for what we describe as "everyday" expenses, though some may occur only every few months. Among these are food, clothing, repairs, medical bills, and all the little things, such as haircuts and newspapers. Since you have full control over a large part of these expenses they can be described as "flexible."

After your pay check has covered the fixed and the everyday expenses, it has to work for you in achieving certain objectives, mainly to bring improved conditions or opportunities into the family life. This is the *plus* side of money management and the reason for much of it.

DEFINING YOUR SPENDING GOALS

You would do well to start your program by setting down your spending goals on paper. This month you will buy certain clothing; this year the new car; within five years money will accomplish certain objectives in education, vacation, debt liquidation, or what not. In Chapter 2 and elsewhere we refer again to the setting of goals. They are of paramount importance because, without them, people have a tendency to fritter money away—and then to wonder why they lack what others have. So—define your goals even before you get down to figuring the dollars and dimes. *The vision of what you want the money to do will help you over any difficult patches that may lie ahead.*

If you are heavily in debt, your first goal will certainly be to get out of it. (See Page 18.) A repayment plan, worked out with outside help if necessary, must precede everything else. All members of the family should account for expenditure until the situation is completely overcome.

THE BUDGET

Smart money management starts with a budget or, if you prefer another name, a spending plan. In the home, as well as in business, the budget is a means of controlling expenses and of directing spending wisely. Many people recoil at the very idea. They think a budget is a strait jacket—something that will tie them down and take all the joy out of living. On the contrary, the budget is a means of releasing money to better use, and of putting the budgeter in control of his fortunes. It is a way out of continual financial harassment, and a tool with which to handle rising costs, taxation, sudden sickness, and other emergencies. It means money at work for you, achieving your objectives, present and future.

At this early stage, the new budgeter should settle questions such as who is to keep the records, who is to handle what expenses, and how personal allowances shall be scaled. (See Chapter 3 for detailed discussion.)

Many families, having discovered the value of methodical financial planning, use it to steer a course throughout life. A civil engineer who began budgeting in the early days of his marriage is still using this method twenty years later. He and his wife have raised two children, planned college education, and bought and sold three houses—each time with profit. In the early days when money was needed to finance a home and car, they borrowed from relatives. Each transaction was businesslike, and at current loan rates. Following his financial program, the young man repaid interest and principal promptly on the due dates. Though income is at a modest level, the family enjoys the newest appliances, has a good car, and can take vacations across the ocean or across the country. "Budgeting takes time," the civil engineer conceded. "But the results are well worth while. We'll never give it up."

Managing money wisely is chiefly a habit, and one you can build into your life. Establishing a good habit isn't necessarily easy; you may have to get rid of poor habits of money management at the same time and so will need to discipline yourself. But the result will repay you handsomely, in cash and in satisfaction.

The budget plan given below covers two classes of people: Those who earn regular salaries or wages (with or without other sources of income), and those whose income is uncertain and irregular.

While the experienced budgeter usually plans ahead for a calendar year (the period we shall discuss below), the new budgeter may prefer to set up a shorter program. If you wish, start with a three-month trial period. You can enlarge it later.

You may find it helpful to do rough planning on large sheets of paper that will not restrict you. Use unglazed shelf paper if you like, or tape sheets together. Later, when you have decided on your personal setup, you can transfer to a suitable columnar book or pages, or rule up a large notebook.

It is a good idea to pencil in projected figures so you can confirm or change them later. If you use ink or ball point for a whole period you are likely to end up with confusion or else feel you have some inflexible chart that is going to tie you down.

STEP I—THE PATTERN OF YOUR INCOME

If you are steadily employed, you can probably forecast your income for the year. You also know what additional sources you usually have, such as *savings bank interest, dividends, regular gifts,* and *bonuses,* and income from *rentals, profitable hobbies, part-time work,* etc.

Draw up your Step I form into fifteen columns as indicated below:

Source of Cash Funds	Jan.	Feb.	Mar.	(etc. ...... Dec.)	Total	Notes
Take-home pay: Husband Wife Interest Dividends Other...						
Total						

Project your figures across the year (or shorter period). If you expect a raise, change the entries *after* you have it. A smart policy in money management is never to spend such money in advance or even to plan on covering essentials with it. Many people get in trouble with credit payments (see Chapter 6), because the money they counted on failed to come through. You play safe when you work on a minimum basis.

You cannot say in advance exactly what your savings bank interest will be. You might pencil in last year's figures as a guide, although with good savings, you may do better this time. However, an emergency withdrawal of savings would mean a drop in interest. Again, it would be wiser not to count on expectations. Other figures may be estimated or based on last year's income, as for instance, profit from a hobby or a rental.

If your employment is irregular, or depends on business profits or commissions, you will probably have to use last year's figures or a reasonable estimate in your projection. The person who receives income in large amounts at irregular intervals is often prone to spending sprees, then has to borrow to meet the inevitable bills. If you are in this category, start now with discipline; be conservative in your plans, basing them on minimum expectations. You may find it helpful to total expected income for the year, divide it by 12, and to allow yourself only one-twelfth for each month. You are then on the same basis as the regular wage and salary earner, but because your total is uncertain till received, you should exercise restraint in spending until you have directed savings into a solid bank account.

Finish up your Step I form now with a line of monthly totals.

STEP II–PROGRAMMING YOUR COMMITMENTS

Draw up a 15-column form similar to that used in Step I.

Fixed Expenses	(January through December)	Total	Notes
Total			

On the left under the main heading of Fixed Expenses, note down this type of obligation:

Additional Federal, state, and city taxes
Mortgage or rent
Repayments of all types of loans and installment purchases
Insurance premiums
Telephone, heat, light, water, etc.
Pledged contributions
Society or union dues
Savings (a *fixed obligation* to yourself and your family) for future
　　goals and emergencies.

You know when these fixed expenses have to be paid. Some are certain in amount and you can project them across twelve months. Some are variable, such as the telephone bill. You can use previous bills or estimate this type of upcoming payment.

Note that Step II does not include department store and similar billing, only installment payments, if any. This step is designed to cover your *fixed expenses* of which regular savings should be a part.

SUMMARIZING STEPS I AND II. ADJUSTMENTS

You now have a total line for your income (Step I), and one for your fixed expenses (Step II). In summarizing, you can use a separate paper if you prefer, but if you have room, save copying by running your Step II totals under those of Step I. Deduct one from the other. *The resulting figure shows what you now have available for your everyday expenses.*

	Jan.	Feb.	Mar.	(etc. . . . . Dec.)	Total
Step I (Total income) Step II (Fixed expenses)					
Available for Step III (Everyday expenses)					

No doubt your Step III line is uneven because you have more heavy expenses one month than another. Perhaps the expenses of some months will be so heavy you are practically in the red for your everyday expenditure. You also see some months show few, if any, fixed expenses.

HERE ARE WAYS TO MAKE AN ADJUSTMENT

Some people make a total of the heavy obligations that only come up about once or twice a year, divide the total by twelve and bank that sum monthly. By so *averaging,* they prepare for vacations, certain taxes, insurance premiums, and educational expenses.

Example:

Total Cost

Taxes
Insurance
Heating
Vacation
Education

_____

Total   ÷ 12 = (amount to be set aside monthly)

However, the experienced budgeter will want to consider each item separately in order to project the figures across the budget form. The civil engineer referred to on page 5, gives this explanation:

"We have averaging in use on several items: heating is one of them. The total cost each year is around $216 and this is budgeted for at $18 per month, although it may, in fact, vary from $4 or less for a summer month to about $28 for a winter month. The same idea is applied to water and electricity costs which, again, vary seasonally.

"Our local taxes are paid three times a year, but we average them to a monthly figure. Insurance premiums due annually are divided by 12."

People with few such fixed expenses—and a young couple both working may not have many—may prefer to even up their adjustment form simply by raising the *savings* on Step II so that Step III comes out to a more or less even monthly figure. (Goals for savings are discussed on page 17.)

Exactly how the juggling and adjusting is done is your personal affair. *The aim is to arrive at a consistent monthly figure for everyday expenses in line with the budget you draw up in Step III.* As you can see, it will be necessary for you to work backwards and forwards on these steps before you can develop the best plan through which you can reach the objectives you have named. (Page 4.)

Throughout your early budget experiments, remind yourself that you will need at least a full year before you can come up with reasonably settled forms and figures. Too many people seeing plans in a book or pamphlet assume they can solve their financial difficulties overnight by filling in the suggested forms. Usually, a personal situation is far too complex for such an easy solution. *The budget works for you when you have worked at it.*

STEP III—THE KEY TO YOUR BUDGET

A period of keeping track of your present rate of expenditure is necessary before you can settle on the most profitable plan for everyday expenses. Only by seeing how much you are presently spending in certain categories can you set up an improved pattern.

A newly married couple will have to set up many aspects of their budget on a tentative and experimental basis, but keeping track of all spending will provide invaluable records. Others not in the habit of noting where the money goes may not enjoy scribbling in a purse or pocket notebook or filing supermarket tapes, but it is absolutely necessary to good money management to find out exactly what is being spent.

Some budgeters, once in the habit of such record keeping, prefer to continue it. Most people find it too constricting and, once they have established a suitable set-aside for a particular category, such as food, will not continue to run the last dime to earth. Plan on at least two months of strict record keeping for all members of the family, and note that if you keep these records in summer your pattern may be different in winter. A budget readjustment may be called for seasonally *within the set figure you arrive at for Step III.*

THE CATEGORIES OF EVERYDAY EXPENDITURE

Base daily accounting on the headings you intend to use when making up your budget. Following is a list of suggested main categories and the types of expenditure which would be entered under each:

Food. In this category, include food bought for meals at home, school lunches, and all meals out. Alcoholic and soft drinks, and candy should be included, also any taxes and tips.

Household Maintenance. Repairs, supplies, paid help or services.

Furnishings and Equipment. This will cover furniture, floor coverings, accessories such as tableware, curtains, and slipcovers, television, radios, etc., cleaning of any items.

Clothing. Dry cleaning, laundry, and charges by tailor and dressmaker would come under this heading as well as garments and the material for making them.

Transportation. Automobile upkeep and operation; commutation expenses, air, train, bus, and taxi fares.

Health Care. Fees for professional services, including hospital; drugs, supplies, and eyeglasses.

Education. Textbooks, supplies, tuition.

Recreation. Entertainment, reading, hobby material, games.

Personal Care. Beauty parlor and barber's charges, toilet items, etc.

Family Allowances. Each person's spend-as-you-please money.

In general, avoid overanalysis. It can prove tiresome and discouraging unless it serves a particular aim. So, separate details only when necessary. The cost of meals out can go in with other food unless you are reporting them as business expenses or you need to track down where the food dollars are going.

Of course, you will need details and receipts of items you may be deducting for income tax, or need to record for inventory or insurance purposes. Too, you may wish to separate cash from check transactions.

METHODS OF KEEPING TRACK

We have suggested spending be noted in a small book or pad carried in purse or pocket. Receipts and store tapes should be placed in a prearranged place in the home, such as a box, a drawer, or on a spindle. Enter these outgoing payments on a form drawn up in accordance with your family situation and need of specific details.

Here is a suggestion:

Date	Food		Clothing		Housing			Transpor-tation		Health		Personal		Etc. ...
	At home	Out	Pur-chases	Cleaning, repairs	Phone	Sup-plies	Furnish-ings	Car	Other	Doctor drugs	Dentist	Allow-ance, hair care	Drinks, tobacco, candy	-- --
Total														

Refer to the list on pages 11 and 12, but work out the full form according to your own type of expenses, the number of people in the family, and the need to subdivide (which should not be carried to excess). Note, for example, the points on which the suggestion above differs from the list. Also, these headings show the telephone under everyday expenses. Earlier, we showed it on Step II as a fixed expense. You can place it as it best suits you, or split the set rental charge from excess charges, especially if you wish to place a limit on family calls.

Since this record keeping is to account for everyday expenses, we omit the Step II (page 8) items, such as rent, insurance, utilities. Nevertheless, you may well want to record them separately so that at the end of a month you can accurately show:

Total family income for January   _____

Total expenditure for the month   _____

(Money in hand? Good! It can satisfy a goal.)   _____

WEIGHING UP YOUR SPENDING

On page 9 you arrived at Income Less Fixed Expenses Equals Amount Available for Everyday Expenses. By averaging, you found you could even up the Step III line. Now you have been keeping a record of your actual spending. Was it in line with your Step III figure?

If you are fortunately not overspending, you now only have to keep on the same track, perhaps making a few adjustments within certain categories. If, even better, you can draw a line under Income

Less Expenses for the month above and show a saving, you have that much more to put in the bank or to satisfy an item on your list of goals (page 4).

But too many people will find themselves overspent. That means they have used money they should have put into savings or have gone to the bank and taken out money already saved or, worse still, they have borrowed to cover expenses. If you are overspent, trim spending for next month. See Chapter 4 on cutting costs. Do not take on more fixed expenses (Step II), such as installment payments. Let the spending goals wait until you have a surplus.

YOUR STEP III BUDGET FORM

After you have been keeping records for a period you can project figures on an annual basis (though you may not find it practical to plan closely for more than two or three months in advance). Below, a form is suggested:

	Jan.	Feb.	Mar.	Apr.	(etc. ...... Dec.)	Dec.	Notes
Food Housing Clothes etc. etc.							
Total							

Through this form you control your budget because, if you keep spending in line with projections here, you are fulfilling your other objectives, covering the Step II fixed expenses, and the savings program (page 17). If you compare a record of what you actually spend with what you should spend to maintain an adequate reserve, you will have a useful guide to help you in cutting back.

At times, of course, your control over Step III expenditure may break down. Unexpected medical bills may roll in, just at the same time you have to pay the plumber, painter, and roofer. *The only sound answer to such emergencies is the reserve in your savings account.*

Until you have that reserve in a substantial condition, set a minimum operational figure for your everyday expenditure, and make the necessary adjustments *within that figure.*

For example, you see a lot of money going under recreation and clothing while members of the family complain new furniture is needed or another car is positively necessary. Here, a family conference may be in order to establish what is essential and what is a luxury. If plans for large purchases are ahead, the family may have to agree to a new ceiling on recreation, clothing, entertaining, or what not. You establish a new budget figure in these categories, and step up savings to meet outright or installment buying.

As we have noted, it may not be practical to budget daily expenditure for more than two months in advance, and sometimes a shorter period is desirable. But when your Step III form is fully developed, you should have established a reasonable sum which, each month, will cover your family's daily needs and take care of department store and professional billing.

The point is that, unless you are heavily in debt and need to take the steps outlined on page 18, you need never develop any sense that a budget is a limiting factor in your life. You are simply using this means to foster a realistic attitude toward money among members of the family and to channel that money toward the needs and aspirations of each one.

UPCOMING VARIABLE BILLS

A hurdle which frequently throws the hopeful new budgeter is the charge account (see Chapter 6). Today people buy—but they do not spend money until the bills arrive, by which time robbing the savings account is the only answer.

You should keep a record of credit spending so that you will be ready for the billing. Note the date each department store or other company usually bills you; if one company bills on the sixth of the month and another on the sixteenth and you are paid twice a month you can set aside the money in your checking account from two pay checks.

If you are already working your budget you will be less haphazard in your buying than formerly, and not buying in excess of planned items, but because people do tend to buy on sight (and sometimes it may be wise to do so), a record of what is being charged (from gasoline to garden tools) will help in adjusting next month's plan to meet the expected bills.

THE DEDUCTION METHOD OF KEEPING TRACK

Once people kept their budgeted money in cash in envelopes or jars. These days money allocated to a certain category may be in cash, a checking account, and a savings account. How can you keep track of your spending?

An idea you may find useful is to set up index cards or pages of a notebook which show the budgeted amount in each category and then to deduct from it as purchases are made. For example, the mother of a family knows that the agreed sum for clothing buying this month is $100. She has cash in hand for small purchases, the rest in checking and savings accounts. Carrying a card in her purse, she marks down a charged coat and dress; her husband reports at night his cash purchase of shirts; a teenage daughter who has been handed cash returns the change and reports the buying of a skirt. Deductions from the budgeted $100 show only a few dollars left. The family can readily see that, except for minor purchases, clothing buying is over for the budgeting period.

A variation of this method is to give each member of the family cards with his portion of the budgeted category on it.

Some budgeters can carry their budget in their heads, but when several members of the family are spending, the deduction method can help to solve problems in money management.

STEP IV—PROGRAMMING YOUR SAVINGS

Saving is not something you do spasmodically—when you find a few extra dollars over on the pay check. It should be an integral part of your program. You use accounts at banks, savings and loan associations, and in credit unions to cover such categories as an emergency fund, upcoming commitments scheduled on your Step II form; short term needs—vacations, gifts, Christmas, etc.; plans for college education, aid to an older relative, a summer home, retirement for yourself, anything you like to name.

Chapter 9 will guide you in selecting your savings establishment. Some will allow customers to open several accounts, each for a specific purpose. Most run Christmas Clubs, but not all pay interest on the deposits. You and your family may prefer to earmark a portion of your regular savings as the Christmas Fund. But those who find themselves dipping too freely into special funds may need the safeguard of the old-fashioned Christmas Club Plan that cannot be drawn upon until the holiday season.

Individuals in the family may want to deposit their personal allowances in the savings bank and to draw on it as they wish. A local savings bank also helps safeguard against too much cash in the house.

Whether you open accounts in several savings institutions or have only one, you can work out the application of your funds on a form ruled into a number of columns. Use a column or so for notes and dates of deposits and withdrawals. Then, across the page, run names of your banks or savings institutions and, under them, the various funds you are, in effect, establishing in each one.

You can then note the amount you are channeling from fixed savings into such funds as reserve, college education, vacation, Christmas, etc. You can also run records of savings which cover your Step II obligations. Probably you will be depositing money needed for monthly bills straight into a checking account. But money for annual insurance premiums; or put aside as car depreciation, school fees, and other less frequent payments, might as well earn interest in a savings institution until you need it. With such planning ahead, you are putting your money to work for you.

If additional savings seem necessary to build up certain funds, a family can adopt its own variations of the piggy bank method. Some people save cents, nickels, or dimes, others empty their pockets or purses of small change each night, still others put aside money received for coupons at the supermarket or what they have saved by "do-it-yourself" instead of using a service. Some savers achieve a glow of satisfaction by taking to the bank money they were tempted to spend on an unnecessary purchase. In time, all or any of these plans add up to dollars for some particular objective.

SAVINGS BANK INTEREST

When you noted down your total income (page 6), you will have put down the interest your savings are earning. Usually, this money will be kept at the bank in order to earn more interest for specific items you are saving for. In practice, therefore, the interest is generally part of savings money rather than available to spend.

HANDLING A DEBT PROBLEM

Are you burdened by past debts? If the bills are not too large, and the creditors are not pressing you too hard, you can probably arrange to work out a regular plan of payments from each pay check. If your creditors understand you are handling your indebtedness systematically, they will probably agree to a certain period of time by which you anticipate clearing the load.

What if the debts are too heavy, the creditors press you, and you cannot handle the problem by spreading payments over several months? Your answer may be to get a "rehabilitation" loan. (See Chapter 6 for advice on where and how you may borrow—and the type of loan establishment to avoid.) Now, with money available, you can pay off your creditors. The repayment of the new loan can be planned on your Step II form.

If neither of these methods will overcome your difficulty; the amount of your debt is too much, for instance, you might try asking your most considerate creditor to help you work out a reasonable repayment plan which would be approved by the other creditors. A sincere intent to repay and a businesslike plan will usually win respect.

Once your system of regular debt repayment is set up, you can plan to reduce overheads by adopting some of the ideas for smarter buying and cutting costs suggested in Chapter 4. See, too, ways to increase income given in Chapter 5.

A certain amount of indebtedness is usual and even desirable in our credit-oriented society. (*Debts plus prompt payment equals a good credit rating. See Chapter 6.*) But if you are constantly having to cover one loan with another, falling short on payments, or committing a fifth or more of your net income to such payments, you should lose no time in getting rid of the burden. *Set down the extent of your problems on paper* and, if necessary, seek outside assistance. A local social service or county extension worker may be able to give guidance. Too, clergymen are usually in a position to channel people to suitable advisors.

The average family will find their answers in adopting a disciplined program of debt repayment, of making extra money, and of lowering expenses.

LOOKING TOWARD EXPANDED LIVING

In this chapter we have given methods and forms which demonstrate how you can keep your records, how you can pinpoint the heavy inescapable expenses, how you can conveniently check the difference between income and fixed outgo, and how you can methodically spread savings to take care of commitments and plans for the future.

We have not made any suggestions as to *how* you should spend or save your money. There can be no generalizations, no "average budget." You do the planning, but in the chapters that follow you will find guidance on buying, on credit and installment purchasing, house purchase, insurance, the stock market, and taxes. The application of that advice to your particular situation is your program for sound money management.

Chapter 2

AN AGENDA FOR YOUR FINANCIAL PROGRAM

ESTABLISHING YOUR NET WORTH	22
A REVIEW	24
DEALING WITH INFLATION	27
YOUR FAMILY RECORDS	28
Keep a Record Book	28
Your Safe Deposit Box	30
YOUR AGENDA AND ITS PRIORITIES	30

Financial independence and security are the goals of most individuals and families in our society. Is this twin goal an objective only the fortunate few can reach? Is there some certain way you can achieve it?

It may as well be said—nothing is sure in this world! Nevertheless, the prizes tend to go to the organizers, the people who map out their course of action and pinpoint the targets.

You can build for the future on what might be termed the Foursquare Program for Successful Living. Here are the four squares and their cornerstones:

INSURANCE —The Social Security Program
                       Life and Annuity Plans, including pension and
                          profit sharing
                       Health and Accident Protection
                       Home and Property Insurance
SAVINGS —Banks
                       Savings and Loan Associations
                       Credit Unions
                       Government Bonds
INVESTMENT—Stocks and Corporate Bonds
                       Mutual Funds

Home Ownership
Business or Professional Enterprises
PERSONAL   —Budgeting
Defined Goals
Family Cooperation
Factor X

Just what is that last item, Factor X? Let it be defined as what you bring to the program yourself. You need to be alert to trends, to plan intelligently with your family needs in view, to organize each aspect of the plan, and yet to remain flexible and be able to adjust when the economy or your personal situation demands a change in course. Factor X is the key to any successful financial program since without *skill in management,* which is what it amounts to, neither a business nor family can achieve its aims.

ESTABLISHING YOUR NET WORTH

No financial program can be made for the future without finding out where you stand today. Depending on your circumstances, you may or may not have made use of the methodical system of planning and spending described in Chapter 1. But now, as you initiate your plan, and annually thereafter, you need to assess your net worth.

Turn to the forms given on the next two pages. They will help you to make your tabulations. Add and delete headings to suit yourself, but see that you cover all items that add to your total worth and every liability against it.

ANNUAL FINANCIAL STATEMENT FOR THE FAMILY

(Date)

ASSETS

Cash on hand $_____
Checking accounts   _____
Savings accounts   _____
Money lent to others (repayment expected)   _____
Value of life insurance (Cash surrender value plus divi-
    dend accumulations)   _____

Annuities   _____

Retirement funds   _____

U. S. Savings bonds   _____

Investments—

    Stocks, bonds, mutual fund shares   _____

    Real estate   _____

    Profit-sharing plans   _____

Your home—full market value   _____

Other property (List such items as)—

    Automobile   _____

    Household furnishings   _____

    Furs, jewelry   _____

    Sports and hobby items   _____

    Clothing, etc.   _____

       Total Family Assets $_____

ANNUAL FINANCIAL STATEMENT FOR THE FAMILY

(Date)

LIABILITIES

Unpaid Bills

    Charge accounts $_____

    Credit card accounts   _____

    Taxes   _____

    Insurance premiums   _____

    Other   _____

Balances Due on—

    Installment contracts   _____

    Loans (from banks, savings and loan associations,

       insurance companies, etc.)   _____

    Other   _____

Mortgages payable on home and other property (or rent)   _____

       Total Family Liabilities $_____

SUMMARY

Assets $_____

Liabilities   _____

       Net Worth of the Family $_____

In completing your statement, you will need to ask questions, do some research. Your insurance agent, your employer, and your bank can give any help you may need in filling in figures on annuities, retirement funds, and U. S. Savings bonds.

Be thoroughly objective when you value property of any kind —home—automobile—household equipment—personal items. What would they bring on the market today? Has your neighborhood depreciated? What effect have new industries or highways in your area had on property values? Your local newspaper's real estate section and advertising are useful sources of information for property prices. An automobile dealer's Blue Book will help you make a realistic estimate of your car's worth—*and it may be less than you think*.

Personal property is hard to value. How much would you ask if you were putting it up for sale? Would you get that price? Clothing and equipment depreciate as styles change; but antiques, paintings, and hobby collections may acquire value. Custom mart advertising and the columns of specialty journals at the library may help you make your assessment.

The value of your stocks, bonds, mutual shares will be easier to assess. *Use today's quotations to get your total.* The fact that later in the year you may take a loss or find your stocks soaring is immaterial.

With your net worth established, you and your family can look ahead and plan for the year. You are in a position to set up *a five-year plan,* as businesses and governments do, and to gear income and outgo to the fulfillment of your objectives.

A REVIEW

How do you stand *now* on the Four-square Program? This is the time to review present status in each category and to define what changes are necessary. We will check over each item. Note down points where your own financial program appears to be weak. References are given to later chapters where full discussion is given.

Insurance. Social Security benefits (see Chapter 14). Ascertain your present standing by requesting the Social Security Administration for a statement. (You may do so once a year.) From your district Social Security office, you may obtain the official Form OAR-7004, which is a postcard addressed and ready to mail to Baltimore, Maryland.

Check over the benefits your family could receive from Social Security if and when certain eventualities occur—disability, retirement, death. With full information, you are in a better position to consider what additional benefits should be provided for your family through private insurance.

Life insurance and annuities. The head of a family should review his policies, asking such questions as these: What will the family live on in the event of my death? What provision is made for the children's continued education, especially for college? What other sources of income are there within the family group? What other potential earning ability?

How much life insurance is necessary? You provide the answer to your situation by a thorough analysis (see page 156). If you conclude you are underinsured, Chapter 10 offers suggestions for you. Toward retirement, you may contemplate annuities; see page 171. Nevertheless, some breadwinners make themselves and their families "insurance poor" by overprotection. That is why we suggest you view the whole situation at one time and *continue to do so annually.*

Pension and profit-sharing. When weighing up your assets, be sure to include your benefits under your employer's plan for pension or profit-sharing, or any provision made if disability forces early retirement. At the same time, you must consider what would happen if you die before or early in retirement. Would your company bear any responsibility toward your widow or other dependents? *If not, you may find it necessary to step up private insurance or earning possibilities.* (Chapters 10 and 5)

Health and accident protection. The group coverage you have at your place of employment or through a union or other organization may not be sufficient in these days of rising medical and hospital costs. Consider your need for a major medical policy or loss of income insurance. (Chapter 13)

Home, property, and automobile insurance. Wherever you live your personal assets are vulnerable to loss by fire, theft, vandalism, natural disaster, and civil disorder. Use the list you made to establish net worth as a basis for a household inventory, to be kept up-to-date as you acquire further items of value, or have reappraisals made because of changed market values. The inventory should be stored away from the articles it describes, preferably in a bank safe deposit box. See page 131 for discussion of insurance for home and other possessions. In particular, consider how you stand on automobile insurance. *Are you adequately insured?* Is liability insurance required in your state? If not, wisdom may dictate your obtaining this safeguard against the possibility of burdensome responsibility for very heavy damages.

Savings. In Chapter 1, it is suggested that you separate (at least on paper) your savings into funds, each one aimed to a certain goal. In addition, you will require a standing emergency fund, possibly also ready money for stock investment. What proportion of your savings should go into so-called "safe" savings (protected by Federal insurance)? What proportion into government bonds, stocks, and mutual funds? While some suggest certain percentages, we believe a categorical statement cannot cover every situation. You, the individual, must decide. (See Chapters 9, 11, and 12.) Nevertheless, you should certainly avoid tying up all your assets in real estate, stocks, and bonds, so that the availability of ready cash depends on a pay check. Preferably keep that emergency fund at no less than the equivalent of six months salary—and readily accessible at a nearby savings bank.

Investment. Chapters 11 and 12 discuss stocks and corporate bonds, and mutual funds. You have an equation to work out: Element of risk in the stock market against loss of dollar value in savings and interest at the bank. Venturing into the market is probably the wrong answer for the young married couple who have yet to establish a full program of regular savings and insurance. In general, fulfill your savings program first.

Home ownership. (Chapters 7 and 8) Your own home is a sound investment which will pay dividends through good maintenance and improvements, but keep a watchful eye on the possibility of declining neighborhood values.

Business and professional enterprises. Investment in some profitable hobby or the development of a small business can be a sound aim, especially with retirement years in view. (See Chapter 5.)

The personal factors are those which we are emphasizing throughout this book, particularly the first three chapters. From the start, we have mentioned cooperation between husband, wife, and family. The overall attitude of you and your family toward money management is far more important than any major or minor event that may throw the budget out of whack. The family who have established *a basic working agreement on money matters* can repair the damage because they understand the elements that go into saving and expanding money to do the work they want it to do.

DEALING WITH INFLATION

A point that is sure to come up in your family discussions is: What will a change of residence, that new car, or an overseas vacation cost when we are ready for it? Will the savings we put aside now decline in value? Will the cost of borrowing rise? Should we buy now—or pay more later?

You know you have to reckon with inflation, that the purchasing power of the dollar continues to decline. For the dollar that bought 90.5 cents worth of goods and gave you some change in 1951, you needed one dollar and 14.8 cents early in 1967. Inflation, sometimes described as "creeping," since the rate has risen at approximately 1 percent a year, has been with us for over twenty-five years; it is now 4 percent, with measures to contain the trend yet to be proven.

The economy, thus, has not been favoring the thrifty. People who put money into savings accounts, Government bonds, or other forms of investment which gave fixed returns have found that their interest dollars can buy less and less. On the other hand, people who have borrowed money to invest in successful enterprises have not only enjoyed that success; they have paid back dollars of less value than they borrowed.

You will have the inflation factor in mind when you set aside money for such future needs as education for the children and for retirement. The chapters on various types of investment indicate the degree to which you can build a hedge against inflation.

Too, there are everyday steps you can take to beat this trend in the economy; you will find them detailed in Chapter 4. The advice given to the person who needs to cut corners is also designed to fight the battle of inflation.

YOUR FAMILY RECORDS

Calculating your net worth has necessitated your referring to many personal papers. Because many people need to organize in this important area, we discuss it below.

Do you know where all your important family records are now? Your marriage certificate, your will, Social Security card? And all the documents connected with your home, insurance, investment, or installment buying? If you know exactly where to find such data, you are more methodical—and wiser than many of your neighbors. All too often, when emergencies arise, vital documents cannot be located. Sometimes they are misplaced through neglect or sheer carelessness; sometimes the one person who knows where the papers are is stricken by illness or accident. The problem can be avoided, as shown below.

KEEP A RECORD BOOK

Family records will, of course, differ according to the assets owned, but the whereabouts of all data should be set down. If a loose-leaf notebook is used, it is easy to have extra photocopies made of all or any of the pages. It may be desirable for duplicate information to be in the hands of married children, or kept at an office. Printed record books are obtainable, but you may prefer to make your own in line with your other financial records and inventories of valuables.

Here are some important items which should be listed with a note of reference about their location:

Certificates of birth; marriage; divorce; death; naturalization. Official documents of life's major events are essential for innumerable purposes, to prove date and place of birth, to obtain American citizenship for the foreign-born, to claim Social Security benefits. If one or other of such important certificates is missing, obtain a certified copy in case it is needed—to collect on insurance, to claim an inheritance, to obtain a passport, or when remarriage takes place. You may not yet know of all the occasions when members of the family will need one or other of these major documents.

If you need a certified copy of a birth or death certificate, inquire at your state or city's central vital statistics office, usually associated with the Department of Health. Booklets (fifteen cents each) on where to send for birth and death, marriage, and divorce records are available from the Superintendent of Documents, Washington, D.C., 20402. They give full addresses and list fees.

Social Security. Members of the family who have cards should list the numbers and where the cards are usually kept. The cards come in two parts, so you may keep the stubs with other important records. Then, if a card is lost, a stub can be mailed to your local Social Security office with a request for a duplicate. Supply name, address, and place of business, in addition to the number, when writing.

Bank accounts. List bank names and addresses with the numbers of savings account books and the names of the members of the family who own each one. Each year banks advertise for missing depositors who have either forgotten their accounts or died without informing their relatives of them. See that the necessary information is available in your family.

Also list the names and addresses of banks where you and any others have checking accounts, and the numbers of those accounts.

United States savings bonds. Maintain a careful record of your bonds, noting full serial numbers, issue dates, and denomination. If the bonds themselves are lost, stolen, or destroyed, send such information at once to the Bureau of the Public Debt, Division of Loans and Currency, 536 South Clark Street, Chicago, Illinois, 60605. You will then receive full information on how to get replacements.

Insurance of all types. Record information about each policy, its number, amount payable, and method of settlement. Include information about any personal coverage at place of business, such as participation in group health, pension, or profit-sharing benefits.

List names and addresses of all companies involved and state where policies are kept.

Credit cards. Because this method of charging accounts is so vulnerable to theft and other loss, you should list all your account numbers and the names and addresses of companies issuing the cards. Usually, you are liable for goods charged in your name until you provide a notice of loss in writing.

Inventory. It has already been suggested that you keep a household inventory in a bank safe deposit box. If you do not have one, use a fireproof box at home. If you file at the bank, you might want a duplicate of your inventory in your record book, so you can see when additions and reappraisals are necessary on the original.

YOUR SAFE DEPOSIT BOX

For a very small sum, often no more than fifty cents a month, a safe deposit box can be rented at your bank. Here, you can safeguard valuable jewelry, stock certificates, deeds, legal records of all types, passports, bankbooks, personal papers, and the above mentioned inventory.

You will have to guard the keys to the box, for you are the sole possessor and you should appoint a deputy who can open the box in case you cannot. Check with the bank on its regulations affecting deputies.

You might also discuss with your attorney the legal implications which might arise if you rent the safe deposit box jointly with your spouse, particularly at time of death.

YOUR AGENDA AND ITS PRIORITIES

You now have before you an assessment of your net worth. It will serve as a guide to what is financially possible for you and the family as you together establish an agenda. The objectives on that agenda, and those you name as priorities, will, of course, reflect your circumstances and what now seems most important to achieve. If you are young, perhaps living in an apartment, home ownership may be the initial goal, together with a sound insurance program. Later, planning for your children's education may be the prior aim. Ultimately, you will be looking toward retirement.

In between come many types of long- and short-term priorities, from new furnishings to vacation travel; automobiles and television, or perhaps dealing with temporary adversity, such as a job loss, accident, or sickness in the family.

Whatever your targets are, write them down, and then *define exactly how you will finance them.* Out of current income, from the savings, insurance, and investment program? Tie your objectives into your savings funds. Some may come within a one-year program. But as you set up those one-year projects, do not fail to look five years ahead. Will you then have increased education expenses? Or a likely commitment to an elderly member of the family?

Think your objectives through, and do not let too many short-term goals absorb your savings while you fail to take note of middle and long range needs. *Plot out the five- and ten-year objectives* so that, in due time, you are making provision toward retirement. Such planning for many people begins in middle life when they purchase a summer home and so locate a second community where they can establish roots in readiness for full-time residence in later years.

You are planning now with finances as they actually are. If certain objectives seem impossible because of limited means, weigh the budget and decide if some areas could stand trimming. Then see Chapters 4 and 5. They provide ideas for cutting expenses and for expanding income.

It might be added that if money management is to be really sound, it needs to be well seasoned with humor and a certain element of relaxation. The people who frowningly deny themselves and their family a minor joy because "it is not in the budget," and the people who cheerfully dump every resolution for a spending spree need to work toward middle ground. As you set up your Four-square Program, see it is built there—in the middle.

Chapter 3

FAMILY COOPERATION IN FINANCIAL PLANNING

WORKING TOGETHER ON THE SPENDING PLAN	34
ESTABLISHING WORKING HABITS	35
HOW SHALL THE BILLS BE PAID?	35
YOUR BANK ACCOUNTS	36
Regular Checking Accounts	36
Special Checking Accounts	36
PERSONAL ALLOWANCES CONTRIBUTE TO FAMILY HARMONY	37
HOW MUCH FOR THE CHILDREN?	38
Covering the Routine Expenses	39
Handling an Allowance	39
Charge Accounts?	40
FINANCING A COLLEGE EDUCATION FOR YOUR CHILDREN	40
Scholarships and Loans	41
The College as a Source of Aid	42
Other Sources of Aid	42
Federal Loans	43
MONEY MANAGEMENT AND THE WORKING WIFE	44
Does It Pay for a Wife to Work?	44
Factors to Be Weighed	45
Child Care Help	45
Day Care, Nursery Schools, Summer Camps	46
Household Services	46
Food	46
Part-time or Temporary Work	46
The Wife's Pay Check	47
FAMILY COOPERATION IS A NECESSITY	48

In putting forward suggestions for your financial program, we have assumed that husband, wife, and family have come to terms, can discuss the situation frankly and can make reasonable, harmonious plans for earning and spending.

This is the ideal situation, but it must be recognized that some families face areas of violent conflict over money. Psychological difficulties may lead to gambling, wildcat investments, or lavish generosity out of all keeping with circumstances. A husband or wife may be a spendthrift or a penny pincher; one may indulge in heedless spending even after agreeing to a plan to pay off debts; another cuts corners and subjects the family to financial squeezing and unwarranted limitation. Such people may well be among those who must eventually have professional advice.

This is a book on money management, not psychological counsel. Where this type of help is necessary it may be found through a Family Service Agency, which can be located through a telephone directory. Where none can be traced, write to The Family Service Agency, 44 East 23rd Street, New York, New York 10010 for names and addresses.

WORKING TOGETHER ON THE SPENDING PLAN

One of the first decisions to be reached in a family money management program is—who will manage what. If you are only just married, you have a good chance to come to an early understanding on this subject—and so to avoid one of the conflicts that endanger marriage. If you are long-married and the division of responsibility is a source of trouble, decide now to start afresh. The following steps outline a reasonable program:

Begin with a working partnership in handling money. The pay check earned by the husband is not his alone—to be doled out as he pleases. His wife earns her share, and often works a far longer day in the home. On pages 44–48 we discuss the role of the working wife and her earnings. Here, we are concerned with the husband's salary which should be used to cover all major expenses for the family. Responsibility for its distribution belongs to both partners. From a joint checking account (see page 37), the husband can handle items such as rent or mortgage, taxes, insurance, and expenses of the family automobile. From the same account, the wife takes over food and clothing expenses, probably the utility bills, and the cost of entertaining at home. List the type of bills faced in your household and decide which items husband or wife will handle. Often the wife will look after budgeting and keep the records of expenditures. Here, much will depend on personal temperament and ability. In contrast to the man who likes to "be the boss" and keep his wife in the dark on finances is the man who hands over his pay check to his wife and lets her return him his lunch money and transportation expenses. Neither make good team members.

Certainly, adjustments will have to be made where the wife is "plain dumb" at figures and extravagant into the bargain, or where the man knows he may spend too much and too wildly. (When the two types combine—outside family counsel is invariably needed!)

ESTABLISHING WORKING HABITS

A preliminary to work on budget and bill-paying is the setting up of the special area in the home where papers are to be kept. If all members of the household know that a certain drawer or portion of a desk is for bills, financial records, checkbooks, etc., there is little possibility of payments being overlooked. Establish your own "in and out" system of bills, from receipt in the mail to payment and filing of your copies for reference, or possibly with income tax papers.

We suggest a monthly basis for budgeting, but you may find it convenient to use pay periods. Whatever system you use, accompany it with a definite set-aside of time to enter figures in your own records and to write checks. If you fail to establish a regular schedule for dealing with your plans, payments, and records, the good management of money is unlikely to happen for you!

HOW SHALL THE BILLS BE PAID?

Paying bills with cash and getting a receipt is becoming old-fashioned in our credit-conscious society. It may be possible for you to settle your telephone bill at a local bank, but for the most part payments are made by checks which, when returned from your bank, automatically become your receipts.

If you are a young person or someone living alone who faces few bills, you can perhaps manage with a savings account only. Your savings institution will issue you the few checks you need or you can buy postal money orders, bank money orders, registered or cashier's checks. Such measures should not be used for long since it is desirable to maintain a checking account for credit reference purposes. (See page 89.)

YOUR BANK ACCOUNTS

In determining the type of checking account to set up at your personal bank, consider the following:

REGULAR CHECKING ACCOUNTS

Use this method if you expect to keep a substantial balance each month and to be active in making deposits and writing checks. The balance you keep in the bank will earn a credit which is applied against maintenance and fees for checks and deposits. Consequently, if your balance is large, there is only a low fee or none at all for account activity.

Banks will supply you with details of their fees for this service, which is suitable for personal, business, and professional accounts.

SPECIAL CHECKING ACCOUNTS

This service is usually the best choice for people who do not expect to maintain a large balance in the account, and who will only write a few checks each month.

A ten-cent fee per check is usual, with a maintenance charge of about fifty cents a month. Banks charging only thirty cents a month are still to be found.

If you have a choice of several banks in your vicinity, inquire about their charges, and extra services, such as checks imprinted with your name and address, and different types of checkbooks.

When you have decided upon the most suitable type of checking account, you may want to set it up at the bank as a *joint checking account,* whereby checks can be made out by either husband or wife. This works well in that each can handle particular areas of responsibility without reference to the other, and gives a sense of ownership to both. A career girl giving up her own salary upon marriage or shortly after does not feel like an unpaid dependent when she handles part of the family finances through a joint checking account.

Note, though, that close cooperation is needed to make the joint checking account a success. Husband and wife must keep each other informed of how the balance stands—or bouncing checks will disrupt the marital harmony.

PERSONAL ALLOWANCES CONTRIBUTE TO
FAMILY HARMONY

A personal do-as-you-please allowance for everyone is a most important factor in family financial plans. No one should have to account for every penny. If one member of the family appears to fritter away his allowance and another hoards it to buy something that seems particularly pointless to everyone else, that is exactly what the personal allowance is for. So—no interference!

What each allowance should be will, of course, depend on family circumstances. This advice only—*even if the budget is very tight, there should still be a little spending money for everyone.* It represents freedom and emotional outlet, which, in the long run, may safeguard other areas of a spending plan.

An affluent family may tend to develop too easy an attitude toward such personal allowances. Because large amounts are available now, it does not say that a widow, a married daughter, or a son who goes his own way will always have such sums to play with. Where the personal allowance can be large, the more reason to study how it can be wisely spent.

HOW MUCH FOR THE CHILDREN?

Not too much, certainly. A too-free handout for Billy and Betty is not going to aid in their mature growth. Though you may have a good income, you do not know what financial problems your children will face. Therefore, a sound training in money values from an early age may well be one of the best gifts you can offer.

But try to follow the happy midcourse between good training and generating anxiety over money. Flexibility may be called for where one child is slower than another in developing understanding on how an allowance may best be spent. Children, even within a family, will differ widely in their perception of money values.

But, although you may avoid the trap of giving a six-year-old five dollars a week for himself just because you can afford it, you cannot ignore the cost-of-living rise at the candy and toy store. The youngsters need more than you had at their age. At four or five, fifteen cents a week is enough, and if it comes in pennies, Junior will think he has a fortune. With ten- or fifteen-cent raises, at eight the child should have fifty cents a week for himself, and so up to perhaps seventy-five cents or a dollar at ten.

While this is free-spending money, the child can be trained to understand the principle of saving for some higher-priced item he wants. If this costs fifty cents and he prefers to spend his twenty-five cents a week on something else, that's his choice, but he should not be given the fifty-cent article. He can save—*or he can earn*. Once he understands *how* he can obtain something for himself, he has learned a valuable lesson and gained a personal satisfaction.

An advance against next week's allowance is not good training for Billy (though his parents may well be borrowing the cost of his home!). Nor is it advisable for him to be given money for doing household chores which he should learn to accept as his own—without pay. Extra money should be given for work he does not usually do—a job you might undertake yourself, for instance.

Some parents, it must be said, feel that a child should receive *no allowance at all without earning,* either at home or by doing chores for the neighbors. Certainly the principle is good, and if you institute it in your family, you will do far better than those parents who willingly hand out on demand.

COVERING THE ROUTINE EXPENSES

Will you add the cost of movies, church contributions, or other week-by-week expenses to the allowance? Often parents prefer to give the extra money as needed until the teens are reached. But if a particular child is ready for the experience, he should be allowed to handle his own finances.

HANDLING AN ALLOWANCE

After ten, the personal allowance will need to rise—so also the money given for specific spending, till you deal with the problems of teenage money management. Your circumstances, and how people live in your area, will influence what you allow, but here is a suggested range: The twelve-year-old gets between one dollar and two-fifty; a year later, a fifty-cent raise, if it can be made within the parent's budget. In some families, the allowance stays at two dollars; if the child wants more he must find ways to earn it. In others, the allowance rises to four or five dollars at fourteen and fifteen, but so do the number of items the child must care for himself.

If you have been letting the children in on family financial discussions, bringing them up to understand where the income comes from, and how you manage expenses, you may save yourself some of the headaches of handling teenage allowances.

Now the growing Billy or Betty not only want all their contemporaries have; they are also bait for advertisers, and want to assert their independence by buying what they please. You will need a specific agreement on what the allowance covers. School lunches, club dues, toiletries, and hobby items are expenses the young person should manage. But start the clothing allowance gradually, with responsibility for shirts and skirts, rather than for essential items such as winter outfits. The youngster who has been allowed to exercise a certain freedom of choice while shopping under parental guidance will later on respond with wiser choices than the teenager whose mother has done all the choosing and buying for him. The temptation offered by consumer goods today is so great the children need an early education in sensible buying.

CHARGE ACCOUNTS?

Definitely not for the teenager, the experts say. Indeed, with the difficulties many parents have in managing credit wisely, why would the child do better? Permitting charge accounts does not provide the necessary lessons for living within income.

FINANCING A COLLEGE EDUCATION FOR YOUR CHILDREN

Planning for a child's college expenses can well begin when the infant is born. Expenses are mounting so rapidly that the average family faces a severe financial pinch as soon as the college years arrive.

The budget program in Chapter 1 calls for savings under the heading of education. If you channel regular payments from your pay check into a savings institution specifically for a college fund, compounded interest will enlarge your savings at the rate of 4½ to 5 percent a year. But inflation eats those saved dollars and with college costs rising at about 5 percent a year, savings alone are not likely to cover your student's education. Certainly not if you have several children college-bound.

See the chapters ahead on *savings bonds, insurance,* and *investment.* All offer possibilities for the college fund. Government bonds are safe, and you may be able to buy them through a payroll savings plan. The stock market is risky, but offers a hedge against inflation.

Insurance (Chapter 10) should, of course, cover the risk of the breadwinner not living to fulfill his savings and investment program for his children. Educational endowment policies force savings, but lack the coverage against death obtainable in a straight life policy.

The latter offers more protection, plus the cash value. You can then borrow against the policy, or obtain funds by turning it in. If your insurance agent suggests buying juvenile insurance for a college fund, explore the idea, but bear in mind that this is generally considered more expensive and carries less benefit.

These avenues of funds anticipate college costs in the future. Say college is no more than a year or two ahead. You and your son or daughter will want to start checking up on the possibilities of scholarships and loans.

SCHOLARSHIPS AND LOANS

You and your college-bound offspring should start to check on scholarship and loans before the student reaches the senior year in high school. While the young adult should do as much of the writing and checking up as possible, especially as far as the college is concerned, you should know just what the possibilities are.

No doubt you will be conferring with the high school guidance counselor regarding the colleges where your student should apply for admission. At this time, inquire about scholarships and loans. Full information should be available to you.

For those who want to follow through with their own investigation of the possibilities, we suggest writing the U. S. Government Printing Office, Washington, D.C. 20402, for a listing of booklets on financial aid to students, or write the U. S. Department of Health, Education, and Welfare Office of Education. From Washington, D.C., or from regional offices across the country, the Office will supply full information in book and pamphlet form.

You can, for example, obtain the booklet "Federal Aids for College Students" which describes the *College Student Guaranteed Loan Program*, primarily for students from middle- or upper-income families; *Educational Opportunity Grants* given to promising needy students; *National Defense Student Loans,* repayable within ten years at interest and again for needy students; and the *College Work-Study* program for students from low-income families. Participating institutions are listed.

Because the range of possible scholarship and loan aid is so wide, you or the student should ask your local library for a current guide to scholarships or buy a copy from a newsdealer or bookseller. *Lovejoy's Scholarship Guide* is useful, and a librarian or bookseller will guide you to other publications on the subject. These include the three-volume reference book, *Scholarships, Fellowships, and Loans,* by S. Norman Feingold.

THE COLLEGE AS A SOURCE OF AID

Here, financial need is the essential criteria coupled with reasonably good achievement potential. A top scholastic record plus evidence of real financial need equals best chance for direct college aid. Help is often given in package form now; part scholarship, part loan (with low interest and long repayment terms), and part campus job. The student should inquire at the colleges of his choice and, offered entrance at more than one, will choose on the basis of aid.

Five-year cooperative work-study programs are available at certain colleges. Earnings from work will substantially defray a student's expenses. The program, which varies according to the college, covers a number of fields of study. Write National Commission for Cooperative Education, 8 West 40th Street, New York, New York 10018, for a listing of colleges.

If you have several children due for college, one after the other, your financial headache might be eased by the selection of a near-home college. A municipal or state college could save on residential costs.

OTHER SOURCES OF AID

If you are an employee of a large corporation or a union member, inquire if either organization offers college scholarships or loans for which your child would be eligible.

Churches offer both loans and scholarships to young members, particularly if they plan careers in teaching, social work, nursing, medicine, and, of course, the ministry. Your minister or the church headquarters office will supply information. Sometimes, also, individual churches will sponsor promising students from the membership.

Local organizations of various types may also help students. Your high school guidance counselor (or Chamber of Commerce) can direct you. So, too, can your state's Department of Education which also may offer scholarships and loans in its own program. Be sure to write the office, usually located in the state capital.

Widows of veterans who died as a result of certain wars should contact their local Veterans Administration office to find out if the veteran's children can receive educational aid. The American Legion and other organizations also grant certain scholarships.

FEDERAL LOANS

Many banks, certain savings and loan associations, and credit unions participate in the low-cost college loan program available through the 1965 Higher Education Act. The student should inquire at his college's financial office for the name of a participating institution near home.

The nonprofit United Student Aid Funds participate as a guarantor in the Federal program. It also has its own program to assist full-time students from any of the colleges participating. Write the organization at 5259 North Tacoma Avenue, Indianapolis, Indiana 46220, for information if your local banks cannot give it to you.

A number of finance companies run education loan programs, but their loans are apt to be expensive. If you plan to use one of these tuition plans, be sure to consider the *true interest rate*. (See page 98.) Work out the interest rate in conjunction with the repayment plan. Question what happens if the student should die, or otherwise fail to fulfill the program. It is unlikely you will find the terms as favorable as those of a bank.

In conclusion, *begin college planning early with savings*. Through your newspaper and other media, keep informed of new developments on student loans and scholarships. Ask at your library to see college catalogs and books specifically on loans and scholarships. There are some unusual opportunities. Delivering newspapers for a year may qualify a boy for aid, and so may your ancestry! Seek out further information on any scholarship that may pertain to your student.

MONEY MANAGEMENT AND THE WORKING WIFE

Here, we are concerned only with the working wife and the money she earns, not with the many other aspects that arise—the psychological effect on her children, her husband's approval, whether she works from economic necessity or for personal satisfaction. The questions that arise are:

1. If there are small children, does it pay for a wife to work?
2. How should a wife's pay check be used?

DOES IT PAY FOR A WIFE TO WORK?

It depends on the individual situation. Will it be necessary to hire someone to take care of the household or the children while the wife is away from the house? If so, *and the wife is qualified to earn a high salary through her profession or career,* the answer may well be *yes;* the expense, and sometimes the difficulty, of engaging a housekeeper may well be justified. When the wife would earn only an average wage or salary, it may not pay to employ a substitute to care for very young children. When the cost of a mother substitute is added to the wife's commutation, lunch, additional clothing needs (and her taxes!), there is too little left over from a run-of-the-mill job to justify the many difficulties involved.

The question is often examined, too, where a couple have the care of an infirm relative, or in families where there is a mentally or physically handicapped child. In many of these cases, it may be advisable to engage specially qualified home help or to place the dependent in special day or full-time care facilities. Whatever extra money the wife can earn is needed to meet expenses; in some cases, there will also be a psychological need to have the diversion of a job instead of full-time care of the dependent.

Factors to Be Weighed

In your situation, there may be many reasons why you want a working husband/wife partnership. Here, we only point out the factors you must weigh in connection with money. Take pencil and paper, and be prepared to analyze these points:

Taxes. Will a two-salary income place you in an undesirably high tax bracket? Frequently, a working husband and wife find that payroll deductions do not cover their Federal taxes on the joint return. The new tax bracket means a substantial outlay when the mid-April deadline rolls around. Consider, too, the additional state and city tax to which you may be liable. You may, however, be among those who can claim a deduction for child care. (See Chapter 15.)

Payroll Deductions. The wife's employer will reduce her pay check, not only by Federal and state taxes, but by Social Security, and probably by group health insurance and a pension plan. Consider the effect of that reduction if the wife only wants to work for a short time to cover special financial needs. But, on a long-term basis, a working wife acquires assets for the family by gaining her own Social Security pension and company pension, and by participating in a health insurance plan.

Other Deductions. Some types of work involve union or club dues. Check this when seeking new employment.

Child Care Help

Remember that your employment of a mother substitute carries more expense than just the woman's wages. Social Security payments are due from employer as well as employee on cash wages of more than $50 a quarter, and you will probably have to pay carfare for a day worker. You may have to provide uniforms, or work smocks. Your telephone bill may increase. (You had better set a rule about calls, though it may not be observed!) The employee may not buy food, or use household appliances and cleaning products as economically (or wisely) as the wife she replaces. Therefore, running expenses for the household increase. *These points carry weight when the wife is not in a high-pay job.*

Day Care, Nursery Schools, Summer Camps

Your family may use all three, whether or not the mother works. But when she holds a job, they will certainly be needed. Ascertain the expenses involved for additional child-care hours, or for weeks in the summer.

Household Services

If the working wife tries to do her home job in addition to her outside employment, the result may well be doctor bills. She can cut down on personal wear-and-tear, but she will raise the family cost of living where she uses outside services for jobs she used to handle herself, such as laundry, self-operating dry cleaning, rug-shampooing, window cleaning, and perhaps even the gardening. And her husband is certainly going to be asked to share more of the burden of household chores. (In fact, he should not have to be asked!)

Food

The working wife does not have time to shop around the various supermarkets for the specials; she may buy more at the expensive but convenient small store. Too, the family may eat out more often. Count on a rise in food costs and on evening or Saturday shopping at the market.

PART-TIME OR TEMPORARY WORK

The housewife may consider this type of work because she thinks that she will also be able to cover most of her usual duties. She should realize that she will still need suitable clothing and that, for only a part-time or short-time salary, she will have the usual deductions from salary and most of the expenses of the full-time worker.

How did you come out after discussing and checking the points we have raised? Can a working wife contribute to your financial program—and at the same time run the household? Weigh the pros and cons of your personal situation, both financial and psychological. If the financial plus is small, but the wife needs the stimulation of outside activity, the decision for her to work may be wise. On the other hand, where the money contribution works out as a definite plus, but the wife is likely to be harried by the combination of job responsibilities and the home, you may be well advised to seek some other way to increase the family income.

THE WIFE'S PAY CHECK

In the average home where there are two pay checks, there are many reasons why husband's and wife's income should be pooled. Mutual confidence is established, and there is none of the "holding out" of "my" earnings—a fruitful source for marital discord.

From her pay check, the wife will certainly have to deduct her additional expenses, such as transportation (perhaps a second car will be needed) and lunches out. Her personal allowance from the check must now cover the type of clothing suited to her job, and all the accessories. She will want money for gifts and contributions, and more for personal spending. Both husband and wife should keep a record of their needs for a while to see just how much a personal expense allowance should add up to.

Where household help is employed specifically because the wife works, the payment is sometimes made directly by the wife before the rest of her money goes into the pool—simply because she prefers to be responsible for her stand-in.

It is certainly desirable that a husband's income should be used to cover the basic expenses—rent or mortgage, utilities, taxes, insurance, and, from a psychological point of view, he may well prefer to handle all these bills himself. When every effort is made to live on the husband's income, the couple are prepared to manage when there is to be a baby, or when, for other reasons, the wife gives up her job. Sometimes, a two-salary income deludes young people into taking on far too heavy a financial commitment; then, when suddenly they are reduced to one salary, they are in trouble.

It is a good idea for the wife's earnings to be directed toward some special purpose. Many wives work specifically to see their children through college; so, after the expense deduction, they put their money into the education fund. In childless families, or after children are grown, the wife's salary can provide the luxury items, special vacations, or be earmarked for the couple's retirement.

FAMILY COOPERATION IS A NECESSITY

In this chapter, we have examined a number of points affecting the family. Cooperation is essential to the successful working-out of these considerations. We emphasize the importance of frequent family discussions to study needs and spending objectives, to reset budget goals, and to get rid of those sore points that fester in too many homes.

Your money management plan can work for you in establishing a genuine partnership in the business of being a family.

Chapter 4

RAISING CASH THROUGH CUTTING COSTS

BUY WISELY	50
Smart Buyer Tactics at the Supermarket	51
Overpricing	52
Can You Believe the Advertisements?	53
Caution—It's a Gyp!	54
Sale Time	56
Thrifty Buys	57
Buying at the Discount Store	57
THE TRADE-IN	58
LET A RENTAL SAVE YOU MONEY	58
RANDOM SPENDING	59
PAY WHAT YOU OWE—AND NO MORE	59
SAVING THROUGH HOME ECONOMIES	60
Cutting Clothing Costs	60
A Do-It-Yourself Program for the Family	61
Comparing Costs	61
FUN FOR FREE	62
A LONG-TERM INVESTMENT FOR YOU	62

You don't need to be told the cost of living has gone up and is going up. A trip to the supermarket, department store, or the receipt of a medical bill tells you more about inflation than all the words from Washington and the reports of the Consumer Price Index.

If your family income isn't keeping pace with this rise—and you have plenty of company if it isn't—you want to know how you can pass your own Anti-Inflation Bill. It can be done in small ways and in large—all adding up to substantial savings, cash you can use for your own family's benefit.

Here are some of the steps you can take to beat the drop in dollar value:

Buy wisely. It pays to shop around. *Be a comparison shopper.* Plan your buying ahead and do not be unduly swayed by advertising and attractive packaging.

Practice economy in the home. Save on utilities, equipment, and in countless small ways.

Adopt a do-it-yourself-program. Have the family handle jobs ordinarily undertaken by service personnel.

We will cover each point in turn:

BUY WISELY

In food and household items—Watch food store advertising and *make out a list.* Stock up on specials if you have the freezer and storage space. But make sure that you and not the store management are in control. See the remarks on advertising below.

Do you know just what you are buying in quantity, or quality, or in nutritional value? By law, labels must provide the buyer with certain information. Compare prices, quantities, and labeling on brand and supermarket products. The goods packaged for the store may be equal in food value and flavor to the nationally advertised products, and you can save considerably.

You should know canning standards and grades of meat, fruits, vegetables, and dairy products so that you have the knowledge you need to buy wisely. Send to the Superintendent of Documents, Washington, D.C. 20402, for price list #86 on Consumer Information. For a few cents you can obtain booklets which will guide you in all phases of consumer interests. For example, ten cents brings the "Shopper's Guide to U.S. Grades for Food" (Catalog No. A. 1.77: 58/3). (In sending for government booklets, note that stamps are unacceptable in payment.)

Many families spend a considerable sum each month on vitamins, health foods, and food supplements. You might save by first consulting your doctor. Ask if any member of your family is in need of these extras. It is nowadays stated that *regular, well-balanced meals* give the average person all the vitamins and nutrition necessary to health.

Moreover, it is not necessary to buy the most expensive cuts of meat, for example, in order to provide nutritious meals for the family. Write to the Office of Information, U. S. Department of Agriculture, Washington, D.C. 20250, for a listing of publications on nutrition—and do not believe all you see in popularized books on diet, etc. The above-named government department warns on worthless diet fads which consume dollars that could have been saved or sensibly spent at the grocery store.

SMART BUYER TACTICS AT THE SUPERMARKET

The bride and the younger housewife are particularly vulnerable to the deceptions of packaging and pricing. Some girls are more experienced in a business office than in a supermarket and when faced with the responsibility of all the marketing they are bewildered by sizes, weights, and prices that cannot be calculated for value without a slide rule. (And these are indeed used by thrifty and experienced buyers.)

Take time to check can and package labels. Note prices on several sizes of the same type of cereal and calculate the price per ounce. The one you regularly buy may not contain the most for the money. The larger size or the several-packs-for-so-much are not necessarily bargains. One cautious shopper who worked out the decimal points found that the two-for-so-much container of bouillon cubes cost more than the smaller, three-for-so-much containers of the same product.

Know the prices of your regular purchases and the usual quantity. The housewife will often pick up a container at a familiar price and fail to notice the small print which indicates the weight (or in some cases, the length) has been reduced. Another manufacturer may offer better value for a similar product.

Sometimes the store is at fault. The product may be marked "so many cents off," but unless the shopper knows the regular price she cannot tell if the store has reduced the cost. One housewife regularly buying loose tea at 85 cents for a half-pound hunted up a supermarket manager to complain the price had not been reduced to 79 cents to justify the big "6 cents off" notice on the package. She bought three more packages of tea over the next two weeks and each time had to find the manager. He had not given instructions for the pricing to be changed, and many customers must have lost the benefit of the sale.

It is not uncommon for the retail price to be put up so that the advertised ten or twenty cents does not benefit the buyer, and the bargain offered may vary greatly from store to store. It is almost impossible not to be taken in at some stage or another in the process of marketing, but the alert housewife will complain to companies, to store management, to city and state government, and to representatives in Congress until all deceptive practices have ceased or are *adequately* covered by legislation. The effectiveness of new laws has to be tested and the buyer must make himself heard when deception reveals loopholes that have yet to be plugged.

Economy is buying the amount *you* need. Some buyers attracted by the bargain offered by a large size will buy it, disregarding their own needs. If you only need a small quantity of some particular product, the large size will only take up closet space, the contents perhaps prone to deterioration or evaporation.

OVERPRICING

The cosmetics industry is one where overpricing is usual, and nothing short of supercolossal. In fact, a high price is said to attract more buyers than a low one. A woman would feel "cheated" if she bought a beauty product, which is advertised to maintain or restore her youth, at a low price. The truth is that the ingredients of most cosmetics are very inexpensive (some can be picked up at a drug store for a few cents), and mass packaging, however attractive, is not expensive either. A woman with the courage to buy her beauty products at the five-and-ten instead of the elaborate department store counter can save considerably—and at no noticeable effect to her appearance.

Cosmetic preparations of one type or another are marketed under as many deceptive labels as food and household items. For example, the shampoo selling for years at "$1.50, regularly $2.50," may not have sold at the higher price for more than a short period when it was first advertised.

CAN YOU BELIEVE THE ADVERTISEMENTS?

The advertising trap is one we all tend to fall into. We enjoy some TV commercials more than the show, a magazine advertisement better than the article alongside. We mentally note to look for that product. Probably we buy it. On store shelves and in windows plastic bottles and snappy packaging tempt our eyes and the buying impulse. How often did you buy a well-dressed container and fail to compare its price and value with similar, less noticeable goods? Did you stop to think if you really needed it? Day after day, through all mediums of communication, we are being invited into an all-color, all-persuasive world of gracious living and told it may be ours —at a price. Too often we do not stop to consider whether the price we pay is worth the value we receive, in terms of necessity, use, or pleasure.

People who can afford to buy on impulse and to splurge on luxury items without a second thought are an asset to our consumer-geared economy. We all enjoy the occasional mad buy. But this book is designed for those who want to manage their finances more effectively. If you need to save money, be wise to advertising in all its forms. It can inform and entertain; it can guide you to a new product or a new house, but *do not let it direct your thinking.* Stay in control. Ask yourself such questions as: Is it necessary? Is it available at competitive prices? Is it effective? Durable?

Note that there are publications which show the results of tests and which make disinterested comparisons of consumer goods. (See *Consumer Reports* and *Consumer Bulletin* at newsdealers and libraries. Too, you can find annual paperback guides on the same subject, and on buying from discount stores.)

Research pays, particularly where expensive purchases are involved. You can curb impulse buying by cultivating the habit of comparison shopping and reading up on value tests.

CAUTION—IT'S A GYP!

You may be too smart to fall for the "inspector" who says you need a new furnace and, amazingly, can refer you to the right man to supply and install it. You wisely do not sign any contract that would involve a less alert person in skyrocketed installment payments for shoddy goods or a so-called "home improvement" job. You stall off these fast-talking hucksters until you have checked with your Better Business Bureau, the local Chamber of Commerce —or local authorities. But you may be a pushover for the soft-sell or the more subtle approach.

You may be taken in by a smooth book salesman who gently frowns upon your disinclination to introduce your children to stimulating knowledge—and so goads you into signing an irrevocable— and wholly legal—contract to buy an encyclopedia set or other volumes you can do without. Too late, you realize the children could well have learned to use the local free reference library instead and saved you burdensome and often inflated charges.

A man eager to advance the education of his children fell for an encyclopedia salesman's line that he was "sent by the school." He began to pay a monthly charge, failed to keep it up, and had his wages garnisheed as a result. Legally he became committed to payments *four times* as heavy as the original (inflated) cost. Moreover, because he had not paid *an additional sum,* the books were taken from his home. This buyer could be you—caught in an unwary moment.

Too, you may fall for a supposed "researcher" who telephones for an appointment to tell you about a famous company's new product. You will get a fabulous bonus for just telling your friends about it, he says. But there's a catch in it. The caller and the famous company may well be strangers, and your pocket will definitely be lighter if you listen to his blandishments.

Sales gyps, ranging from out-and-out fraud to the delivery of substandard merchandise or services, are countless. Watch for books and magazine articles that will inform you on rackets and protect yourself against con men and women of all kinds in the following ways:

Beware the person who calls, telephones, or writes offering *something for nothing*—a prize, just a few moments of your time, nothing to buy . . .

If an "inspector" calls, do not be convinced by a badge. Shut the door on him while you telephone the city office or utility he is supposed to represent. If he is genuine, he will not object to your precautions.

Don't accept the verbal promises of salesmen in or out of stores. See that any payment plan or installment contract offered for your signature *carries the same promises*. You have no redress if it does not.

Don't be hustled into signing documents. Read the fine print and if you do not understand it, don't sign. Some checking-up may be in order.

Never sign a document which has blank spaces on it. See that any details that have to be typed or written into a printed form are completed to your satisfaction before you sign.

Telephone or call at a Better Business Bureau when you suspect sharp practice.

If door-to-door solicitation is a trouble, advise your local authorities. In some areas, complaints from residents have resulted in the banning of all such callers who lack a license.

Beware the "fantastic bargain" advertising, and the salesman who tries to switch you from this particular offer. "It's not so much of a buy. Let me show you something better." He will—and the price will be a gyp.

Sometimes unsolicited items appear in the mail. You didn't order them, but the bills keep coming. The best way to deal with such merchandise is to return it to the Post Office, unopened, "Refused —Return to Sender" marked on it. (Repack opened packages.) Inform your Better Business Bureau and ignore the letters which may follow.

Children sometimes get involved in unwanted subscriptions or not-so-free offers when they send in coupons. But, since binding contracts cannot be signed by minors, the parents are under no obligation to pay for unsolicited items. Return, as above.

Americans are traditionally charitable, and their willingness to give lines the pockets of swindlers who sometimes even use the names of well-known persons on the letterheads of their "organization." Fund raisers have been known to absorb all but a tiny percentage of offerings running into millions. See that your giving is directed to worthy causes you know something about, probably through your place of worship, your community, your personal work as a volunteer, or because it is nationally known.

SALE TIME

Be on the alert when you go to sales. They can be your dollar-saving friends if you use them to full advantage—and don't let them take advantage of you. Watch for advertising, but go to the stores with a clear idea of actual requirements. At a sale, you are usually buying on a "no return" stipulation, so don't get carried away and buy a wrong size or unflattering color simply because it's cheap.

The smart mother of a family is wise to seasonal sales; she makes last year's spring outfits and hats do till after Easter when the clearance sales begin. Winter clothing is best bought after New Year, and the swim suits following the Fourth of July.

Apart from storewide seasonal clearance sales, the city and suburban buyer will find constant markdowns of quality clothing at high-class stores. National brands of clothing and all types of commodities will be advertised from time to time. You can secure good buys then. Much supposed bargain merchandise is specifically manufactured for "sales." Watch, therefore, for markdowns *from what you would have paid elsewhere or earlier*.

The secret of smart sales buying is to *note down what you really need* before you go to the store—and to keep to those requirements in whatever you buy. The hope that if-the-shirt-won't-fit-Dad-it-will-fit-Johnny or that the bargain rug will probably go all right with your color scheme is likely to steal dollars that could have better been spent on full-price goods. Your neighbor, or a thrift shop, may benefit from your too-hasty buying! You won't.

THRIFTY BUYS

You may be fortunate when you visit a thrift shop yourself. Those run by charitable organizations or commercially offer a perpetual sale. An excellent way to furnish a child's room or a rumpus room is to buy at such outlets and do a refinishing job at home. Too, many towns have "exchanges" where children's outgrown clothing is sold. You can take in your family's clothing, cleaned and in good order; if it is sold, you get the sale price less a percentage. You have the opportunity to buy other clothing in nice condition for your own family.

BUYING AT THE DISCOUNT STORE

Again, you can save if you are wary and demanding; if you know that *exactly the same article regularly sells elsewhere at a higher price.* A common policy at the discount store is to tempt you in with an advertised "loss leader." This bargain may be genuine, if you are not subjected to the "bait and switch" tactic described on page 55 (but note that other merchandise you may buy at the same time may possibly be substandard or available elsewhere at the same price).

Here is one gimmick, a variation on "bait and switch." Recently, a well-known discount store in the New York area advertised at an amazingly low price a blender said to be manufactured by a company known across the country. One woman hastening to the sale found a number of disgruntled buyers at the display. Reason: the blender was a substandard product practically guaranteed to fall apart at the first blending. Nearby, she noticed a display of better quality blenders at a much higher price.

While the store did not have a fast-talking salesman at hand to push the switch from the poor-quality advertised product, the effect was the same. The woman, too smart to buy herself, saw several people (not to be disappointed in their purchase of a blender) take a higher priced one to the check-out counter.

Discount stores, like others, vary. Only personal experience can pick out the most responsible. At some you can take away your purchase in factory-sealed cartons; the manufacturer, not the store, stands behind guarantee and service. You get a substantial price reduction on a costly appliance in return for "no credit" and the trouble of carrying away and installing your buy personally. (Today, some large discounters even offer credit.)

If you want some major appliance, decide on the brand, model, and year of the item and check around. You may find the discount store offers a genuine bargain—for cash; you may prefer to have a favorite department store stand behind the purchase, and to charge it; you may discover a local store's price compares well—and the owner offers you convenience, personal attention, and repair service during the guarantee period. The judgment—and the decision is yours—*just keep your head.*

THE TRADE-IN

While you may be well aware of the value of the trade-in when you buy a car, do not overlook smaller items that may be acceptable. Take, for instance, a typewriter. You may see a favorable price quoted at a large store where trade-ins are not acceptable. A reputable small dealer in your town may quote a slightly higher price, but he may allow you a sufficiently good margin on a trade-in to put you ahead—and you got rid of your old machine.

Check on this type of possibility with other equipment.

LET A RENTAL SAVE YOU MONEY

Many families will pay a great deal for certain types of equipment which will rest in attics, basements, and closets most of the year. Before you buy a rug shampooer or camping equipment for a family trip next summer, consider renting.

When the question of buying some expensive item comes up, the family should consider the number of times it is likely to be used and also how soon it is likely to become obsolete. If you can find a reliable renting source for what you want, your pocket may be considerably better off.

Check the yellow pages of your telephone book under *Rental Service* and inquire at your local hardware and department stores. Your friends may be able to name some good sources for rentals.

RANDOM SPENDING

In Chapter 1, we suggested keeping account of your spending for a period, at least. If you have carried out this project faithfully, you will be well aware of the amount of money that has been casually spent by members of the family—especially if teenagers are involved.

People buy readily at the five-and-ten, the newsdealers, and at drug, cosmetic, and toiletry counters. If money isn't doing a good job in your family, look to these loopholes.

PAY WHAT YOU OWE—AND NO MORE

If you are not careful when you pay cash or sign to have items or services charged, you may lose out. A watchful eye on the cash register when the supermarket purchases are being rung up can save dollars over the year. More particularly, see that sales slips for charges are correctly completed before you sign them.

Recently, Mrs. West, a suburban shopper, was asked to sign for her several charged purchases before the clerk had filled out the cost. Mrs. West refused to do so until the bill was completed. Checking it before she signed, she found a $5 error. This mistaken charge might have been overlooked when the final statement was paid, or if found would have been troublesome to straighten out with the computerized billing department.

Sometimes an unwary customer may be charged the regular price for an item instead of the advertised sales price. The clerk's error may well be unintentional; the loss is still the customer's.

SAVING THROUGH HOME ECONOMIES

When you use your household equipment and appliances properly and to full advantage, you are cutting costs. The devices give the service you require; you avoid repair bills. Be sure to follow manufacturers' instructions for use and care—and see that the members of the household understand them, too. Care is an important economy. Overloading breaks down the washing machine, the full dustbag prevents the vacuum cleaner from doing its job, the motor-driven device will fail through lack of oil. When saving money is important, you cannot afford to be careless in the little things which, neglected, can build into big repair jobs.

Do you keep fuel costs low by conserving heat? Fuel is a householder's major single expense, and in building or buying you surely will investigate a house's heating system (and air conditioning) thoroughly and see that the necessary insulation is installed. Perhaps, too, you attend to plastic calking and weather stripping to prevent leaks and drafts from cracks and spaces around doors and window frames. But do you watch the little things as well? See to it that the family closes doors and windows? Or do you leave the damper open in the unused fireplace and never close the entry to the unheated attic? Do members of the family use radiators for stacking magazines so that heat—and money—is lost? Everyone should co-operate to pull draperies and shades so that cold air is kept out; the thermostat setting should be lowered at night, and when the room where it is located is aired.

Adopt cost-cutting practices for air conditioning, too. Waste spells cost and you should inform yourself of the simple, everyday actions that will prevent loss.

CUTTING CLOTHING COSTS

Here is a routine to get the most out of clothing buys, especially with a growing family. Keep a box or drawer space for garment tags that recommend special cleaning methods, note which item each refers to so you can follow manufacturer's instructions when necessary; attend to stains and repairs without delay; hang—and air—clothes after wear, shoulders lined up with the hangers and fasteners closed; avoid overcrowding a closet rail; store only cleaned garments, and protect against moths; provide drawer or box space for woven garments that might drop if they were hung.

If the family can be trained to cooperate, clothes should not only survive longer but may be good for thrift shop sale when outgrown—a double saving.

A DO-IT-YOURSELF PROGRAM FOR THE FAMILY

Today, the time-pressured American pays for services and for things once made at home. He pays substantial sums annually for appliance repair, housepainting and plumbing jobs, and for garden care. But what if money-saving is an essential in your household? Can you and the family cut down on expense-making spare time activities, such as movie-going, the ball game, entertaining, or whatever goes in your household that consumes both time and money? The hours saved can be applied to projects that save money. (And if the children learn to find the work pleasurable, they will not feel "deprived.")

There is no lack of instruction available, in pocketbooks, monthly magazines, in the library, on specific subjects. If you don't know how to build cabinets, refinish furniture, repair chairs, remodel clothes, or raise your own fruits and vegetables, you can obtain "how-to-do-it" information easily and enjoy a new hobby while saving money. Check, too, on classes available in your neighborhood. If you send for the government price list mentioned on page 50, you will find available a number of useful booklets for the handy homeowner.

Comparing Costs

Plans to save money by "do-it-yourself" are valid only if you first compare costs. Is it really cheaper to bake, sew, or make, say, a bookcase? Only through estimating such factors as cost of materials, need for professional finish, your own competence, time, and working space can you learn which types of home jobs pay off in savings.

For example, day or weekend-old bakery goods on sale at a supermarket may be cheaper than baking and may save time for the mother of a large family. But making the draperies and slipcovers could prove a saving. A reasonably handy man or woman can fix leaky faucets and deal with a balky tank or drain. But better call the plumber for the frozen pipes.

FUN FOR FREE

Recreation is often costly to a family who have not explored the many opportunities their area offers for free or low-cost entertainment. City and suburban residents often overlook the many possibilities in their area, ranging from museums, some with special sections for children, to a parade or guided tours of great stores and buildings; in a port such as New York, a visit to liners or to a visiting aircraft carrier. (New Yorkers can contact the Navy Public Affairs Office, Third Naval District, 90 Church Street, New York, New York 10007 regarding fleet vessels.)

The homes of famous men and women are open to visitors. Seeing them, students gain a sense of the real past—not one pictured on a screen.

Across the country, visitors can drop in at the plants of great companies (*though advance notice is preferred*) and watch the production of many of those items familiar from store shelves and television commercials. Check the yellow pages of your telephone book and call up companies which make products of particular interest.

Local Chambers of Commerce and state information bureaus issue free brochures and you can always get initial information from a library. Take it from there—and cut down on commercial entertainment costs.

A LONG-TERM INVESTMENT FOR YOU

Saving—as a consumer—is a lifetime job for the millions of Americans who find personal financial gains constantly eroded by inflation and increasing family responsibilities. The old saying *Money saved is money earned* is worth remembering. If you invest on the stock market, you may receive dividends or lose your shirt. Cash gains will definitely come your way if you buy expensive items after you have compared values in the stores and after you have checked such publications as *Consumer Bulletin* and *Consumer Reports;* when you watch advertising for sales and information, but develop a block to impulse buying and the persuasion of Madison Avenue; when you know what you want and see that you get it at the best price possible.

It is not easy to observe discipline in buying and to develop immunity to advertising appeal. The average consumer wants to be persuaded—and it is a chore to build up a home reference library of buying tips and impartial consumer or government reports. But if you find it worth while to study for some business or profession, or to spend time on sports and hobbies, you will begin to work out a family dollar-saving plan based on your own buying needs.

A good point to remember is that while there are certain civic and governmental protections for the consumer, that person is still very much on his own. The alert man or woman who demands quality, questions price, and reports attempts at fraud is benefited financially and helps to improve consumer standards and knowledge at the same time.

Chapter 5

HOW TO INCREASE THE FAMILY INCOME

IDEAS FOR A SECOND INCOME   65
VITAL FACTORS TO KEEP IN MIND   67
YOUR PERSONAL ATTITUDE   68
PUTTING MONEY-MAKING IDEAS TO WORK   69
STEPS TO BE TAKEN   70
TAKING YOUR IDEA TO MARKET   71
SELLING BY MAIL   72
YOUR OBJECTIVE—PROFIT   72
A WORD OF WARNING   73
WORKING FOR OTHERS   74
OUTSIDE EMPLOYMENT   75
ESTABLISHING YOUR OWN BUSINESS   76
    Raising Capital   77

Is there a gap between your income and outgo? Do your future needs or special plans call for money you do not presently see in the budget? If so, how can you supplement the family income?

The purpose of this chapter is to suggest ideas to you, mainly for the type of work that can be done from or near home, and possibly may be developed into a personal business. That aspect is further discussed on page 76. Suggestions are also given on outside employment.

IDEAS FOR A SECOND INCOME

You may already have some hobby or interest you can expand into a money-earning project; your business training or mechanical ability might earn after hours; your home, garden, or special equipment offer possibilities. Whatever it is you do, the choice is personal, according to need and ability. There are as many opportunities as there are individuals; you may be one who can touch a commonplace idea with unique creativity and go on to make a substantial income. From small beginnings—*renting a room, commercializing a talent,* or *rendering a needed service in the community,* people have entered into apartment ownership, developed large mail-order businesses, and become presidents of their own companies.

If you are not immediately sure of the right idea, stimulate your thinking through reading up on profitable hobbies, and along the lines of your particular aptitudes, whether a facility in talking (an asset in *selling* or *lecturing*), or *mechanics,* or just plain *sewing* or *mending.*

Whole books are written on this subject, with full bibliographies to guide you to further reading, and into action. Your local library, with its informed staff, is invaluable to you. We shall also give some other sources of information, and as you follow up one, you will learn of others. If you are determined to increase income from home, you will surely find the right means.

In this chapter, we can do no more than suggest a very few of the ways people have used to earn from a sideline. Here are some of them:

Your Part-time Project	*Possible Markets*
Teaching your talent or skill to individuals or classes	Students in the home; leading an adult education class; joining others to form a school
Using your talent (singing, lecturing, entertaining, etc.) in the community	Restaurants, hotels, clubs, groups, churches, local radio and TV stations
Using your training, skill, or interests to render personal services	Repairs of all kinds in your home or where needed; mothers' or invalids' helper; running children's library; boarding plants or pets; walking dogs; shopping for shut-ins

Raising fruits, flowers, mushrooms, etc., keeping bees for honey	Direct; roadside stands; through local retailers; mail order
Raising and breeding animals, birds, fish; Raising for produce (as eggs, goats' milk for invalids), fur, etc.	Direct; through classified advertising; pet stores; mail order
Cooking, candy-making, kitchen products of all types	Direct, mail order, retailers. Catering services to individuals, groups, offices, for parties
Products, crafts items, jewelry, woodwork	Direct, mail order, retailers

VITAL FACTORS TO KEEP IN MIND

Your object is *to increase the family income*—not just to cover the expenses of some time-consuming project—and certainly not to lose money.

Ask yourself the following questions and give much thought to the answers:

Who needs talent, product, service, or accommodation? To earn, you must offer something others want, or will want, and this may mean tailoring your personal wishes to please a demand.

How can my offer be marketed? By what means will you bring your idea to the attention of the potential market? Here, you start to reckon *cost.*

How does location affect my plan? Ideas good in one area court failure in others. Take this factor into full consideration; but because no one offers such an idea in your area may be the very reason that you should. Watch that fine line between venturing where others dare not—and finding a gold mine; and undertaking a project where no market exists.

How much will I make? Right from the planning stage set the costs of running your enterprise against what you expect to make. *Profit*—and that is what you want—is only the *excess over expenses,* a point too many home-enterprisers forget. Full discussion follows on page 72.

Have I the time needed? Probably, if you are retired, semi-incapacitated, or young and unmarried. The person with a full-time job and the mother with small children must consider if their proposed idea can be scheduled in spare time or if it would prove a burden on health and temper. It is true, too, that otherwise busy people can find time when they are determined to achieve an objective. Many will sacrifice leisure pursuits. But, because "second-job" people may feel strain, their new activity should be pleasurable.

What obstacles do I face? Think these through and list them. Competition is certainly one. You may have to come up with a superior product or service, or cut your profit, even to get a toe in the field. A new slant would help—or maybe you should try a less crowded enterprise. Consider, too, all personal factors, such as lack of cooperation in the home, and if more capital than you have would be required. (In general, the person eager to make extra money is limited to starting in a small way, which is not necessarily an obstacle but rather an opportunity to test market possibilities.)

YOUR PERSONAL ATTITUDE

Only you can decide what you can offer, and *your own attitude may be far more important than actual skill.* Project a modest talent with confidence and enthusiasm; undertake a service with willingness to meet the needs of others, and you open a door to success. Leave a greater ability undeveloped, or a highly original idea unproclaimed; you earn neither dollars nor kudos and confer benefit on no one.

People who have felt short on talent and personal skills have successfully capitalized material assets. Some have *rented rooms* in the home *as offices* for doctors, lawyers, authors, and real estate or insurance agents; some have looked over *junk in the attic* and seen the nucleus of an *antique store;* more than one person has transformed a *collection of old recipes* into a *highly salable cookbook.*

PUTTING MONEY-MAKING IDEAS TO WORK

Here are three real-life examples. A childless housewife, a widow with young children, an elderly man successfully earn through such diverse means as running a *typing service,* operating as *a caterer,* and selling both *commercial* and *fine art.*

Rose Shapiro, whose salesman husband had an uncertain income, decided to operate a *typing service* from their apartment in an outlying suburb of New York City. She culled the names of professional people, small firms, one-man businesses, etc., from the telephone directory and mailed out announcements. She also advertised in local newspapers. At first, she handled the work herself. Now, with a group of women working for her in their own homes, she has, in effect, placed a typing pool at the disposal of her clients. She serves a wide area in the county and her main job is to drive around making pickups and deliveries. Mrs. Shapiro uncovered her profitable market with a modest investment in advertising.

Linda Tracy, a widow left with young children to bring up, recognized a potential market in a well-to-do community where people entertained a great deal. She would offer a catering service for parties, weddings, and gala occasions. Like Rose Shapiro, she began by mailing announcements to potential customers and by advertising in the local paper. Soon, word spread about her skill in cooking and her pleasant and efficient service. Out of her home kitchen, Mrs. Tracy built up a highly successful small business, now with its own premises and mobile staff of assistants.

Albert Helwig, who retired after years in an advertising agency art department, found he and his wife needed a supplement to their present income. So, from his home in a city suburb, he developed a number of greeting card designs which he took or mailed to companies which bought from free-lancers; he canvassed small firms in the area for advertising art jobs; he increased his "fine arts" output to sell more at local art exhibitions and from displays at a restaurant; he sought assignments to paint pictures of people's homes and landscapes from their favorite photographs.

STEPS TO BE TAKEN

None of these people began with heavy financial outlay. The two women made their initial lists of possible customers by checking social and business news in local papers and by browsing through telephone directories. Mr. Helwig checked in stores for the type of cards various companies bought and wrote to the Greeting Card Association for lists of those which bought from free-lancers.

How did Mr. Helwig know about this association where he could obtain market information? He talked to a local greeting card store owner. He could also have found the address through a telephone directory, or through a magazine, such as *The Writer,* which lists markets for greeting card verse.

Initiative is your great asset in launching any home enterprise and, like these people, you have to dig for information and your customers. Both may turn up through unexpected channels.

Look for publications covering your interest: *hobbycraft, animal raising, woodworking,* etc. In most reference libraries you can check *The Readers' Guide to Periodical Literature* and *N. W. Ayer & Son's Directory of Newspapers and Periodicals.* Because you should have up-to-date information on your project, be sure to check this source for titles of publications.

Talking to people will put you in touch with information, ideas, and criticism. You will have to distinguish between the pessimistic types who see insurmountable obstacles in every setback, and those who can alert you to factors you may not have taken into consideration. See that your advisor is qualified. Your local Chamber of Commerce will prove helpful. *It is, of course, essential to see your city, town, or village authorities.* Not only can they give you valuable general information, but they will tell you how zoning and other regulations affect your plans. Before plunging into an enterprise, you certainly need to check on the law. For example, control over the preparation of food is exercised not only locally, but by the Federal government through the Food and Drug Administration.

TAKING YOUR IDEA TO MARKET

We have seen how three people went about marketing their diverse wares. What other means are there to *market a skill, service, or product?*

Locally, there is always the *telephone* which is sometimes used to initiate an approach, sometimes to follow up on a mailed announcement. Your area may have a *customer's market type of publication,* made up entirely of classified advertising, through which you can reach the public. Inquire at your newsdealer. You may be able to *post notices* on company, organization, or church bulletin boards, or in stores. If your community has no regulations against *house-to-house selling* you can use this approach.

If you have items for sale, such as *jewelry, fine sewing, workshop products,* or *kitchen products,* ask local stores to buy from you. Some may purchase outright; others will suggest a consignment basis; that is, you share a portion of the price with the seller, or take unsold goods back.

Women should seek out the address of their nearest "Women's Exchange." (Try the phone book or the Chamber of Commerce.) The exchanges customarily sell "on consignment." In New York State, the Department of Commerce runs a Woman's Program. Information and assistance is available on all aspects of selling a product or service, or in starting a shop. Find out if your state now has such a program.

The Small Business Administration, a branch of the Federal government, has offices in main cities of each state. Write the one nearest you, or to Washington, D.C., asking for titles and prices of their booklets and guides (many are free). You can get information on licenses and regulations, financing, management, record keeping, pricing, selling, advertising, and other aspects of part-time and small business.

SELLING BY MAIL

Selling goods, services, and information by mail is "big business," but there is room for you, if you are willing to pay for advertising. If you have fine homemade wares for sale in quantity, space in a national homemaking magazine may be worth the investment, especially at the Christmas season. Most people will start with local newspaper advertising and, with suitable enterprises, expand to nearby radio and television stations. Frequently, they can also enjoy the publicity of a news story.

Often the lone individual will sell through a mail order house which will catalogue novelty and other items and sell by "direct mail" (approaching potential customers through the mails with advertising), or "mail order" (advertising in the press). If your product or service justifies it, you can enter the direct mail field yourself by buying lists of names from brokers.

Read up on all phases of marketing before venturing deep. There are books on retailing, direct mail, and mail order. Here again, the Small Business Administration can provide booklets and advice.

If you are barred from running a mail order business from your apartment or house because of the terms of the lease or local zoning regulations, the use of a Post Office box number may overcome the difficulty.

YOUR OBJECTIVE—PROFIT

Whatever your venture—*repairing toys, television,* or *watches; raising animals* or *produce; remodeling furniture,* or *running a telephone answering* or *party helper service*—you are in it *to make a profit,* so do not lose sight of this objective because you like your sideline work. However, you should enjoy whatever you undertake, particularly when you run it as a sideline. Pleasure in the work for itself is a guard against depression when the start is slow, business lags, or you run into personal and outside difficulties. Nevertheless, enthusiasm—that invaluable asset—should not blind you to the question: *Am I making money?*

From the start, maintain accurate records that will prove the point. Set down whatever costs are involved—for materials, for improving facilities, for expert advice. You will need these records for your tax return (see Chapter 15); you need them to be your own cost accountant.

Say the materials you buy for some craft item cost you fifty cents, and you sell for one dollar. Profit—fifty cents? Not if you have mailing or advertising costs; have spent time and money on the telephone; used extra light and power; certainly not if you could have used your time to earn outside through employment.

When you have fully considered your own *costs,* you should add a fair hourly or daily rate for your *time.* You should check the price of similar products and services. Will people pay a little extra for yours? Yes, if it is unusual, particularly skillfully made, offered with special personal service, or exceptional in your area. No, if it is commonplace, "homemade," in the worst sense, or something that can be better handled by big business.

With time, experience, and increased volume, you may be able to cut costs and so increase profit on an item or service which rendered small profit in the first place. *Investigate pricing thoroughly* before you start, trying to steer between "cheapness," which devalues your product or service, and a figure no one will pay. (Ask if you would pay it yourself!)

The publications you read may guide you to business associations and councils which give advice on pricing. For instance, a craftsman may inquire of The American Craftsmen's Educational Council, Inc., at 29 West 53rd Street, New York, New York, which will give much helpful information. Check, too, on advertising of products, services, and manufactured items for general guidance on current prices.

A WORD OF WARNING

Before we discuss working for others, a word of caution should be added on fraudulent business opportunities. If you want to earn extra money, yet are undecided on the means, you may be scanning the advertisement columns for ideas. You read of some attractive goods or device that will earn you substantial sums.

A reply to your inquiry may bring an avalanche of mail or a salesman to your doorstep. You could be asked to invest in some equipment through which you can earn at home; you might be told you need only "refer" some offer to your friends; or a certain franchise will make your fortune. Too, you may learn of certain courses which will teach you to make an income as a writer, artist, or what-not. How do you distinguish genuine business or teaching offers from out-and-out frauds?

Observe certain rules: proceed slowly, refusing to be pressured into action; investigate thoroughly—if necessary seeking the advice of your Better Business Bureau or a lawyer; and, most important of all, *sign nothing,* until inquiries are complete. You may be told of some free offer you will miss by delay, but that "miss" may be well to your advantage. The outfit wants your money; it isn't out to help you earn any.

Genuine correspondence schools rarely *guarantee* sales to their students. Beware of the school that does. Also of the "publisher" who will make your book a best seller if you will only pay the costs. Often he is a printer; certainly he will not have the usual channels of distribution. (If you really do have a best seller, you can be sure a top-notch publisher will pay you for it.)

WORKING FOR OTHERS

From home, you can make money by working part-time for others. Watch classified advertisements (or place your own) to uncover local opportunities for selling insurance, or encyclopedias, or cosmetics. There are party plans for selling kitchenware, gifts, and cosmetics. Women often enjoy this mode of selling. A good way to enter is through the recommendation of a friend in similar work. You learn, firsthand, about the company, and you get tips on handling your first assignments.

People who work during the day can moonlight as collection agents for delinquent accounts, doing bookkeeping for small businesses, or selling by telephone. The telephone can be the means of earning in innumerable ways; in your own business as, for instance, in setting up an answering service, and in working for others in selling or in research.

Research offers opportunities to the woman who cannot commit herself to long-term employment. Market research firms (listed in the yellow pages of the telephone directory) customarily employ free-lancers who work for one day or for several, sometimes for longer periods, gathering information which is used by advertising agencies, manufacturing companies, publishers, and others. The job calls for tact, patience, and legwork and involves interviewing people, often housewives. Some researchers have connections with several survey firms, others work for only one or two. Temporary office work is also available to analyze the results of surveys.

Both men and women interested in this type of work should check classified advertising under Market Research.

OUTSIDE EMPLOYMENT

A dependable source of additional income is available to any member of the family willing to take a job in office, store, or plant. Classified employment advertisements cover every type of opportunity; some open to teenagers working part-time, some to retired people. For the most part, the wife and mother is the person who undertakes to be the second wage or salary earner in the family.

Getting a job involves these steps: 1. Assessing ability. 2. Possibly taking classes in learning new or improving old skills. 3. Checking classified advertising and/or visiting an employment agency. 4. Sending out letters or telephoning for an interview.

If you are new to business or out of touch with today's requirements, turn to your public library. The librarian will direct you to books on part-time jobs, submitting résumés, and, for the housewife, on successfully managing both home and employment.

If local classified advertising does not offer a suitable opportunity, you can do more than advertise in the "Employment Wanted" column. You can write to firms in your vicinity inquiring about upcoming vacancies. State your skills and say whether you want full, temporary, or part-time employment.

If direct efforts fail, both part-time and temporary employment are obtainable through agencies. Some specialize in such opportunities. An agency is entitled to a fee, often one week's salary, but the fee will vary according to the type of job offered. Sometimes, even for temporary jobs, the prospective employer will pay the fee.

When dealing with an agency, check the financial arrangements at the start. Usually, the fees are posted in the office, and in most states they are regulated by law. An agency that does not give a satisfactory answer about charges is best avoided.

ESTABLISHING YOUR OWN BUSINESS

Your own business may develop as the expansion of a part-time home enterprise, or from the desire to be independent of an employer. You may have a new product to market, a new service to render, or you may want to take over a going concern.

Whatever your reason for wanting to start your own store, shop, plant, or other business, make sure that you are first well acquainted with the type of responsibility you are acquiring. While much of the information we give for the part-time enterpriser applies to you, you will want to delve deeper. For example, in addition to the printed information supplied by the Small Business Administration office nearest you (see page 71), you may wish to join one of their workshops where the specific problems of the business owner are thoroughly analyzed.

Acquaint yourself with the law regarding the sole proprietorship of a small business. You are personally responsible for all business losses and liabilities (including those incurred by your employees); this means that your property, savings, and monies from other sources may be reached by your creditors for settlement of business debts. You must consider, too, that your illness or death might end operations. Would your family be protected financially? Check, also, on the change in your Social Security status.

In a partnership, where you and one or more partners contribute skills or capital, all share losses and profits, both of which are reported on personal income tax returns. Advantages and disadvantages of a partnership are similar to those of a sole proprietorship. In addition, however, business debts incurred by partners endanger your personal assets unless you insure against the eventuality.

You can organize a corporation and so protect your personal assets, but such a venture is more complicated and costly. Thoroughly explore all the aspects of establishing a business through inquiries, reading, and in consultation with a lawyer or certified public accountant before you take any irrevocable steps.

You may, of course, invest in a franchise, *after the most thorough investigation;* your lawyer's advice is essential. You can start your exploration by picking up a free booklet from the Small Business Administration. When you operate under a franchise you gain the advantage of a "company name," its advertising, and services. You will still have to carry many of the responsibilities of a proprietor, such as providing capital and real estate.

RAISING CAPITAL

We will assume you have a certain amount of capital and a sound project. To raise additional funds, see your local banker first; probably he knows you and if your reputation in the community is good, he will give you a favorable hearing.

But you shop for money as for other commodities and you want the most favorable rates. A large bank outside the community may have a department that specializes in loans to the small businessman.

The Small Business Administration, an agency of the Federal government, may provide you with a direct or immediate participation loan if you can satisfy their office that you have an eligible enterprise. You must first endeavor to raise money privately. Send first to the SBA for their guides on sources of capital. Their free and low-priced publications are invaluable to the small business man or woman seeking advice on management and financing.

If you approach some private company for a loan, you may find some offering reasonably priced credit, others which are undoubtedly "loan sharks." Do not enter into any contract without legal advice.

If you are a veteran—or the unmarried widow of one—inquire of the Veterans Administration if you can qualify for a direct loan, or can obtain a private "GI loan," as is usual.

See, too, the section of Chapter 6 dealing with borrowing. Books specifically written about the establishment of small businesses are available and will guide you with complete details on sources of capital.

Your best friend, however, is your own good standing and ability to raise money from personal sources. But if friends and business connections become your backers, you will still need the services of a lawyer to ensure that proper agreements are drawn up.

Chapter 6

BUY NOW—AND BE READY TO
PAY LATER

YOUR CREDIT RATING	80
YOUR CHARGE ACCOUNT CREDIT AT DEPARTMENT STORES	81
CENTRAL CHARGE PLAN	83
THE REAL COST TO YOU	83
CREDIT CARDS	84
Loss of Credit Cards	85
Insurance	85
INSTALLMENT BUYING	85
The Installment Contract	86
Signing an Installment Contract	87
YOU NEED A LOAN	88
Credit Ratings and Loans	89
Insurance Loans	90
Comaker or Cosigner Loans	90
Insurance of Loans	91
LOANS AT THE SIGN OF THE GOLDEN BALLS	91
BANKS	92
USING STOCKS AND BONDS AS COLLATERAL	93
BANK CREDIT PLANS	94
CREDIT UNIONS	95
THE SAVINGS BANK	96
SMALL LOAN COMPANIES	97
THE LOAN SHARK	97
CREDIT COSTS AND TRUE RATE OF INTEREST	98
Types of Loans and Ways of Stating Interest	99
Table of True Annual Interest	103

Today, it is the rare person who does not use credit in some form or another. People who say they always pay cash almost certainly use credit for their utilities and to pay their doctors and dentists. Credit for the consumer, a pleasant-sounding term for a state of debt, is so readily available now it can be ruin or boon depending on how it is used.

As long as you recognize that credit represents a debt you have to pay, and you are prepared through your financial planning to pay within the stated time, you can enjoy immediate possession of department store goods, plane tickets, gasoline in your car, and countless things and services merely by showing a card and signing a bill.

Credit, of course, represents trouble if you lose sight of your obligation to pay. With so many desirable material goods available, people from all walks of life are tempted to buy now and worry later —and they do. Families in suburban communities with more than average incomes are as vulnerable to serious debt involvement as the immigrant city dwellers who have signed up for time payments they are unable to meet.

YOUR CREDIT RATING

Your standing as a good credit risk is a major asset, and you protect it by the prompt payment of your bills. You can build up your standing over the years and take it with you across the country. From coast to coast, credit bureaus pass along information and confirm— or deny—your ability to meet your obligations.

Once your credit is established as good, there will be less investigation when you apply for new types of credit. At the outset, the department store, the bank, or finance company will require you to fill out a form and to satisfy an interviewer as to your character, your financial resources, and your capacity to pay. You will be called upon to give the name of employers, past and present, to state your salary and other income, and to give details about home mortgages or rent.

See to it that your answers to questions will stand investigation. If you fail to give full or truthful information, you will damage your credit record—and that is a fatal step in financial mismanagement.

YOUR CHARGE ACCOUNT CREDIT AT DEPARTMENT STORES

There are several types of charge accounts of which the most usual is the *Open or Regular Account*. You buy from stores in person, by mail, or by telephone without down payment or service charge. But the statement which you receive is invariably marked "Payable within 10 days of receipt of statement." In practice, this works out as a 30-day period, and some stores will—protestingly—carry unpaid balances forward for several months for the customer with a good credit rating. Ultimately, of course, they will threaten to sue—and you should certainly settle the account in a hurry to avoid such proceedings. In the meantime, you are likely to have been labeled a poor risk at the central credit bureau.

Other stores will impose a service charge on the past-due balance, but this would depend upon the type of contract you signed in the first place. If you and your family find it hard to settle regular charge accounts in 30 days, you can open a service charge type of account.

Titles of accounts vary from store to store and it is not always possible to say which title fits which method. Some retailers combine different forms of payment into their installment contract. For example, one national company's *Revolving Charge Account* contract permits the customer three choices. He may pay within 30 days, no penalty, or, if he fails to so pay, he automatically becomes liable for a 1½ percent charge on his outstanding balance. He then remits whatever installment payment is due according to a set schedule. That is, if he owes $50, he may have to pay $10 a month, but if he runs his account to $200, he pays $20. He can also pay in advance.

Another form often described as the *Revolving Credit Account* works this way: The customer agrees with the store credit department on an amount to be paid monthly. The store then sets a limit on what he is allowed to buy, so that the amount outstanding will not exceed the original set level. This type of account is helpful to those who are too easily carried away by the array of merchandise in the store and the magic-wand effect of the words *"Charge it!"* Debts above the agreed amount must be paid *immediately*.

The *Retail Installment Credit* agreement of a famous coast-to-coast store operates as a Regular Charge when the bill is paid before the next statement date. Otherwise, the customer has to pay a service charge of 1½ percent per month and at least ⅛ of his current balance. Ten dollars is the minimum monthly payment.

The *Flexible Charge Account* of one New York City store operates as a Regular Account or as an approved limit type of account. The customer pays according to schedule. Here, if he owes $50, he pays $10; if he owes $200, he pays $40.

The *Optional Account* of a well-known Western store also can be used as a Regular Account, or the customer pays according to the current extent of his debt. When his balance is $50, he pays $5; when he owes $200, he pays $10. He, of course, pays the 1½ percent per month charge.

This charge is usual in the retail business on bills to $500. Over that amount, it is reduced to 1 percent a month. Note that 1½ percent a month is 18 percent a year, a fact many people tend to overlook.

One difficulty that arises in these multiple-type agreements is that the customer who mailed his check to settle on the regular 30-day basis may get a bill with a 1½ percent service charge. Reason: his payment did not reach the company's accounting department before the next billing period. If this happens to you, write the store at once. Otherwise, your further purchases will only extend the amount of the service charge debt you do *not* owe.

Note that this kind of interest billing is *actually built into some Revolving Charge Account agreements*. The customer's partial payments are *not* deducted when interest is computed.

Many companies as well as department stores set up "Easy Payment Plans," which do not have the optional regular account feature. The customer pays a presettled amount each month until the specific merchandise is paid for. The time periods of installment contracts (also see page 86) will vary and the "carrying charges" also. You must also keep well in mind the percentage you would actually be paying. Your pocket might be better served if you get a loan (see page 88 to 98) in order to buy the goods outright.

CENTRAL CHARGE PLAN

In many areas a *Central Charge Account* plan is in operation. Participating merchants send details of bills to a bank in the vicinity which acts as a clearing house. It collates all the different bills one customer owes into a monthly statement. The customer either pays in full or in agreed-upon monthly installments for ten months, plus service charges. Check on what those charges will be.

THE REAL COST TO YOU

Charge accounts and installment buying are a convenience—for which you pay, not only in service charges, which are stated, but in hidden costs. Pricing takes into account the cost of operating the regular accounts, and the cash customer pays that price, too. When you deal with the established department store you have certain privileges, such as returning goods without question, first announcements of special sales, and the general happy status of a charge customer. You get lower prices and less service at other types of stores. (See Chapter 4.) In general, running a department store Regular Account which you pay when due is worthwhile. It helps to establish credit status and offers many conveniences. When you start to incur interest charges, stop to think if they are really necessary. Perhaps you only need to work out your problems with the aid of the forms in Chapter 1, spreading savings ahead to enable you to meet bills promptly. Think about it—and that true interest rate of 18 percent a year. What you save by paying promptly could add up to a useful sum in an education or vacation fund.

CREDIT CARDS

The credit card is designed as a tempter. In the store you will charge merchandise you might have done without if cash were demanded; in the restaurant you think "why not?" and order a particularly expensive meal. After all, payment will not be due until next month.

The person concerned about the good management of his finances will treat his numerous cards as the convenience they are—and keep some account of how much he is charging, where, and when. If his wife does the same, the couple know how much will be needed to cover the inevitable billing. Those whose bills are running too high should preset their credit card buying at a specific level each month.

If you do not know just how and when you are going to pay for the merchandise, services, entertainment, or travel charged, you should get yourself on a strictly cash basis until you can bring better order into your financial affairs.

Some invitations to use credit are, in effect, invitations to take a loan at a high interest rate. Do you need this type of advance? Some people enjoy the apparent status of card flashing and easy credit. The purveyors of cards cater to that weakness. Since discipline and control are part of your money management program you can afford to pass up "status" for security.

Nevertheless, the "I always pay cash" man is at a disadvantage. He has failed to establish his credit, and when the time comes for him to take out a loan he does not have the necessary background. The thoroughly honest, prompt-pay man is as disadvantaged as his constantly indebted neighbor who is tagged as a poor credit risk.

Plainly, the smart money manager uses credit cards instead of paying cash. *But he does so knowing that he could have paid cash if he so wished;* and he does not charge items or services he would not otherwise have bought.

We do not list all types of credit cards; they are too numerous to mention, besides being well known through advertising. Billing is either through a specific company, as when you charge at a department store or buy gasoline, or may be consolidated, as when you use one type of card for services or purchases of a widely varied nature.

Some organizations issuing credit cards do so on payment of an annual fee; they will add a service charge on delinquent accounts. Your need for such services in the course of your business or social life will dictate whether or not you apply for membership. If and when you do so, weigh the specific charges made by the particular organization or club against your expected benefit from the services offered.

Bank plans are discussed on page 94.

LOSS OF CREDIT CARDS

What if you lose credit cards? Since they are as good as cash, you might consider insuring against this eventuality, particularly if you are apt to lose things. But you do not have to be "loss prone" to lose credit cards by theft, and many go when a wallet or pocketbook is taken. Your credit cards may then go on a spending spree unless and until you notify the issuing companies. (See Chapter 2, page 30.) You are required to report loss *immediately in writing* to protect yourself against misuse, but for speed also use telephone or telegram.

INSURANCE

Credit card coverage may be bought separately or, in some cases, added to personal policies such as homeowners or casualty policies. You may at the same time acquire other benefits, such as insurance against loss on altered checks, but you may also have to prove that you handled your cards with due care and immediately reported loss. Inquire about company rates and requirements, which vary widely.

INSTALLMENT BUYING

One of the most important points about your savings program is that it enables you to pay cash for the goods you want instead of paying someone else additional money for a loan or time plan. This is where your planned goals serve you. You decide that next year you will have a new car, or a refrigerator-freezer. You could go out and obtain the desired goods now at the cost of installment payments, or you could save the money at approximately 5 percent interest per annum until you had the purchase price. Here, you would have to weigh your actual need of the item—essential now or desirable sometime; the pace at which you can save (your work on Chapter 1 provides an answer here), the interest rate at the savings bank weighed against installment charges—and the possibility of a rise in price. You should be aware of the economic factors currently obtaining so that if, say, the price of certain appliances is rising, a good installment contract is worth more than saving against a rising tide of costs. See Chapter 4 and keep informed on consumer trends in making your decision.

THE INSTALLMENT CONTRACT

We give some warnings about installment contracts here and in Chapter 4 in order to alert readers to the possibility of fraud and of becoming involved in deliberately inflated but legal commitments.

We hope, of course, that you will be doing business with ethical establishments. But even when you are so doing, you still have to be alert and to bear in mind such points as:

Your ability to make a substantial down payment. A large initial payment will reduce the spread of payments and the charges you would be paying. If you do not have the means to make that large down payment, should you be undertaking the installment payments?

What will your other commitments be during the period you would be paying on time? Have you left yourself a cash margin for emergency? Certainly it is not possible to safeguard against all eventualities, but it is the too heavy load assumed for too long a period that drives many families to seek Family Service advice.

The repayment period. Interest charges mount up during the spread-out paying period. Such advertising as "Easy terms! No down payment, three years to pay" may involve you in a prolonged and inflated debt. Choose to pay as quickly as you can. The shorter the period of repayment the lower the overall cost.

SIGNING AN INSTALLMENT CONTRACT

Whether a contract is offered to you by a ready-money lender, or by a store where you wish to buy "on time," or by a door-to-door salesman, you should know that this person or his company is likely to sell the installment contract to a third party.

That third party may be a bank or a sales finance company and the matter may well be in order. You pay on time; no trouble, no comeback. But when you do not pay, *the buyer of the contract has the legal rights set out on that contract*—he may repossess the property, take over your security, have your wages garnisheed, or take you to court. You have signed; you are definitely committed to whatever terms you so accepted. It behooves you, therefore, *to know what you are signing for, to know what will happen if you fail in payment.*

Since your legal commitment will be *what the contract says* and *not* what the salesman or lender says (unless those statements are written into the contract), your first step is to read the fine print of the contract before you sign it and to see that full information is given. Examine these points:

Does the contract spell out in detail what you are buying? The price of the merchandise or the amount of cash lent? What your allowance is from trade-in (see page 58) or the sum of the down payment? The total of your debt and how payments have been divided? The number of your installments and when they occur? Importantly, what are the credit charges?

What happens if you cannot pay? Are the goods repossessed? If so, are there terms under which you can redeem them? What are the details on nonpayment penalties? Note repossession of the goods may not relieve you of commitment to pay.

Can your pay be attached if you fail to meet installments? Does the contract include an assignment of part of your wages?

Has the salesman or lender filled out all the spaces in your contract? Sign nothing till blanks are satisfactorily completed or you may become liable for charges or goods you did not consent to accept.

To whom are you to make your payments? You may suppose your contract to be with a certain store or dealer when, in fact, you will be dealing with the bank, finance corporation, or central organization who has bought up the contract or acts for your merchant or lender.

Will the monthly payments completely cover your indebtedness for the goods or loan, and interest? If not, you might find a lump-sum balance still has to be paid, and without delay. This type of provision is being eliminated by merchants and lenders of good standing, but may still occur and prove a trap for the unwary and ill-prepared customer. Check for it.

Credit laws vary considerably from state to state. Inquire if your state's Banking Department issues information for the consumer. The position in New York is defined in the booklet "Know Your Rights *when you buy on time*," obtainable from the New York State Banking Department, 100 Church Street, New York, New York 10007.

When you have signed your contract, make sure you have a copy and that you keep it safely for reference.

Changes designed to protect the consumer are taking place in both federal and state laws. Be alert for these developments and see that you receive all the protection the law affords in your credit dealings.

YOU NEED A LOAN

Don't buy at the first stall is still good advice when you want *to buy the use* of someone else's money to meet an emergency; to purchase a house, a business, a car; to finance education, or to replace a pile of small bills by one large one.

If you are not presently wanting to buy—i.e., borrow—money, don't think this section isn't for you. Sometimes money is needed in a great hurry and if you are reasonably well informed on lending establishments and their terms, you can hasten to the one most likely to meet your need.

The uninformed, worried, and hurried borrower is the most likely person to buy himself more financial trouble in the shape of an unnecessarily expensive loan. In his fear, he may even fall into the hands of a "loan shark."

First, we will examine the preferred attributes of the borrower, then the types of lending institutions and their practices.

CREDIT RATINGS AND LOANS

Your personal credit status is what enables you to borrow at the most reliable establishments at the most favorable rates. A person whose credit record is blotted by slow payments or nonpayments knows he is unlikely to get a favorable reception at the personal loan department of the neighborhood bank.

What people do not always realize are the other factors which weigh for or against them. You are rated on such factors as:

Your job and how long you have held it

Your home-ownership, or standing as a tenant; your neighborhood

Your marital status and the number of your dependents

Your present (and possibly your future) financial obligations

The usual state of your bank balance

Your reasons for seeking the loan

The ubiquitous credit cards may give you the feeling that you have unlimited credit, but you will find that a prospective lender will analyze you, your current situation, and your prospects before he agrees to lend you money. Expect to be questioned by a reputable lender. A loan too easily extended may well mean that you are about to be bound by excessive interest charges. Protect yourself by enhancing your credit rating and by shopping around before you buy a loan.

However, a reliable and well-intentioned borrower through no fault of his own may not find it possible to "buy" at the most reasonable source. He may be young, only shortly settled in a job, and unsettled in his living quarters. He may have paid cash too long; he might be a new arrival in this country. Though he may have to borrow from a small loan company, he can choose a reputable one (see page 97) and begin a good credit rating by fulfilling his obligations promptly.

INSURANCE LOANS

Life insurance policies differ as fund-raising vehicles; the type of policy you own may make a ready loan available to you. Read up on your policy; cash value and loan rate will be stated.

If you want the money briefly, this can be a quick, low-rate, true interest method of obtaining money. Write your company, giving your policy number, and state how much you want. (You can borrow most of the cash value.) Usually, a check will be sent within a few days, no questions asked, and you can repay on a system convenient to you. There are no extras on an insurance loan. At, say, 6 percent, you may appear to have a bargain.

But—of course, there is a BUT—you reduce your family's protection against your death by the amount of the loan and the interest charges. The very lack of pressure to repay an insurance loan is not in its favor on a long-term basis. By constantly postponing full discharge of the loan, you shoulder the burdens of a running debt and heighten the risk of being underinsured. You also lack that cushion of financial assurance your insurance policies offer should you have to meet an even greater emergency.

Insurance companies do not encourage loans on policies and if you require an extended and sizable loan, you would protect yourself better by offering the insurance policy as collateral for a bank loan.

COMAKER OR COSIGNER LOANS

If you, through no fault of your own, do not have an established credit rating, raising a loan may be difficult. Here, your resource may be a person who has the required financial standing. If you can find such a friend or relative to *cosign* a note at bank or finance company, you get your loan. Your *comaker,* who personally believes in your integrity and ability to repay, has taken equal responsibility for settling with the lender if you should fail to do so.

INSURANCE OF LOANS

With many types of loans you automatically acquire life insurance —for which you may or may not pay directly, according to your source. The life insurance buys protection for the lender against your death and consequent inability to pay the debt. It may sometimes appear that you are getting a particularly good deal—a competitive rate of interest plus insurance. A closer look at the terms of the contract may prove otherwise. You and your family would derive no personal benefit from the insurance—except for the coverage of the debt in case of death, and taking full cost into consideration, the overall contract is no bargain.

You may be offered "free insurance," which is part of the deal, but the cost may be built into the interest charge you will pay. Sometimes, in addition, you will be offered the benefits of accident and health insurance for "pennies a day." Should you protect your responsibility for the loan to this additional degree? Before doing so, check on whatever coverage you already have in case of accident or disability and what the general state of your finances would be in such an eventuality. If your loan is heavy and your overall situation would be weak in case of health breakdown, the insurance may be well worth while.

LOANS AT THE SIGN OF THE GOLDEN BALLS

The sign of the three golden balls, hanging over dingy stores on back streets and in run-down neighborhoods, has denoted the local pawnbroker to generations of borrowers throughout the western world.

In twentieth-century America, the dusty little shop has, in many places, blossomed into handsome establishments run by corporations. The principle of lending remains the same. The customer takes his security, in the form of jewelry, furs, a camera, a musical instrument, etc., to the pawnbroker; in return, he receives a loan and a receipt. If he is unable to pay back the loan, plus interest, he will never return to redeem his pledge. In time, the article will be sold and the pawnbroker gets his money back.

We hope that you will never need the pawnbroker, but if you ever use such services, seek out the reputable man who allows you to seal your pledge of jewelry in a bag or to write the serial number of equipment on your receipt. When you make a pledge of this kind, you have to guard against substitutions by a dishonest employee.

Interest rates vary, perhaps as low as 2 percent a month—or they may be five times higher, but they end with the month in which the customer repays his debt.

"No questions" is the rule at the pawnbroker's and, for the short-term need for ready cash, the establishment still has a place in the complex society of today.

BANKS

Once chiefly interested in lending money for business purposes, the commercial bank today is a prime source of personal loans, generally given at advantageous rates. In general, when you need a loan, you should approach a bank first to check on its terms and your eligibility. Depending on your area and requirements, the interest rates will vary, but you will get the more favorable terms when you put up collateral, such as stocks, bonds, insurance policies, a savings bank passbook, or execute a chattel mortgage on your car. (Passbook loans on your savings account are discussed at page 96.)

You do well to deal with your bank for loans. When you meet their repayment terms, which are rigid, you establish a good credit relationship. The bank has, of course, checked your credit record and established the good purposes of your loan.

Banks vary in their interest rates for different categories of loans. In the New York City area "signature" (unsecured) loans of up to $5000 are obtainable for emergencies, including hospital and dental expenses; vacations and Christmas shopping; hobby equipment and debt consolidation, etc. The scope is wide, and you can apply for the loan by mail or even by telephone.

Automobile or boat loans are offered up to $5000 with three years to pay. Property improvement loans (also see page 131) range from $100 to $15,000 and terms may be spread over as long as seven years. Education loans, which are insured, are available from $300 to $15,000.

Business loans, of course, continue to be big bank business. With a sound commercial or professional purpose, you can approach a bank for a loan—perhaps $100,000 or more, and you might have five years in which to repay.

If a veteran of World War II or Korea, you may still be eligible for a G.I. Business Loan. While your first approach would go to the local office of the Veterans Administration you would probably find the bank makes your loan through its participation in the G.I. Bill lending program. Terms are better than those offered to other borrowers.

Once again, it must be said that because of the variation in terms offered, you should shop several banks for the specific loan you want.

USING STOCKS AND BONDS AS COLLATERAL

If you own stocks and bonds and you need a loan you have ready security for a bank loan. The bank holds your stocks against cash, and you sign a "time note." This note may become due before you are ready to repay, but if your securities still have high market value, you will probably be able to have your note renewed. You only pay interest.

You should be alert, however, to several factors in this type of loan. You do not get the current market value of your securities as a loan. The bank will offer less, a protection for both against possible decline in value. You will not be asked to put up additional security or have your note recalled unless the stock drops to below the actual amount of the loan.

Say you cannot pay the loan, but the market is good. The value of your stock soars. You are in luck. The bank will sell all or part; it collects the debt, you collect some profit.

Your pledged stocks and bonds still bring in your usual dividends, and these may help to offset the cost of your loan.

Of course, when you repay a loan secured by stocks and bonds, they are returned to you.

BANK CREDIT PLANS

Currently, bank credit plans blossom overnight. They vary in detail, but not in substance—the people who use them will pay interest, and that adds up to good business for the banks.

One plan establishes the borrower's right to credit of up to $5000. The borrower does not actually receive any money. He makes use of the available credit whenever he pays his bills with the special checks issued to him. He pays a monthly interest charge on the amount of credit he actually uses, and for the checks. As he repays the amount borrowed plus interest, he establishes his right to use the credit again.

Another system does not require special checks. A borrower of good standing may write a check for more than he currently has in his account. But, because he has arranged for the bank to set up a credit reserve of between $400 to $5000, his check is met. In *multiples of $100,* the bank will move money into his otherwise overdrawn account. The borrower repays on a 12- or a 24-month basis, plus a monthly interest charge of 1 percent *on the daily unpaid* balance. If he repays in less than a month, the interest is proportionately reduced. If he does not call upon the reserve by overdrawing his account, he incurs no liability for interest charges. (He pays the regular bank charges the bank imposes for checks and service.)

In both of these credit plans the borrower must meet standards of credit eligibility similar to those required by a bank in making conventional type loans. The loan proceeds are not turned over to the borrower under either of these plans. Instead, the loan comes into existence when the arranged-for credit is used—by the writing of a check.

In another type of plan, banks issue credit cards honored by participating merchants in an area. The statement of your various bills comes to you from the bank and if you pay within a stated period, there is no penalty. However, the plan also works on a budget basis so that you can spread payments over two years at an interest rate of 1½ percent a month on your unpaid balance. The bank is, of course, running a plan similar to a department store charge account, but through the participation of dozens of merchants and services in a specified area. Moreover, it will issue loans between $25 and $150 to its cardholders without a loan application.

The loan application can be dispensed with because, in the credit card plan as with the special check and reserve accounts previously described, the bank customer has had to fill out a detailed application form in the first place. In reality, he is processed like any other type of borrower although he does not get a loan as such. With a regular bank loan the borrower describes his purpose, which must be approved. Under these other systems he spends or charges as he pleases.

Details may differ from one area of the country to another, but variations of these plans are widespread today and new developments may be expected in the computerized society.

CREDIT UNIONS

Members of credit unions save by purchasing shares in the association. Out of the accumulated savings fund, loans are made to members of the credit union. The law permits unsecured loans up to $750 and adequately secured loans in larger amounts, depending on the size of the credit union. Repayments are made periodically, according to an agreed-upon schedule, but they may not extend over five years. A credit committee elected by the members of the credit union passes upon the applications for loans. Interest on these loans must not exceed 1 percent per month on unpaid balances inclusive of all charges incident to making the loan. Each credit union fixes its own interest rate within this limit. Where the interest rate is 1 percent per month on balances, no other charges for the loan may be made. On a Federal credit union loan of $100 which is repaid in equal monthly installments, the total cost at the maximum interest rate would be:

$ 5.50 for 10 months
6.50 for 12 months
10.50 for 20 months
12.50 for 24 months

The charge for the loan often includes insurance that automatically liquidates the debt if the borrower dies or becomes permanently disabled.

THE SAVINGS BANK

We have suggested your using your own money at the savings bank or savings and loan association rather than running up credit charges. But what if you need money quickly, for an emergency or for an especially good buy, and you stand to lose a quarter- or a half-year's interest by early withdrawal of your money?

A loan on your passbook may be a good answer. The savings bank will advance you the sum you need at a comparatively reasonable rate, currently about $2.88 a year per $100 discounted (which equals simple annual interest of 5.4 percent). Other institutions offer non-discounted passbook loans, charging 1 percent more than their interest rate on savings.

You are required to repay your loan in monthly installments over one to three years at some banks. Other banks leave the manner of repayment largely to the discretion of the borrower. Self-discipline is important here lest the interest charges mount up.

When you make a passbook loan, you have the advantage of not losing the interest accumulated on your savings. Withdrawing savings prior to an interest payment date may result in forfeiture of the interest for the entire period on the withdrawn amount. It may be more economical to postpone the withdrawal and make a short-term passbook loan instead. After the interest is paid, you make the withdrawal and repay the loan with interest. Note that the interest is tax deductible.

If interest has just been credited to your savings bank account, a withdrawal of the needed sum, rather than the loan, would certainly be to your advantage. True, you don't have to repay your account, but if you intend to practice good money management, you will.

SMALL LOAN COMPANIES

Here, we discuss licensed small loan companies, which probably means that they are reputable and operating within state law. (Most, but not all, states provide some protection for the borrower.)

You will, no doubt, find it easier to walk into your friendly small loan company—open long after the banks close and on Saturdays, too—and to walk out with a $500 loan than you would to get the same money from a bank.

But in return for speed and lack of intensive questioning, you will pay their high interest rates. These may vary. The true interest rate of, say, 3 percent a month, comes to 36 percent a year; this is an expensive loan.

Nevertheless, the small loan company can assist the person without a credit background to consolidate debts and thereby to improve his future standing. Some will provide competent budgeting and counseling services which are of real benefit to people who cannot see their way through a difficult financial situation.

In general, go to the small loan company only if you cannot get a loan from a lower-rate source. If you do so, check on the company first. This can be done through the local Better Business Bureau.

THE LOAN SHARK

You already know that the reputable loan company operates under state license, which gives varying degrees of protection to the borrower. The loan shark operates for his own benefit, or possibly for that of a larger and altogether sinister organization. In these days he may set up shop in attractive surroundings which are likely to lull the borrower's suspicions.

Since we cannot list every device an unscrupulous lender might use, we can only urge the prior checkup as above, and to be aware of the following possibilities:

You may be asked to sign papers in which there are blank spaces.

You may not be given copies of all the papers.

You may not get a chance to read the fine print; an additional document you did not see may be among the carbon copies.

The amount of the loan may be overstated.

The date of the loan may be incorrect.

The charges may be exorbitant—and they may skyrocket further in mysterious ways if you get yourself involved.

The person who has become involved with a loan shark does not get free easily. Some who have borrowed have accepted lifelong shackles. They fear to go to the District Attorney lest strong-arm tactics be used against them—and sometimes these fears are realized. The threat alone is a burden no one should carry.

Our suggestion—manage your money so that, when you need to borrow, your credit is good at reputable sources. Your own handling of your finances is your best protection against involvement with shady characters.

CREDITS COSTS AND TRUE RATE OF INTEREST

The complex nature of contract terms and credit charges confuse the average buyer or borrower. He does not fully understand what he is actually paying for his installment purchase or loan in terms of true annual interest. Like other merchants, those who extend credit advertise their wares in the most favorable terms. When the merchandise is money, this means showing as low a cost as possible to potential consumers of credit. One way to make the interest rate appear low is to state the monthly rather than the annual rate. Another method is by advertising only the dollar cost of a loan with no indication of the true annual interest. Beginning July 1, 1969, the new Federal Consumer Credit Protection Act will generally require credit merchants to disclose the annual percentage rate.

If a person making a loan realized that a loan quoted as $6 per $100 per year would actually cost him 12.5 percent annual interest, he might reconsider his need for the loan. He might decide to borrow for a shorter period or he might shop around for credit from a cheaper source. If it was stated clearly that a purchase on a revolving credit plan could add an additional 18 percent to the price of the merchandise, a purchaser might well postpone the purchase until he himself had saved the price to pay cash.

There is a variety of credit offered consumers under the guise of it costing "only 6 percent per $100 per year." Until legislation makes it mandatory for all credit merchants to disclose true annual interest, a buyer, to protect his pocketbook, must be able to translate the credit terms and determine for himself the true cost of borrowing.

Credit is available from various sources, banks, finance companies, credit unions, and retail stores, to name the most common. If you decide to buy on credit or to borrow money, you will want to know how much it is costing you to use the lender's money—both in terms of dollars and rate of interest. Then you can compare the varying prices of credit and be able to buy and borrow at the lowest cost. Or, you might find that you cannot afford to use credit—the price may be beyond your means.

TYPES OF LOANS AND WAYS OF STATING INTEREST

Using credit is an everyday fact of life for millions of Americans. When you "buy now, pay later," "charge it," buy "on time," "use a 'payment plan'" and whenever you take out a loan—you are using someone else's money—and usually paying for the use of it. How much it costs depends on the terms of the credit agreement.

Simple interest. A loan at simple interest at 6 percent a year means that you pay six cents a year for each dollar you borrow. If you borrow $100 at 6 percent for a full year and do not have to make monthly installments, you would have the full use of the money until the end of the year. At the end of the year, you would repay $106.

You would then be paying a true annual interest of 6 percent. If you repaid the loan in six months, the interest would be half, or $3. Six percent simple interest comes to ½ percent a month.

A simple interest loan is available from few sources, and usually requires good collateral in the form of a savings passbook, life insurance policy, real estate, etc. The most economical loans you can make will probably be a first mortgage loan or one against your life insurance or bank account.

Unpaid balance—monthly interest. Credit unions and small loan companies, as well as retail merchants and banks on certain types of charge plans, quote charges as a percentage of the balance unpaid each month. Multiply the monthly interest by 12 to arrive at annual interest.

Monthly rate	True annual rate is
¾ of 1%	9%
⅝ of 1%	10%
1 %	12%
1¼%	15%
1½%	18%
2 %	24%
2¼%	27%
2½%	30%
2¾%	33%
3 %	36%
3¼%	39%
3½%	42%

As you repay the amount borrowed, the size of the loan decreases. For example, say your unpaid balance is $120 and is repayable in 12 monthly installments at 1 percent per month. Figure your interest charge on the unpaid balance at the end of the month as follows:

Divide $120 by 12 to find the amount of principal you must repay each month:

$$\$120 \div 12 = \$10$$

Determine the 1 percent a month interest charge payable on $120, your unpaid balance at the end of the first month:

$$\$120 \times 1 \text{ percent} = \$1.20$$

Your first payment is $11.20; $10 principal and $1.20 interest.

Subtract your monthly principal payment from the balance:

$$\$120 - \$10 = \$110$$

The second month you would repay $10 of principal and 1 percent interest on your remaining balance of $110 or $1.10. The second month you pay $11.10.

Figure your payments of principal and interest this way each month. Remember, your principal payment remains the same; the interest charge decreases as your unpaid balance gets lower. Your final payment of the loan will be $10.10.

This $120, 1 percent a month loan, actually costs 12 percent per year in interest; in dollars it costs $7.80.

Add-on loan. On an add-on loan, the interest charge is added to your loan or purchase. On a 6 percent per $100 loan for a year you have to repay $106. If you make monthly repayments, as is usual, you do not have the full use of the money for the entire year. Month by month, you have less, but you are still paying on $100 at 6 percent a year. If you repay the $100 plus 6 percent interest in 12 monthly installments of $8.83 each for a total of $106, your true annual interest is 11.1 percent, almost double what you thought you were paying. If your repayments are scheduled over 18 months, you would be repaying $109 (6 percent per year for 1½ years). Your monthly payments would be lower, $6.05 per month; your true rate of interest would be higher, 11.4 percent.

Discount loan. On a discounted loan, the bank discounts or *deducts* the interest in advance. On a $100 discounted loan, instead of $100, you are handed only $94. On a loan for a year quoted as 6 percent per $100 you have to repay $100. Each monthly installment comes to $8.33. Your true annual interest is 11.8 percent. If you repaid a $100 discounted loan over an 18-month period, the true annual interest would jump to 12.5 percent.

The discount method actually works out to a higher rate of interest than the add-on loan. The reason: the same $6 of interest is a larger share of $94 than it is of $100. Roughly, true annual interest on such a loan to be paid back in monthly installments over a year is about double the amount stated.

You can determine true annual interest by applying the following formula:

$$\text{True Annual Interest} = \frac{2 \times \text{number of installments in year} \times \text{\$ cost of loan}}{\text{Amount of loan actually received} \times \text{Total number of installments} + 1}$$

Say you take out a loan of $1000, quoted at 6 percent per $100, discounted, to be repaid monthly over two years. This means you receive only $880. $120 is the cost of the loan. You figure the true annual interest by applying the above formula as follows:

$$\text{True Annual Interest} = \frac{2 \times 12 \times \$120}{\$880 \times (24 + 1)}$$

This works out to 13.1 percent true annual interest.

Or, say you plan to purchase a washing machine costing $300. The dealer offers you $25 for your old one as a trade-in and quotes you a price of $36 to cover carrying charges to finance the purchase over an 18-month period. You can determine the true annual rate of interest you would be paying by applying the formula:

$$\text{True Annual Interest} = \frac{2 \times 12 \times \$36}{\$275 \times (18 + 1)}$$

The finance charges on the washing machine would come to 16.5 percent in true annual interest.

The following table shows the true annual interest rate for a $100 loan at various rates. You can compare the higher cost of a discounted loan as against the add-on loan. You can also see how the length of the period of debt and frequency of installments increases the rate of interest.

TABLE OF TRUE ANNUAL INTEREST
ADD-ON LOAN

Amount of Loan Proceeds	Rate per $100 per Year	Cost of Loan in Dollars	Number of Monthly Installments	True Annual Interest Rate
$100	$6.00	$9.00	18	11.4%
100	6.00	6.00	12	11.1
100	6.00	5.00	10	9.1
100	5.00	7.50	18	9.5
100	5.00	5.00	12	9.2
100	5.00	4.17	10	7.6
100	4.00	6.00	18	7.6
100	4.00	4.00	12	7.4
100	4.00	3.33	10	6.5
100	3.00	4.50	18	5.6
100	3.00	3.00	12	5.5
100	3.00	2.50	10	4.5

DISCOUNT LOAN

Amount of Loan Proceeds	Rate per $100 per Year	Cost of Loan in Dollars	Number of Monthly Installments	True Annual Interest Rate
$91.00	$6.00	$9.00	18	12.5%
94.00	6.00	6.00	12	11.8
95.00	6.00	5.00	10	9.6
92.50	5.00	7.50	18	10.2
95.00	5.00	5.00	12	9.7
95.83	5.00	4.17	10	7.9
94.00	4.00	6.00	18	8.1
96.00	4.00	4.00	12	7.7
96.67	4.00	3.33	10	6.3
95.50	3.00	4.50	18	6.0
97.00	3.00	3.00	12	5.7
97.50	3.00	2.50	10	4.7

Chapter 7

WHEN YOU RENT, BUY, OR SELL
YOUR RESIDENCE

CITY OR SUBURB	106
RENTING AN APARTMENT	107
RENTING A HOUSE	108
WHAT YOUR LEASE SHOULD INCLUDE	108
BUYING A HOUSE	109
BUYING A COOPERATIVE APARTMENT	110
A CONDOMINIUM	111
IS A LAWYER NECESSARY?	111
THE ROLE OF A REAL ESTATE BROKER	113
GET AN EXPERT'S OPINION	114
OLD VS. NEW	114
THE CUSTOM-BUILT HOUSE	115
RETAINING AN ARCHITECT	116
YOUR GENERAL CONTRACTOR	117
SELLING YOUR HOME	118
INCOME TAX CONSEQUENCES OF RESIDENCE SALES	119

A family looking for a place to live generally has a decision to make on the location: city, suburb or outlying area; type of house or apartment; type of financing, purchase or rental. Before the search is begun, serious thought should be given first to the needs, interests and convenience of family members; then to capital in hand and prospective income and earnings for future years.

If your family is young and growing, an area within safe walking distance to good schools, safe play areas, and a place of worship should be preferred. Try to find out something about the people in the community. An area where most of the residents have grown children, different interests and attitudes from yours and incomes in a much higher or much lower range could be an unhappy choice. Investigate accessibility to shopping, job location, costs of transportation, travel time for work and whether a car is essential to get around.

CITY OR SUBURB

The past ten years have brought about a marked increase in the number of families who have settled outside of city areas. Economic prosperity enjoyed by more and more American families has fostered the urge to seek the "better living" of suburbia. City noises, congestion, traffic, polluted air, high rentals, expense and inconvenience connected with owning or operating a car in the city, extra sales taxes and city income taxes have contributed to the exodus from metropolitan areas.

Families look to suburbia for more living space at very little if any extra cost. Generally, areas outside the city have cleaner air, are nearer to beaches, lakes, golf courses and tennis courts, and offer a bit of nature and greenery at the doorstep. For the family with young children, the suburbs offer less crowded schools, generally with higher educational standards, more protected play and recreation areas for children, and a wider opportunity for adult members to make friends and take an active role in community and civic affairs.

On the other hand, living in a city better suits the needs and interests of other families. If family members are all adult, they will generally prefer the city. They can get to a theater, concert, museum, art exhibit, and other places of interest with less time, effort, and expense from a city home than from one in a suburb. Working members may even be able to get to work on foot. At least, they will be able to get there by bus or rapid transit and avoid the inconveniences and expense of commuting. Families living in the city find that owning a car is not necessary. It may even be a nuisance. Taxis, buses, and other public transportation are generally adequate. You do not have to meet railroad time schedules or frustrating parking and highway traffic problems to get into the city. You do not have to be driven to or from the train every day for work.

Many families who move to the suburbs for the advantages it offered their children while they were growing up return to the city after the children leave the family home and establish themselves elsewhere. Senior and soon-to-be senior citizens whose children have left the family home find they can more conveniently enjoy in the city the interests they developed over their years in the suburbs. They relieve themselves of burdensome high taxes for schools they no longer require, of commuting pressures and responsibilities of home ownership. Most find that the general inflation in the real estate market gives them a profit when they sell their home. Investing the proceeds in a city cooperative or condominium avoids tax on at least part of this gain.

RENTING AN APARTMENT

When you rent an apartment, either in the city or a suburb, you are generally relieved of responsibilities for most repairs and maintenance expenses. You can go away for as long as you please without concern, by merely turning the key in your door lock. You have no worries about whether the water pipes will freeze or the furnace will break down. Your major and only responsibility for the apartment is to pay the rent when due. (Under many landlord-conceived leases, paying the rent is about the only thing you can do without violating some provision of your lease!)

When you rent the place you live in, you have more flexibility than when you own it. You can leave when your rental term is up. Your responsibility is definitely ascertainable in advance and is a fixed amount each month. With your landlord's consent, you can even give up your tenancy during its term with no further liability. However, this depends on your agreement with your landlord. You may continue to be liable for rent until the expiration of your term if the apartment remains unoccupied or your successor defaults.

If you are in a community where rent is controlled and you are in a rent-controlled building, you are protected against rent increases at the landlord's will. Generally, you will occupy your apartment as a month-to-month tenant after your lease expires. You can terminate your tenancy without further obligation by complying with the local law provisions relating to termination. But your landlord cannot force you to get out except as local law may provide for particular situations.

RENTING A HOUSE

Renting a house generally means greater responsibility for maintenance than renting an apartment. You will probably have more space to live in, a front lawn and backyard. But you may have to take care of the grounds, pay the cost of heating and garbage removal (where this is not offered as a public service). However, this is a matter of agreement between you and your absentee-owner. The limits and extent of your responsibilities should be negotiated in advance and clearly set out in writing. Local laws require that leases for more than a certain period of time must be in writing. Even if local law does not require your agreement to be in writing, you should insist on this course. It will avoid future misunderstandings of the term, your rights and responsibilities and those of your landlord.

WHAT YOUR LEASE SHOULD INCLUDE

A residence lease should include the following provisions:

The term of the lease, with specific beginning and termination dates.

A description of the property rented (including garage, if any).

Responsibilities of each party for repairs, replacements, alterations, and maintenance.

Services to be provided by the landlord (heat, gas, electricity—if included in rent—elevator service, storage space).

Equipment to be furnished by the landlord (stove, refrigerator, air conditioning, etc.).

Amount of rent payable, and when it is to be paid.

Rights of tenant regarding installation of electric or mechanical equipment (air conditioner, humidifier, connecting TV aerial to outside antenna).

Rights of tenant to make changes in decor.

Rights of tenant to assign or sublet lease.

Conditions under which security deposited is to be returned or credited.

Rules and regulations regarding tenants' use of the apartment and building. For example, restrictions against uses of elevators, halls, or other communal areas, if any, for baby carriages, children's bicycles, etc.

If you are a month-to-month tenant under operation of local law, be sure to check what notice, if any, you are required to give your landlord before vacating your apartment so that you will be relieved of further responsibility for rent. In areas where there is no rent control, your landlord can generally ask you to vacate or pay an increased rental when your lease expires.

BUYING A HOUSE

Say that in your search for a home, you have to decide between an attractive apartment and a small house. Both offer adequate room space, but the house offers a garage, front lawn, and backyard as well. You compare the apartment rent, plus rent for garaging your car, with taxes, heating costs, mortgage payments, insurance, and general upkeep of the house. You should include an estimate for repairs and redecoration. Take into account the down payment you will have to make on buying and expenses of closing title and moving into the house. The house appears more costly, but you get more for your money. And, under a long-range analysis, the house will probably turn out to be less expensive because of the economic advantages home ownership offers. These are (1) tax deductions, (2) build-up of equity, and (3) possible increase in value.

Tax deductions. When you pay interest to a mortgagee, and taxes on real property, you become entitled to a tax deduction for the amounts paid in arriving at your income tax liability. Say, for example, the rental of an apartment is $110 a month. You find a small house for $16,500 on which you can make a down payment of $1650 and get a 30-year mortgage. Your monthly payments for interest, principal, taxes, insurance, and heat are $125 a month. In the first five years of ownership you will enjoy tax deductions worth more than the $15 you pay over the cost of renting the apartment.

(If you are a veteran, local law may provide you with a partial exemption from property taxes. This will provide a reduction in the amount of monthly payments you will have to make to the mortgagee.)

Build-up of equity. Each payment you make to the mortgagee includes an amount that reduces your indebtedness under the mortgage. In the first five years of ownership you have paid $1000 off on the mortgage. Thus, the payments are a form of savings. Many a homeowner has financed his child's college education by refinancing the home in which he has, over the years, built up an equity.

Increase in value. If real estate values continue to rise as they have in the past, and there is no indication of a reverse trend, your investment could be further enhanced.

BUYING A COOPERATIVE APARTMENT

When you buy an apartment in a cooperative building, you pay your proportionate share of mortgage payments, taxes, and maintenance and operating costs of the entire building monthly, like rent. The amount is therefore dependent to a large extent on the size of the unpaid balance on the building mortgage, and the general condition of the building. If the mortgage is low and the building modern and in good condition when you buy, your monthly carrying charges will be lower.

What you get when you buy a cooperative apartment is stock in the owner-corporation. If you want to sell your apartment and the shares of stock, your buyer must generally be approved by the co-op's board of directors which undertakes responsibility for management of the building. Demand for co-ops has increased materially in and near large cities. The risk of tenants defaulting, and of increased costs to remaining owners, is very low.

In comparing the cost of carrying a co-op apartment with rent, remember that the co-op gives you tax benefits, like home ownership. You are entitled to deduct the amount you pay for your share of real estate taxes and interest on the building's mortgage.

A CONDOMINIUM

When you buy a condominium you get legal title to an apartment in the building and an interest in the land and all improvements which you hold in common with the other apartment owners. The condominium is a cross between owning a home and a cooperative apartment. You are free to put your own mortgage on your apartment. If there is a blanket mortgage on the whole project, you assume a proportionate part of that mortgage up to the unpaid part of your purchase price. You pay the proportionate share of real estate taxes allocable to your apartment. Like a home or cooperative apartment owner, you can deduct mortgage interest and taxes paid on your income tax return. But unlike cooperative ownership, you are generally free to sell or lease at any price to anyone—subject in some instances to first offering the unit to the other owners at your asking price.

The tax deductions allowable to owners of cooperative apartments and condominiums, like home ownership, may enable you to buy an apartment for less overall cost than rental of a comparable one. The facts and figures should be analyzed carefully. Too, ownership of a co-op or condominium, like a home, allows for a build-up of equity as a form of saving.

IS A LAWYER NECESSARY?

Yes. You should retain a lawyer as soon as your offer for the house of your choice is accepted. The purchase of a house generally represents the most expensive buy of your lifetime. It is economically unsound to "do it yourself" to save a lawyer's fee.

Many brokers ask buyers for a down payment as a "binder," usually $25 or $50. Such binders are often construed as contracts without giving the protection a contract provides. It is better practice to sign nothing and make no payment. The seller's lawyer can get a contract up in a very short time. Tell the seller to have his lawyer get in touch with yours, and the contract can be signed within a few days. At that time you will make your down payment, usually 10 percent of the purchase price.

Your lawyer will see that all the terms and conditions of the sale are included in the written agreement. If you cannot complete your purchase unless you are able to secure a satisfactory mortgage, your lawyer will try to get such condition stated in your contract. If the seller offers certain personal property with the house, such as appliances, garden equipment etc., your lawyer will see that you get title to this personal property with the house. A seller rarely gives anything not specifically provided for in the contract.

Some home buyers are under the illusion that the attorney representing the mortgagee will look out for their interests as well, and that a lawyer is an unnecessary expense. This is not so. The lawyer for the mortgagee is there to protect the lending institution, not you. If there is an encroachment or easement turned up on the title examination, such fact will affect your interest as owner but will not deter the mortgagee's lawyer from going ahead to give you the mortgage. The mortgagee's interest for the amount it advances will be adequately secured despite this encroachment. But this might affect the marketability of your title. If there is an open assessment against the property, the attorney for the mortgagee will not concern himself about who pays it, or if it is paid. But your lawyer will try to get the seller to pay at least a part.

If the seller has failed to complete certain work called for by the contract as of the closing date, the attorney for the mortgagee may not be concerned. But your lawyer will, for your protection. He will try either to get a part of the purchase price put "in escrow" pending the seller's performance or make some other arrangement for your protection. He might get an agreement that the seller can have the balance that is in escrow provided he completes the work on or before a certain date. On his default, the money would go to you for you to have the work done. If the seller has made representations as to construction your lawyer will try to get them in writing, for your protection in your investment.

A lawyer's fee for the contract and closing will vary, according to locality and the amount of work and perhaps price of property involved. It could be from $100 up to $500, or in certain localities, it might be one or two percent of the price. Find out in advance what your lawyer's fee will be.

THE ROLE OF A REAL ESTATE BROKER

You do not incur any liability for broker's commissions when you consult a broker about buying a house. His sales commissions are payable by the owner who makes him his agent to sell his house. Consulting a local broker, who generally knows most of the houses that are on the market in his area, will save you a lot of wear and tear and expedite your search for a home. An active real estate broker generally knows the actual sales prices of homes comparable to the one you seek. A reputable broker will tell you these prices to guide you in your offer. He knows what lending institutions will finance the purchase of the house you choose, what the lending institutions look for in issuing credit on mortgages, how much an institution is likely to lend, and where you can get an FHA or VA mortgage, if you qualify. Brokers are generally more expert than a layman in the art of negotiating between a buyer and seller, and know how to keep open negotiations after a buyer's offer of less than asking price is rejected by the seller.

On the other hand, don't rely implicitly in a broker's sales talk or enthusiasm for the house he wants to sell. There are some things you should check. Have an independent expert examine the property. Check for yourself the location of the school your children will be eligible to attend. You may choose a house because of the educational standards of the nearby schools—only to find out a child at your address has to attend another school. Check also at the school on the availability of bus transportation. You may be just outside the one-mile or other distance limit. Your neighbor's child may be entitled to bus transportation, while yours may have to walk or be driven to school.

GET AN EXPERT'S OPINION

After you find the house you prefer above others, and the price is in the right range, get a building expert to examine it for you. His fee will probably be between $25 and $50, but will be worth it. He will check construction, insulation, the roof, the water pipes, the heating system, and tell you whether there is any evidence of termite infestation—a hidden danger in every house. He will give you an idea of annual heating costs and what repair and maintenance costs you should anticipate. He might recommend additional insulation for savings in heating costs, or other work on the house that will insure years of low maintenance charges. If any costs are to be incurred along these lines, you should take them into account in financing your purchase.

OLD VS. NEW

When you buy and move into a new house you find everything bright, fresh, clean, and modern. You may even have had the opportunity to choose some of its features, such as wallpaper, flooring, fixtures, etc., but only up to the amount the builder has allowed for these. This is generally so when you buy a home from a builder who shows you a "sample" house and then finishes your house accordingly. Anything you want that costs more than the amount the builder has allowed will be put in at your expense.

Builders of new houses usually provide a bare lawn and no landscaping. They do not put in storm or screen windows or doors. You will have to take these items of expense into consideration over and above the down payment for the house. You will also have to weather the frustrations resulting from "bugs" in construction.

When a house is new, and until it is "broken in," doors and windows may stick, outside steps may crack, heating and hot water systems may need constant adjustment, and the settling of the house may mean repainting or papering of walls and tile repairs in bathrooms. However, you will be able to finance the purchase of a new house more easily than an older house. You can get a 30-year mortgage more easily on a new house than on an older one, and on a smaller down payment.

On the other hand, an older house has other advantages. It usually has a warmth, charm, and at least appearance of, if not actual, sturdiness not found in new homes offered at comparable prices. The older home will probably save you the expense of lawn, landscaping, screen and storm windows and doors. If the house is in a well-established neighborhood, the schools are not as likely to become overcrowded or inadequate as quickly as in the new development areas. Property taxes will probably not increase as quickly as in new communities. But an older house may need modernization, particularly in the kitchen. It might need a wall knocked down to make way for a "family room." You may have to repaint or redecorate even before you can move in. You will need capital to do this. If this will make the cost of the old house more than a comparable new one, and you do not have the ready cash for modernization, it would not be wise for you to buy an older house.

One other consideration you should not overlook in choosing between a new and an old house. Make certain the older house is in a neighborhood that is not deteriorating or becoming commercial in character. If it is, your chances of getting your investment back will not be as good as from a new house that is comparable in cost.

THE CUSTOM-BUILT HOUSE

Few houses are perfect for every family. You might find the right house, but the location may not please. The custom-built house is the answer for the family that wants a modern home, designed to their wishes, desires, and specifications, in the neighborhood they choose and on the lot they select.

Steps to take. The first step you take as a prospective builder of a custom-built house is to buy the land. Check zoning laws before buying to make sure you can build a residence on the size lot you are planning to buy. Local law may require that building lots be a minimum area. Make sure yours is at least that size. Check also to make sure nearby property is not zoned for commercial use or any use that would reduce the value of your property.

Have a lawyer represent you on the purchase of the land to make sure your title is good and marketable before you go ahead with building plans.

Your next steps should be taken only after a long period of thought, study, and inquiry into experiences of others who have built custom homes. Examine books, pamphlets, magazines, and newspaper articles on home-building. Attend home-construction shows and exhibits. In every way you can, learn about new ideas in home-building, new time- and labor-saving devices. Look into ideas for built-in lighting that is functional and attractive, in place of traditional lamps, fixtures, and chandeliers. Look into ideas of built-in furniture, particularly adaptable for children's rooms. Look into modern wall-oven units, revolving kitchen shelves that disappear within the wall, mirrored closet doors in bedrooms, different types of heating and air-conditioning units, sliding walls, ramps instead of stairs, and possibilities for expansion of the basic house to be built.

RETAINING AN ARCHITECT

Your next step should be to retain an architect to guide you with design and to oversee construction. His fee could be as much as 10–15 percent of building costs. This may seem high, but what you pay for his services could be offset by savings he effects for you in design or construction, or in both areas.

Expert advice in the blueprint stage of building can help avoid the disappointment many homeowners feel in their finished homes because they visualized something different. And changes, the prerogative of every individual who builds, can be made at little cost in the blueprint stage. The same changes can be prohibitively expensive if made later on, during construction.

An architect is like good insurance. He has the techniques and knowledge required to deal with contractors. The average man does not have this, and cannot tell, as work progresses on his house, whether his plans are being carried out as he anticipated.

YOUR GENERAL CONTRACTOR

After your plans are crystallized with your architect, your next step is to hire a general contractor. He carries out your plans and specifications as drawn by the architect and undertakes to give you a completed house. The contract price can be fixed at a stated amount, in which event you will be liable over and above that figure only for extras you request, or consent to at his suggestion. Or, in the alternative, you could enter into a "cost-plus" contract. In this case you assume the cost of all materials, labor, and other services the contractor provides, plus a stated fee. The fee can be either a lump sum or a percentage of building costs (10 to 20 percent).

You could be your own contractor. But to undertake this without being thoroughly familiar with building codes, regulations, permits, and insurance required would be a foolhardy venture. You would probably end up spending more than you anticipated saving. If your budget does not allow for an architect, you could find a standard plan in a magazine, at a home show or a building supply company for a house that meets your requirements within the applicable building codes and regulations.

If you want the contractor to guarantee fulfillment of his contract he will generally do so by posting a bond, for which you are expected to pay. If you know the contractor's reputation to be good, the bond is probably not necessary.

The prefabricated house. The expanding prefabricated housing industry has indicated it can deliver attractive homes at low cost. More than 4 million Americans now live in such homes. The houses can be purchased at various stages of construction or completion. You can buy the house in factory-shipped parts and hire a contractor to put them together for a completed house. Or you can hire the contractor to do part of the work, and complete construction on a do-it-yourself basis. The amount you will have to pay to the builder will depend on the degree to which the house has been completed on arrival at the site from the factory, and the amount of work you want the builder to leave for you to do.

Before you buy a prefabricated house (they are available now even at department stores), check these points:

1. Will you be able to get financing? Some agencies do not lend money on prefabricated houses. For example, the FHA has restrictions against financing certain types.

2. Compare the total costs with the charges of a building contractor to put up a comparable house. Be sure to include in your estimate the costs of "extras" such as fittings, piping, the heating system, sewage disposal, all labor costs, and the transportation cost of shipping prefabricated parts to your building site.

3. Check local zoning and building requirements to make sure the house you plan to put up meets specifications in the law.

The 10 percent cushion. Whether you are going to buy a house already built, are going to build a custom house, or are going to put up a prefabricated house, you should have a "cushion" of at least 10 percent for unanticipated "extras." Every home owner will attest to the need for resorting to such reserve before he is settled in his new home.

SELLING YOUR HOME

When you list your home for sale with a real estate broker or a local Real Estate Board you have to pay the broker a commission if he finds a buyer who is ready, willing, and able to buy the house on the terms and conditions you offer. Sales commissions vary with localities. Generally they run around 6 percent of the sales price. If you are able to sell without the services of a broker, you save this commission, and can take this into consideration in fixing your price.

An active broker can help a seller in many ways. He knows what a fair price is for the house, on the basis of other sales of comparable houses in the locality. He has a good idea of how much local lending institutions will advance on mortgages, and the prevailing terms offered. He is better versed in the art of negotiation than a layman. He is in a better position than the seller is to keep negotiations open even after a prospective buyer's offer of less than asking price has been turned down—in case you have a change of heart and want to reduce the price.

INCOME TAX CONSEQUENCES OF RESIDENCE SALES

If you sell your principal residence at a profit after owning it for more than six months, and you are under 65, you can avoid capital gains tax on your profit if you meet certain Treasury tests. You must buy and use a new principal residence purchased with the sales proceeds within one year before or after the sale of the old residence, or, if you build a new residence, within one year before or 18 months after the sale of the former residence.

If you are over 65 when you sell at a profit, you can avoid payment of tax on your gain completely if the adjusted sales price of the house is not over $20,000. If over $20,000, a proportionate part of the gain can be taxfree.

Chapter 8

FINANCING YOUR HOME

INITIAL EXPENSES ON BUYING A HOUSE	122
CHECK LIST ON BUYING FAMILY HOME	124
FINANCING YOUR MORTGAGE	126
OBTAINING A MORTGAGE	126
TERMS OF PAYMENT	127
OPEN-END MORTGAGE	128
PREPAYMENT	128
MORTGAGE-REDEMPTION INSURANCE POLICIES	129
SECOND MORTGAGES	129
VETERANS	129
FHA MORTGAGES	130
FHA HOME IMPROVEMENT LOANS	131
INSURING YOURSELF FROM PROPERTY LOSSES AND CLAIMS OF OTHERS	131

There are a number of yardsticks or guides offered by economists to help you determine how much you should pay for a house on the basis of your income. One is that your monthly payments for interest, taxes, insurance, and mortgage payments should not be more than your net weekly take-home pay. Another is that you can usually afford to pay 2½ times your family's gross annual income for a family home. If you have small children or dependent parents, you may have to keep under these guides. On the other hand, if your outlook for additional earnings or income is promising, or you have savings into which you can dip for a larger down payment (to reduce monthly mortgage payments) or for improvements you anticipate you will have to make to the house, you probably could afford to pay more.

INITIAL EXPENSES ON BUYING A HOUSE

There are certain items of expense connected to the purchase of a house in addition to the down payment on the purchase price. First, there are moving expenses. In this connection, consider the necessity of cleaning furniture and drapes, or redoing or buying new furnishings, remodeling that might be necessary to suit your needed space, and costs of appliances and garden equipment you will need.

Then there are closing costs, the expenses connected with obtaining title to the house. Closing costs are estimated, on a nation-wide survey, to come to about $500 on the purchase of a house for about $20,000 and securing a $12,000 mortgage on it. These costs will include the following items:

Survey. Most lending institutions insist that the buyer provide it with a survey. The survey shows up encroachments against the boundary lines of the land sold. For example, if a neighbor had put up a fence that goes over on your property line, an up-to-date survey made by a qualified surveyor will show this up. If the property has previously been surveyed, the title company that insures the mortgage or title will bring it up to date at little or no charge. If a new survey is necessary, it can cost anywhere from $25 to $200.

Title Company Insurance. The lending institutions generally insist on title insurance before they will advance mortgage money. This is paid for by the buyer. It certifies the title of the seller for the mortgagee. If you, as buyer, want similar insurance for yourself, the title company will issue an owner's policy to you for not too much more than you have to pay for the mortgagee's policy ($35 or $40 more). The policy for the mortgagee can cost from $75 upwards. For example, cost of insurance for a $30,000 mortgage would be around $125.

Other Insurance. One of the items of expense you should count on in buying a home is fire and/or comprehensive homeowner insurance. At the very least, you will have to provide your mortgagee with a standard fire insurance policy to protect its investment in your property. The standard policy covers against loss to the building by fire and lightning. The mortgagee may insist on additional coverage for windstorm or other casualties. (Fire insurance does not extend to the land.)

A homeowner's policy is the type of policy most commonly in use. It is designed to provide insurance for the mortgagee and full protection for the homeowner in one contract, at lower cost than a series of separate contracts. It can include, in addition to protection against fire loss for both mortgagee and homeowner, insurance for household effects lost, stolen, or destroyed both in and away from the house; protection against claims for personal and property injuries, and losses for vandalism, water damage, etc. The cost of the premium for this insurance will vary according to the type of the house, the extent of the coverage and the location of the property. Cost is generally lowered if a "deductible" feature is included, insuring for loss only in excess of the first $50 or $100.

Homeowner policies can generally be bought for one year, three years, or five years. The longer term protects the owner against an increase in insurance rates during the term and premium rates are lower. Ask your broker to list separately the cost of the basic policy you have to provide for the mortgagee, and the cost of additional or extended coverage available to you.

Mortgage Expenses. Although the bank or other lending company may not charge you a specific fee for giving the mortgage, you will nevertheless have certain expenses in connection with obtaining it. You will probably have to pay the mortgagee an appraisal fee ($25 to $50). You will have to pay its attorney a fee for drawing the mortgage and other legal papers ($75 to $150). You will have to pay the recording fee for putting the mortgage on record (about $6 to $8). And if local law has a mortgage tax, you will have to pay that tax. (In New York, this tax runs $5 per thousand of the face amount of a mortgage.) These expenses are in addition to the cost of survey and title insurance.

Ask about these items in advance. The appraisal and legal fees may be included in a flat fee charged for giving the mortgage. You should know exactly what your expenses will be and what they are for before you commit yourself.

Lawyers' Fees. When you retain your lawyer to represent you on making the contract of sale, ask him what his fee will be for that and for the closing of title. This fee could be between $100 and $500. It might be one or two percent of the purchase price.

Advance Payments on Adjustments. On the closing of title, certain adjustments are made on taxes, insurance premiums, etc. If you buy subject to an existing mortgage, interest must be adjusted. Generally, as buyer you will have to be prepared to pay in advance up to six months' real estate taxes and, to protect the mortgagee, insurance premiums up to three years.

A buyer of a moderate-priced house should figure on $350 to $500 in closing costs. When you buy a house on which there already stands an existing mortgage, a good part of the closing costs are saved. Moreover, the mortgage interest rate is probably lower than the rate you have to pay for a new mortgage.

CHECK LIST ON BUYING FAMILY HOME

You usually will find two or three houses in the right price range, each of which may meet most of your requirements. However, none may meet all of them. You must make a comparison of the good and bad features of each and resolve your decision by a compromise. Here is a check list of some of the points you should weigh:

Size and expansion possibilities. If the number of rooms is adequate now but might not be after a few years, is there room for expansion? Will zoning laws permit you to expand the house?

Topography of the lot. Is there sufficient level ground for the play area you require? Will abutting property make necessary a retaining wall? Is drainage adequate?

Public utilities. Will you have to maintain a well, or does the public authority supply water? Is garbage and trash removal a public service? Are the public roads near the house kept clear of snow and ice by a public service? What are the zoning laws in the immediate and neighboring vicinity? A home near an area zoned for commercial or industrial use will not be as desirable on a resale, and will depreciate more quickly in value.

Is the house near a traffic center, a main highway, or a transportation center? Traffic noises may make a home less desirable on a resale. But it must be weighed against the advantages of easy travel to work. Is the cost high for public transportation to work, shopping areas, places of entertainment and recreation, etc.?

Will you need a car to get yourself and your family to daily pursuits?

Is the house within walking distance of schools, place of worship, playgrounds, and shopping areas?

Are there sidewalks for children who walk to school?

Do zoning laws protect the neighborhood from deteriorating?

Are the schools crowded? If they are, you can be sure your taxes will be increased to provide for new schools.

Are there sewers, or other public improvements in the area for which your house is likely to be assessed?

Have you gone into and around the house on rainy as well as dry days to look for water seepage, cracks in masonry around window sills and in the basement?

Will your car fit into the driveway and garage?

Is the electricity amperage adequate for the electric dryer, air conditioner, and other equipment you may wish to install?

Is the water pressure adequate?

Is the heating and hot water system a costly type? Is it in good condition?

What about other houses in the neighborhood? Are they maintained with pride of ownership or are they run down? You will not enjoy your home or obtain a good resale price if it is the best kept house in a neighborhood of rundown houses.

Is the neighborhood stabilized or improving?

Is industry creeping toward the neighborhood?

Do the grounds require immediate planting, a lawn or landscaping, a retaining wall?

Is the price comparable to sales prices of similar homes in the area?

Is the house one that will be easily resold for at least what you pay for it?

Is the local government a good one?

FINANCING YOUR MORTGAGE

The purchase price of your house, over and above the down payment, is financed by a mortgage. The lender is the mortgagee. In consideration for the money advanced to you to enable you to pay the balance of the seller's price, you pledge the house and land as security for repayment of your loan with interest. A mortgage is payable in regular installments, monthly or otherwise, over a stated period of years. Most mortgages are payable over 15, 20, 25, or 30 years, but the term could be more, or less. You will be required to maintain adequate fire insurance, pay taxes promptly, and keep the house in good repair for the protection of the mortgagee's interest.

The monthly payment you agree to make will include interest on the unpaid balance of your loan and a payment in reduction (amortization) of the loan. It may also include an amount to be held in escrow for payment of real property taxes as due. Although your unpaid balance is reduced by each payment, your monthly payments do not change. But the way your payment is allocated does change. As your balance is decreased, the interest due from you is proportionately reduced. This allows for a larger portion of each payment to be applied toward reduction of the loan. In the first years of a mortgage a greater part of each payment goes for interest. In the later years the greater part goes toward amortization.

OBTAINING A MORTGAGE

Mortgage money can be obtained from commercial or savings banks, savings and loan associations, life insurance companies, and other lenders, including individuals.

The amount of money you can obtain depends on such factors as the availability of money in the market, your credit, the age and condition of the house and its current market value, the number of years over which the loan is to be repaid, and the rate of interest called for.

TERMS OF PAYMENT

The longer the period over which your mortgage has to run, the more total interest you will have to pay. However, your monthly payments will be less if repayment is spread over a longer period. This may better suit your budget.

Say you can get a $10,000 mortgage at 6 percent interest to be paid off over 10 years. Monthly payments to amortize the loan will be $111. If the term of the mortgage is 20 years, payments will be $72; if 30 years, $60. These amounts will include interest on the unpaid part of your mortgage loan until the debt is fully paid off.

Rates of interest vary in different localities. You will generally find, however, that most major lenders in a given area offer home mortgages at similar rates. Nevertheless, a difference of a fraction of a percent can mean an overall saving of several hundred or more dollars. For example, compare the monthly payments you would have to pay to amortize a 6 percent mortgage with a 6½ percent and 7 percent mortgage similar in term and amount.

Monthly payments required to amortize $10,000 mortgage:

	10 Years	20 Years	30 Years
6% rate	$111	$72	$60
6½% rate	113	75	63
7% rate	116	78	66

Note that the figures above are for interest and amortization only. The mortgagee may require you to pay a stated amount each month toward real property taxes into an "escrow account," from which taxes will be paid by the mortgagee. This monthly payment is subject to change in amount if taxes are increased. In any event, you must count on this, too, as a carrying charge of owning your home.

The larger your down payment the smaller your mortgage loan will have to be, and the less its cost. The average down payment on the purchase of a home is 25 percent, and the mortgage loan 75 percent of the price of the house. However, you should not be influenced or misled by averages. Shop for the lowest rate you can get. Make the largest down payment you can afford. And if your goal is to reduce monthly carrying charges as rapidly as possible, try to repay your mortgage in the shortest possible time.

Keep in mind always that the interest you pay on a mortgage loan is deductible for income tax purposes. The actual cost of a higher interest rate may be less than appears at first when you take into account this tax deduction over the mortgage term. It is only the *interest* portion of each installment that gets this treatment.

OPEN-END MORTGAGE

An open-end mortgage is one that provides that, during its term, the owner can ask for an additional advance to increase the unpaid balance for an extended period under the terms of the original agreement. This provision can be of great value in the later years of a mortgage, when the additional money might be needed to finance a child's education, to make major improvements, or for other purposes. The original face amount of the mortgage is generally the ceiling for the total of new and old loans. The mortgagor usually grants the additional loan if the value of the property, the owner's credit, and other circumstances warrant it. Even if an increased rate of interest was a condition for the extension, it would be less costly for the homeowner than refinancing through a new mortgage.

PREPAYMENT

When negotiating for a mortgage, it is a good idea to get the privilege of prepaying it, preferably without a penalty. Some lending institutions will allow prepayment on payment of 1 percent (more or less) of the unpaid balance due. If you have surplus cash over your family needs and want to cut monthly living costs, it might be to your advantage to prepay the mortgage even on payment of the penalty. In times when mortgage money is tight, the mortgagee might waive the penalty and gladly accept your prepayment without it.

MORTGAGE-REDEMPTION INSURANCE POLICIES

It is possible to buy at relatively low cost an insurance policy that is specially designed to pay the unpaid balance due on your home mortgage on your death. Payment of a mortgage on a family home will eliminate a major expense for those surviving, and might even enable them to remain in the house indefinitely. In any event, the surviving family would not be under pressure to sell at a forced price. If they decided to sell, the entire sales proceeds would be retained, since the property would be free and clear of the mortgage.

SECOND MORTGAGES

Where you do not have the cash necessary to pay the difference between the amount of the primary mortgage and the purchase price, you may be able to get the cash by obtaining a second mortgage on the property. Second mortgages generally bear higher than normal interest rates and other charges that are and will continue to be burdensome. Except in special circumstances, a second mortgage should not be resorted to by a buyer unless his earnings clearly allow for these payments in addition to all other carrying charges projected.

Interest paid to a second mortgagee is also deductible for income tax purposes.

VETERANS

If you are a veteran, check with your local Veterans Administration about your eligibility and opportunity to get a VA mortgage, or a VA insured mortgage. Such a mortgage will generally run for a longer term, and at lower interest rates.

FHA MORTGAGES

An FHA mortgage does not represent a loan from the Federal Housing Administration. The mortgage is obtained from a private lending institution, but this government agency insures the lender against loss in case of the homeowner's failure to repay it. Lenders are willing to accept smaller down payments, a lower interest rate, and to lend their money over longer periods because of this guarantee. FHA charges an insurance premium of ½ percent per year on the unpaid balance, included in the monthly payments the mortgage calls for.

When you buy a home and plan for an FHA-insured mortgage, the FHA will make a complete review of your ability to meet the mortgage obligation. This credit review is made after the bank or other lending institution willing to make the loan submits your application to the FHA. In addition to appraising the property, the FHA will consider your estimated continuing, dependable income, estimated prospective monthly housing expenses, and estimated living costs, debts, and other financial obligations.

Although government agencies are trying to process applications for home loans more expeditiously, these applications necessarily involve a great deal of paper work. It takes longer to get a government-insured loan.

An FHA mortgage provides the homeowner with a certain feeling of security not usually associated with bank or other corporate mortgages. FHA's policy is to see that every effort is made to avoid foreclosure of insured mortgages where the owner is suffering a hardship because of unfortunate circumstances beyond his control. Lenders are encouraged to wait as long as a year from default before beginning foreclosure, to suspend payments or reduce the amounts temporarily, or to modify the terms for payment of the unpaid balance within the owner's ability to meet them. If the lender is unwilling to enter into an appropriate "forbearance" arrangement with the homeowner, the FHA can ask it to assign the mortgage to it, so that it can work out relief provisions suitable to the homeowner's circumstances.

FHA regulations also include special relief provisions for military personnel.

FHA HOME IMPROVEMENT LOANS

The Federal Housing Administration offers several insurance programs in financing home improvements. In addition to interest there is a ½ percent FHA insurance premium, similar to that payable on mortgage loans. Here, too, the loan is obtained from a private lending institution and is insured by the FHA. The lender may impose a closing charge, inspection fee, and other fees and charges that will vary from one locality to another. The bank or other lending institution which makes the loan will give you these charges. You should have the figures before you commit yourself to the loan.

INSURING YOURSELF FROM PROPERTY LOSSES
AND CLAIMS OF OTHERS

Mishaps appear to happen to the other fellow, but you are as prone to them as any other person. Fires, storms, floods, or other casualties may damage or destroy your home. You may be struck by a car, or you may strike someone. A burglar may steal valuables from your house or vandals may ransack your home while you are away. A guest may trip on a rug in your living room. Any one of these accidents may involve you in costly litigation and damage claims. Insurance is the best financial protection against these potential losses and liabilities.

You can buy separate policies to meet the risks to which you are prone. You can buy separate policies protecting against fire, burglary, theft, and personal liability in case you injure someone. There are "floater" policies to insure against loss of such property as jewelry and furs. Generally, the more economical policy is the comprehensive policy such as that offered homeowners that combines insurance for fire loss, burglary and theft (even away from home), and personal liability. Similar comprehensive policies are offered to apartment house dwellers. There are also, of course, separate automobile insurance policies which the law of your state may compel you to carry.

We do not intend to describe the various types of policies which are available. A competent, well-informed, and reliable insurance broker can give you all the information necessary provided you inform him of your needs. But what we want to underscore is the advice to carry adequate insurance on your home. Your largest single property investment subject to loss is your home. According to insurance men, homeowners are negligent in insuring their homes. They fail to increase their coverage as property values increase. They also forget to consider home improvements in their estimate of the home's value. Consequently, when a loss does occur, they discover that they must pay a substantial part of the loss themselves.

Although the insurance should reflect market value, an estimate of market value may be inadequate if it does not also reflect replacement costs. Here, it is advisable to see that your policy provides an 80 percent clause, even if your state does not require such a clause. Under this clause, claims for partial losses are paid in full, provided the amount of your insurance is at least 80 percent of the total replacement value of the property. If you are underinsured, only a proportionate part of your loss is paid, less depreciation. The depreciation reduction could cut your insurance award to a minimum. The extra cost of this feature is not expensive, considering the protection it gives you.

If you took out insurance when placing a mortgage, the bank required you only to take insurance to protect its loan. Check to see that you have additional insurance that protects your investment or "equity" in the property. On the other hand, do not overinsure your house; do not include the value of the land, the foundation, and underground installations.

Keep an inventory of all your furnishings and household property. In case of a loss, it will provide you an excellent basis on which to claim your reimbursement. As you add new property to your house, increase your insurance coverage.

If, unfortunately, a loss does occur, take steps to reduce the damage. Do not sign any document offered by an adjuster until you are convinced that it accurately reflects your loss. Bring in your own appraiser. The adjuster works for the insurance company, not for you. Do not be rushed into a settlement. If you meet a deadlock, perhaps your agent can help you settle the case or request a special review.

Chapter 9

HOW AND WHERE TO SAVE YOUR MONEY

COMMERCIAL BANKS	136
SAVINGS AND LOAN ASSOCIATIONS	137
MUTUAL SAVINGS BANKS	137
CREDIT UNIONS	139
WHICH BANK SHOULD YOU USE?	140
YOUR BANK ACCOUNT CARRIES CERTAIN RESPONSIBILITIES	142
WHAT YOU SHOULD KNOW ABOUT UNITED STATES SAVINGS BONDS	143
Types of Savings Bonds	145
Freedom Shares	148
Tax Aspects of Savings Bonds	149
Check Your Old Bonds	150

Money, its value and availability, is at the forefront of much of the world's attention. The balance on the seesaw between supply and demand for funds has been mainly on the side of demand.

This growing demand has made the saver and his nest egg a fit subject for wooing by commercial banks and other savings institutions. Higher interest rates, added insurance protection for savings, new types of accounts, savings bonds and savings certificates, golden passbooks, and gifts are being offered as enticements to savers.

A more dispassionate view of savings institutions and the types of accounts and methods of savings available may prove helpful.

In deciding where to place your money, you can choose between savings banks, savings and loan associations, commercial banks, and credit unions. In addition, your savings may go into savings bonds or certificates sold by banks, as well as many other forms of investment: government bonds, securities, real estate, etc.

COMMERCIAL BANKS

Many commercial banks maintain savings, time deposit, thrift or special interest accounts and are the largest holders of savings in this country. In some communities, a commercial bank is the only institution in the area that accepts savings.

Interest paid by commercial banks on savings accounts varies; it is usually lower than the rate offered by other savings institutions. Commercial banks, however, offer certain banking services not available at other banks, for example, checking accounts, to name the most popular. Checking accounts earn no interest; rather, the owner of the account usually pays a monthly maintenance fee in addition to charges for checks drawn and deposits made to the account. Christmas Club accounts are available at commercial banks as well as at other banking institutions. These usually earn no interest. Recently, some banks have begun to pay interest on Christmas Club accounts; the rate, however, is lower than that paid on regular savings accounts. It is, therefore, necessary to ascertain the precise arrangement and nature of the account you open.

Although the commercial bank interest rate may be lower than that offered by other banks for savings accounts, commercial banks pay higher interest (often 5 percent and better) to purchasers of their savings bonds, savings certificates, or certificates of deposit. Some can be bought in units of $100; other banks may set higher minimums, $500, $1000, or even more.

Some commercial banks in New York currently offer these three types of bonds at 5 percent interest, compounded daily, yielding 6.5 percent average yearly interest if bond is held for ten years.

Growth Bond—Sold in amounts from $100 to $100,000. For example: $5000 bond; value at end of five years—$6420; at end of ten years—$8243.

Income Bond—Interest paid either monthly, quarterly, or annually; similar to U. S. Series H bond except that interest rate is 5 percent as compared to 4.25 percent Treasury rate; minimum denomination $2500, Treasury minimum, $500.

Discount Bond—Similar to Series E bond, except higher interest rate prevails; minimum bond $100 face value, Series E minimum, $25.

The holder is permitted to select his own maturity date, to change the method of interest payment, or redeem the bond without penalty upon 90 days notice.

SAVINGS AND LOAN ASSOCIATIONS

Savings and loan associations are an old American institution dating back to 1831. Over 40,000,000 people have savings accounts at the more than 6000 state or federally chartered savings and loan associations in all 50 states.

Fundamentally, savings and loan associations operate in the same way as the mutual savings banks. A good many pay passbook savers the maximum rate of interest allowed in the state in which they operate. In some states, the rate has been as high as 5.25 percent.

MUTUAL SAVINGS BANKS

Although mutual savings banks have been in existence in this country for more than 150 years, there are still many states in which these institutions are not permitted to operate. Government regulations restrict the maximum interest rate banks are allowed to pay on savings accounts. The maximum is currently 5 percent. Some savings banks pay the maximum, others pay less. Mutual savings banks also offer other services such as late banking hours one evening of the week, banking by mail with free postage for depositors, Christmas Club accounts, and, in certain states, savings bank life insurance.

Some banks offer packaged savings plans, which combine a savings account with life insurance and purchase of U.S. savings bonds.

Under a triple package plan, all three are obtainable through regularly made deposits in the bank.

One bank, calling their plan a "triple thrift superhighway to financial security" illustrates the results of regular deposits for ten years:

$5 A WEEK

Starting Age	Cash in Bank	Savings Bonds (Face Value)	Decreasing Term Insurance (Initial Amount)
20	$1910	$500	$10,000
25	1880	500	10,000
30	1830	500	10,000
35	1740	500	10,000
40	1570	500	10,000
45	1500	500	10,000
50	1070	500	10,000

$10 A WEEK

20	$3900	$500	$30,000
25	3820	500	30,000
30	3670	500	30,000
35	3370	500	30,000
40	2870	500	30,000
45	3000	500	20,000
50	2150	500	20,000

The cash in bank figures do not include the interest that the savings earn.

The term insurance decreases in coverage to 90 percent in fifth year, 70 percent in tenth year. However, the policy pays cash dividends and can be converted to permanent insurance without medical checkup or may be kept in force 10 additional years at the same premium.

A packaged plan can be worked out calling for deposits at other intervals, such as monthly or semimonthly. Instead of term insurance, a plan can be arranged with straight life or 20-payment life insurance. Or, a savings plan may include only two˙ of the elements, omitting either the insurance or the savings bonds.

CREDIT UNIONS

Credit unions are a special type of institution for savings. They are private organizations, owned and operated by the members, persons in a closely knit group, such as employees of companies, labor unions, teachers, fraternal or social lodges, etc. These cooperative credit societies encourage the members to save systematically and offer free life insurance and low-cost unsecured loans to shareholders.

One of the prime incentives to employees to open up a credit union account at their place of employment is the opportunity for systematic savings via regular payroll deductions. Another incentive is that free life insurance may be provided for the credit union shareholders. The availability of free life insurance acts as an inducement for shareholders to maintain a balance in their credit union accounts even though interest paid on credit union shares is generally less than that offered by other savings institutions. The insurance maximum is $2000 and covers the life of the credit union member. The actual amount of insurance coverage, however, depends on the balance in the account and the age of the saver. On shareholdings purchased before age 55, the amount of insurance matches dollar for dollar the entire balance in the account, up to the $2000 maximum. The insurance covers only half of deposits made from age 55 to 65. However, the saver remains fully covered for shares purchased before he reached age 55.

Membership in a credit union is restricted to persons having a common bond. The bond need not be one of employment. It could be, for example, a common occupation, a group within a well-defined neighborhood, community or rural district, or it may be members of a church, fraternal society, farm organization, or the residents of a natural trade area of a rural community or rural district.

More than 22,000 credit unions having 16 million members operate in the United States. About half of these are under Federal charter and are supervised by the Federal Government through the

Bureau of Federal Credit Unions; however, they are not Federal agencies. The others operate under state credit union laws. (See page 95 for credit union loans.)

The major disadvantage to saving money in a credit union lies in the fact that savings shares are not insured as are deposits in other banking institutions. Another possibility is that a company credit union might be forced to liquidate if, for example, a company in which members were employed were involved in a merger or moved its place of business to a different locality. Shareholders would run the risk of having to wait for their money. Also, if there were a strike, the company credit union would be subject to great pressure. Without pay checks, the shareholder-employees, in need of funds, could put a dangerous strain on a credit union's resources. During a lengthy strike, one company credit union did not permit withdrawals, but instead allowed limited borrowing against money on deposit and carried loans that were technically in default.

WHICH BANK SHOULD YOU USE?

The interest rate alone is not the sole criterion for people in their choice of where to maintain a savings account. Convenience banking near one's home or office, using one bank for checking and for savings, are factors that often determine one's choice.

These important points should be checked before opening an account.

Safety of your savings. How will you be protected against loss of your savings? Membership of a bank in either the Federal Savings and Loan Insurance Corporation or the Federal Deposit Insurance Corporation guarantees the safety of your savings. Each is an instrumentality of the United States Government and insures up to $15,000 of your savings in an account. An individual may have only one account insured up to $15,000 in a single institution.

However, where state laws permit, two or more persons may have individual insured accounts of $15,000 each and, in addition, have an insured joint account. In this way, a husband and wife may have insured accounts in one bank totaling $45,000:

$15,000 insurance protection on wife's individual account;

$15,000 insurance protection on husband's individual account;

$15,000 insurance protection on joint account of husband and wife.

It is also possible to have additional insurance protection when savings accounts are owned in conjunction with one's children or other relatives.

If your funds exceed the insurance limit, you should maintain accounts at more than one savings institution to assure complete insurance protection for all your savings.

There is no cost to the individual saver for this insurance protection. Rather, each member bank pays premiums directly to the insuring corporation.

In Massachusetts, Maryland, and Ohio, savings are protected by state insurance agencies.

Compounding of interest. Two banks may pay the same rate of interest. Nevertheless, your savings might earn more money in one bank than they would in the other. The reason: Some banks compound interest more frequently than do others.

Many banks compound and pay interest four times a year. At a 5 percent interest rate, it would take 14 years for money to double.

Regular monthly deposits in a savings account paying 5 percent interest, compounded quarterly, would grow as follows:

If you deposit monthly	$25	$50	$100	$200
In 5 years you deposit	$ 1,500	$ 3,000	$ 6,000	$ 12,000
With interest you have	1,706	3,412	6,825	13,650
In 10 years you deposit	3,000	6,000	12,000	24,000
With interest you have	3,893	7,787	15,575	31,151
In 20 years you deposit	6,000	12,000	24,000	48,000
With interest you have	10,292	20,585	41,175	82,351
In 30 years you deposit	9,000	18,000	36,000	72,000
With interest you have	20,809	41,621	83,250	166,504
In 40 years you deposit	12,000	24,000	48,000	96,000
With interest you have	38,095	76,196	152,407	304,819

Withdrawals—penalties and restrictions. Banks can legally require thirty days notice of withdrawal from its depositors. Some banks impose a service charge for each withdrawal over a prescribed number.

Find out if it is the bank's practice to require notice before making a withdrawal. Ask whether it places any restriction or penalty on the withdrawal of funds, such as not permitting withdrawals within a certain period of time after an account has been opened. Inquire if it imposes a service charge for extra withdrawals. It is also wise to check on how withdrawals can be made. Will the bank honor a request for withdrawal of funds by mail? This is particularly important in today's mobile society, with the frequent transfers of company personnel and their families.

Some years ago, a large commercial bank followed the practice of imposing a charge if a bank check was requested by a depositor withdrawing funds from a savings account. Make sure your bank invokes no similar penalty.

Loss of interest. Ascertain the bank's timetable for paying interest. Then you will be able to time your deposits to earn the maximum interest. A few banks pay interest from the day of deposit to the date of withdrawal. Some banks pay interest on deposits made within the first ten days of the month from the first of the month. Money deposited after the ten-day grace period may not begin to earn interest until the next period. If funds are withdrawn from the bank before the end of the interest period, the entire interest for the period on the withdrawn amount may be lost. (See page 96.)

YOUR BANK ACCOUNT CARRIES CERTAIN RESPONSIBILITIES

Do not be misled into thinking that a bank passbook is sufficient and perpetual proof of your ownership of funds on deposit at the bank. It is not. Every state, to some extent, practices escheat, state seizure of property with no apparent owner. One of the most common forms of escheat is acquisition by the state of unclaimed bank deposits.

How can such a thing occur? Enticed by a premium offer, someone opens an account at a distant bank, places the passbook in a "safe" place, and forgets about it. The birth of a baby inspires the opening of a now long-overlooked bank account. A husband or wife starts building a private nest egg in a secret bank account, the evidence of which is tucked away at the bottom of a little-used drawer.

Depending upon the state in which the bank is located, an account that has been dormant for a number of years becomes vulnerable to the laws of escheat. In New York, the time is 10 years. If a bank fails to reach a depositor through the mails at his last known address and through advertisements and public notices, it must turn the funds over to the state after 10 years, in accordance with state law. Once the money has been handed over to the state, securing its return is quite costly.

To safeguard your savings, you should keep a record of all your accounts, the number, bank and location (see page 29). At least once a year, have the bank interest entered in each passbook you own. If you move, notify every bank in which you have an account of your new address.

Another little publicized fact is that savings accounts dormant for a number of years may cease earning interest. In addition, a bank may, under its rules, pay no interest on balances below a set minimum, which minimum can change without a depositor's knowledge.

WHAT YOU SHOULD KNOW ABOUT UNITED STATES SAVINGS BONDS

United States savings bonds play an important role in the financial security programs of millions of American families; more than $50 billion worth of these securities are currently outstanding. The popularity of savings bonds as a form of investment reached a 10-year peak in 1966; sales of Series E bonds alone were the highest since the end of World War II.

In addition to patriotic reasons, people have been attracted to investing in savings bonds for one or more of these reasons:

1. Savings bonds are considered to be a riskless investment because they always can be redeemed at a stated value on demand after two months from the issue date; they are considered a safe investment because they are backed by the credit of the United States government.

2. They are a "liquid" reserve, quickly and easily translated into dollars and cents when needed.

3. Unlike other types of investments, they are not subject to market fluctuations; they are never redeemed for less than the amount invested.

4. Interest on savings bonds is not subject to state or local income or personal property taxes.

5. The Federal income tax on Series E bond interest can be deferred, and the annual increases in value need not be reported on the Federal tax return until the bond is cashed.

6. If savings bonds are lost, stolen, or destroyed, they can be replaced without cost.

7. Savings bonds are easy and convenient to buy. They are sold at neighborhood banks. Also, many corporations have established payroll savings plans; an employee can buy bonds regularly merely by authorizing his employer to make automatic deductions from his pay check.

8. Savings bonds have proved to be a popular form of gift. Giving a $25 bond as a wedding present is probably considered to be less impersonal and more thoughtful than a gift of cash.

On the other hand, there are certain disadvantages to savings bonds as a form of investment:

1. Although the Treasury has several times in the past and again in 1968 raised the interest rate for savings bonds, bond rates have always lagged behind savings bank rates. When the savings bond rate in June 1968 was increased to 4.25 percent, New York savings institutions were offering their customers 5 percent; California banks advertised 5.25 percent interest.

2. Although people are given the choice of reporting Series E bond interest annually on their Federal income tax returns, it is more usual for people not to make this election, but instead to defer the reporting of interest. As a result, when funds are needed

and the bonds cashed, all the accumulated and current interest becomes taxable in one year. If this occurs in a high income year, the resulting tax may prove to be onerous.

3. Savings bonds cannot be used as collateral and cannot be pledged. If the money is needed, the bonds must be cashed and an immediate tax incurred not only on the current, but also on any accumulated interest on which tax has been deferred.

4. Compared to other investments, such as securities or real estate, savings bonds offer neither growth potential nor capital gain possibility.

Over the last several decades, this country's economy has expanded greatly. Stock market and real estate investors have seen their properties grow in value. On the other hand, the United States dollar, in terms of buying power has deteriorated in value. The dollar today buys less than half the goods and services it purchased in 1941.

A person who bought a $1000 savings bond in 1941 for $750 and cashed it in 1968 would have $1700. This $1700, however, has half the purchasing power it would have had 25 years before.

This lack of growth potential, coupled with inflation, is considered the greatest disadvantage of savings bonds as an investment.

TYPES OF SAVINGS BONDS

Following is a brief summary of the types of savings bonds currently being sold.

The Series E bond is the type most widely held.

1. *Price.* 75 cents on the dollar of maturity value. $18.75 becomes $25 at maturity, $37.50 becomes $50 at maturity, $56.25 becomes $75 at maturity, $75 becomes $100, etc.

2. *Maturity date.* Seven years from issue date.

3. *Interest.* Beginning June 1968, 4.25 percent if held to maturity; lesser yields if redeemed at earlier dates. (A schedule of redemption values from issue date to maturity appears below.)

4. *Redemption.* Bond can be redeemed for cash at any time after it is two months old without notice, and at stated redemption values at most banks and other financial institutions.

5. *Negotiability.* None.

6. *Eligibility as collateral for loans.* None.

7. *Purchase limits.* $20,000 maturity value ($15,000 issue price) per investor per year.

8. *Denomination.* $25, $50, $75, $100, $200, $500, $1000, $10,000 (maturity value).

9. *Registration.* Must be in registered form and may be registered in the name of a single owner, adult or minor, with or without beneficiary, or in co-ownership form.

10. *Extension.* If an owner does not wish to cash a savings bond at maturity, he may hold it for an additional 10 years after the original maturity date and earn interest now yielding 4.25 percent per year compounded semiannually. Series E bonds issued between May 1, 1941, and May 1, 1949, have been given a second ten-year extension period.

The following table shows the cash redemption value of a $100 bond from issue date to maturity, for bonds bearing issue date of December 1, 1965, and after.

	Redemption Value During Each
Period Held	*Half-Year Period*
Period after issue date	
First ½ year	$ 75.00
½ to 1 year	75.84
1 to 1½ years	77.28
1½ to 2 years	78.80
2 to 2½ years	80.40
2½ to 3 years	82.08
3 to 3½ years	83.84
3½ to 4 years	85.68
4 to 4½ years	87.56
4½ to 5 years	89.48
5 to 5½ years	91.44
5½ to 6 years	93.44
6 to 6½ years	95.52
6½ to 7 years	97.68
Maturity value (7 years from issue date)	100.00

The rise in the interest rate as of June 1, 1968, from 4.15 percent to 4.25 percent will apply only to bonds that are held to maturity or beyond. The added .10 percent increases the maturity (or extended maturity) values of the bonds effective June 1, 1968. An E bond purchased after June 1968 will be worth $100.64 at its maturity seven years later.

The Series H bond is a current income bond, on which interest is paid by check semiannually. The H bond is a companion to the E bond, but there are some important differences. It is priced at par, or face value, and is redeemable at par. While the interest schedule corresponds closely to that on the E bond, the interest on the E bond accrues to maturity; on the H bond it is paid every six months by check. The smallest denomination H bond is $500 (against $25 for the E bond).

The H bond is for the individual who can invest in $500 blocks and who wants a current income.

Here is a summary of its terms and conditions:

1. *Price.* Par or face value.

2. *Maturity date.* Ten years from issue date.

3. *Interest.* Varying semiannual interest checks to provide an investment yield of about 4.25 percent per year, if held to maturity; lesser yields if redeemed at earlier dates.

4. *Redemption.* Bond can be redeemed for cash at par on one month's notice at any Federal Reserve Bank or branch or at the United States Treasury, but it must be held at least six months before it is redeemable.

5. *Negotiability.* None.

6. *Eligibility as collateral for loans.* None.

7. *Purchase limits.* $30,000 per investor per year.

8. *Denominations.* $500, $1000, $5000, and $10,000.

9. *Registrations.* Must be in registered form and may be registered in name of a single owner, adult or minor with or without beneficiary, or in co-ownership form.

10. *Extension privileges.* H bonds issued between June 1952 and May 1959 may be retained for an additional 10 years.

Here is a table showing you the schedule of semiannual interest checks on H bonds of several denominations:

SEMIANNUAL INTEREST CHECKS ON H BONDS

Bonds Bearing Issue Date of December 1, 1965, and After	Denomination			
	$500	*$1000*	*$5000*	*$10,000*
First check (after 6 months)	$ 5.50	$11.00	$ 55.00	$110.00
Next check (1 year)	9.70	19.40	97.00	194.00
Next 18 checks	10.75	21.50	107.50	215.00

An increase from 4.15 to 4.25 percent in the interest rate paid on H bonds effective June 1, 1968, will be realized in the final interest period when bonds are held to maturity.

FREEDOM SHARES

Freedom shares, the popular name for the new United States savings notes, are an innovation in Government securities. They can be purchased only in conjunction with Series E and H bonds and feature a higher rate of interest and a shorter maturity period.

Summary of terms and conditions is as follows:

1. *Price*   *Face Amount of Freedom Share*

$20.25	$ 25.00
40.50	50.00
60.75	75.00
81.00	100.00

2. *Maturity date.* Four and a half years from issue date.

3. *Interest.* On Freedom shares issued after June 1, 1968, 5 percent compounded semiannually when held to maturity. A $100 Freedom share would be worth $101.16 when it matures in 4½ years.

4. *Redemption.* Freedom shares can be redeemed after one year from date of issue.

Since they first went on sale on May 1, 1967, the earliest redemption date for any Freedom share is May 1, 1968.

5. *Purchase limits.* Freedom shares may be purchased only in combination with E or H bonds of the same or larger face amounts. They cannot be bought by themselves. For example, you can buy a $25 Freedom share with an E bond of like amount at a cost of $39; $18.75 for the E bond and $20.25 for the Freedom share.

There is a limit of $1350 (face amount) of Freedom shares that can be purchased by one person in one calendar year. The purchase of Freedom shares is further restricted within the following periods of time: weekly limit—face amount that can be purchased is $25; bi-weekly or semimonthly, $50; monthly, $100.

6. *Registration*. The same form of registration must be used for the Freedom share and E or H bond purchased in combination.

7. *Taxation*. You must use the same method of reporting interest on Freedom shares as you use for reporting E bond interest.

TAX ASPECTS OF SAVINGS BONDS

There is flexibility with respect to the reporting of E bond interest on the Federal tax return. Either you report the fixed increase in value on your return each year, or you may defer the reporting of interest until you cash the bond or until the bond finally matures, whichever is earlier. If you own bonds which have increased in value in prior years and you make an election to report the annual increases this year, you must report the total of all these increases in value, that is, you must include all accumulated interest on all the Series E bonds you hold on which tax has been postponed. And, once you make the election to report annual increases, you must continue to do so unless you get Treasury approval to change your method of reporting.

Interest earned on Freedom shares must be reported according to the method used for reporting E bond interest. If you report E bond interest annually you will also report the interest on Freedom shares on your yearly return. Similarly, if you have deferred the reporting of E bond interest, you will likewise defer the reporting of Freedom share interest.

Tax deferral of savings bond interest can be advantageous if payment of tax on accrued interest is postponed to a low income (low tax-bracket) year, such as after retirement. Since future tax rates and circumstances cannot be accurately predicted, tax deferral of E bond interest can prove to be disadvantageous.

Income tax can be saved in this way:

E bonds can be bought and registered in the name of a minor child.

The child files his own tax return and lists the increase in bond value as income, together with an accrued E bond interest from bonds previously owned. If the child's entire income is under $900, he owes no tax. This return signifies an election and establishes intent. No further return need be filed while the child's annual income remains under $600.

CHECK YOUR OLD BONDS

In an advertisement, a large investment firm once pointed out the amazing fact that American investors at that time were holding almost half a billion dollars worth of Government securities on which they were earning no money whatsoever. This points up the importance of checking old savings bonds, such as A to D, F and G, J and K bonds which are no longer on sale.

Series J bonds that are presented not later than six months after maturity may be exchanged for H bonds without incurring a tax liability at the time of the exchange. The tax liability on any accrued interest on such J bonds can continue to be deferred. The proceeds of other matured bonds, Series F, G, J, or K, can be reinvested in either E or H bonds, but no income tax deferral privilege applies.

All Series E and Series H bonds now outstanding continue to pay interest. A holder may exchange E bonds for H bonds with continued tax deferral on accrued E bond interest.

Chapter 10

YOUR LIFE INSURANCE PROGRAM; ANNUITIES

FIRST STEPS IN YOUR PROGRAM	152
THE INSURANCE COMPANIES AND THE POLICIES THEY SELL	153
THE INSURANCE AGENT	154
WHAT TYPE OF INSURANCE DO YOU NEED—AND WHEN?	155
HOW MUCH INSURANCE DO YOU NEED?	156
TERM INSURANCE	158
WHOLE LIFE INSURANCE	159
LIMITED PAYMENT LIFE	161
ENDOWMENT	161
BASIC LIFE CONTRACTS NOW ARE COMBINED	162
FAMILY INCOME	164
FAMILY MAINTENANCE	165
FAMILY PLAN	166
MAIL ORDER INSURANCE	166
SAVINGS BANK INSURANCE	167
GROUP LIFE	167
BENEFICIARIES	168
GI INSURANCE	169
PAYING YOUR INSURANCE PREMIUMS	169
THE DECISION IS YOURS	169
THE LANGUAGE OF LIFE INSURANCE	170
ANNUITIES	171
Types of Annuities	172
Buying Annuities	174
Problem of Inflation Can Be Met With Variable Annuities	175
Should You Buy an Annuity?	176

For the man or woman with dependents, life insurance is a keystone in a money management program. Its major objective is to protect the family at time of death; it can also provide a basis for loans, either as collateral or in borrowing from the insurance company (page 90); too, it may be used in financing retirement (page 261).

Life insurance is tax protected. The face amount payable on death can be received by a beneficiary free of income tax. If insured had no incidents of ownership in the policy, such as the right to name beneficiaries or take a loan on its cash surrender value, the proceeds are also freed of estate tax.

FIRST STEPS IN YOUR PROGRAM

You should buy insurance with the same caution and comparison that you would employ in buying any other major asset, such as a house. When you buy property you will probably approach several real estate agents; you will view a number of houses before making your choice. Why buy life insurance differently?

Many people, indeed the majority, play a passive role and let themselves be selected as "prospects" by a neighborhood insurance representative; by a relative who has recently become an insurance agent or broker; or by a company advertisement which has hooked them into coupon-signing without too much—or any—forethought.

You can decide to practice your smart consumer tactics instead. Begin by quizzing your friends. From them, you obtain the names of companies and some firsthand experiences of their dealings. But, while you make a note of recommended companies, remember that you are not likely to buy the same types of policies your friends have bought; your situation is different and you want general guidance only.

You will also note the names of advertised companies and those which have agencies in your neighborhood. Preferably, drop in at the offices to get an impression of how the organization does business and to obtain some information. Undoubtedly you will be bombarded by agents, but you should certainly resist pressure to sign up until you have compared the life insurance plans offered by several companies.

Moreover, when you have decided on a particular policy, you should not sign until you have thoroughly examined all the clauses and made sure that you understand what is contained in the fine print. If the agent from whom you propose to buy the policy will not provide you with a sample copy, go to another agent.

THE INSURANCE COMPANIES AND THE POLICIES THEY SELL

For your own protection you will want to do business with a well-established company and to avoid those which have yet to prove themselves. The giants of the insurance industry do not necessarily offer the most reasonably priced insurance. In fact, a small company may offer you a better deal, but you should check on the company's background. Make sure it is not a newcomer with a similar name to one well known. See remarks on page 166 regarding mail order insurance.

Basically, two types of policies are available through two types of company (though there is some overlapping). A *stock company* issues nonparticipating policies, which means that you do not pay as much as you would for a similar policy issued by a *mutual company* (usually identifiable by the word "mutual" in its title).

In the case of the nonparticipating policy, the company has set the rate *at what it expects the insurance to cost*. In advance, you know exactly what you will pay for your coverage.

In the case of the participating policy, the company has fixed premium rates *in excess of what it expects the insurance to cost*. Why then should you consider this type of policy? In the long run it may prove less costly than a nonparticipating policy because you will receive dividends after the first two or three years. The dividends are not taxable; they are refunds on your premiums made when the company's actual operating costs are known. The amount of your annual dividends will, of course, vary with company decision and profit. In prosperous times, your company's participating policy may pay good dividends, but an economic slump might mean small, or even no, dividends.

Company policies differ on payment of dividends, some tending to increase them in the later years, thus benefiting the long-lived, long-paying insured person. If you have a participating policy, you can accept dividends in a number of ways, from cash payment (which would enable you to build your regular savings account) to buying additional insurance. *Be sure dividends are paid to you as you want* and not automatically applied by the company to the purchase of extra insurance you may not need.

THE INSURANCE AGENT

As noted on page 167, savings bank life insurance is available in certain states on a come-and-get-it basis, but the vast bulk of life insurance is sold by agents. These men are sometimes employees of a company and may or may not receive a salary in addition to commission. Usually, they are self-employed and work only for commission. (Bear this factor well in mind and ask yourself if the insurance the agent is advising for you is the protection your family requires, or if it just pays him better.)

When you consider the great importance of life insurance to the security of your family, and the amount of money you will invest, you certainly want to be personally satisfied with the individual who will be making far-reaching recommendations to you and to have some background information on him.

If you can interview several company representatives and let them suggest certain life insurance planning for you without committing yourself definitely to any one, you will be in a favorable position to judge both the variations on basic policies offered and the men who describe them to you.

If an agent has been advising and selling to your friends for some years, you know he is no fledgling, but if you are dealing with a man unknown to you, find out how long he has been in the business. While it may be agreeable to give some young fellow a start, let him practice on the less knowledgeable; you prefer to know that your man is experienced, at least four to five years as an agent, and if he can add "C.L.U." after his name, you can be assured he is a Chartered Life Underwriter, having successfully completed examinations and other requirements set by the American College of Life Underwriters.

Beware the man who insists that only some high-priced combination policy will suit your family's needs. It might make you "insurance-poor" the rest of your life, while he gains good commission. Beware, too, the man who wants you to drop some other company's policy to take his. This unethical gambit, known as "twisting," has resulted in loss for many people who allowed themselves to be persuaded into dropping policies they had for years. If you meet with this ploy, take the opportunity to review thoroughly what your original company offered and, if changes seem justified, see what they can suggest to meet your present needs. Only if careful investigation proves that the agent had a valid point should you let a former policy lapse in favor of a new one.

It should be recognized that an agent may be perfectly sincere in his recommendations to you since he himself is likely to be very well indoctrinated by his company, but what he offers is not necessarily right for you. Provide your own clear-cut ideas on the insurance you should have.

WHAT TYPE OF INSURANCE DO YOU NEED—AND WHEN?

In general, your need begins with your financial responsibilities to others. When a young couple first marry, they may live in an apartment and both have jobs. Their money is better directed toward the savings bank than into life insurance unless either must contribute toward a dependent.

The real need for life insurance usually begins when the first child is expected. Soon, the wife will give up her job; the young husband wants to provide for her and for his child's upbringing in case of his death. At this point he may take out *convertible term insurance* (page 159). If his wife has reasonably good earning potential of her own, his main concern will be for the child's care and education.

The need for life insurance becomes greater as the family increases. The wife is less likely to return to work while the children are young; the couple probably decide they need a house of their own. Now the husband must cover his responsibilities as home owner in addition to the needs of his family. He can combine straight life with decreasing term under a *combination family income policy* (page 164) to protect wife, children, and the mortgage. At this point, the breadwinner will probably find he needs certain supplementary contracts (or riders). Of particular importance and value is the *waiver of premium* rider. Should the husband suffer total and permanent disability, the insurance premiums themselves are protected; the company will pay them.

A desirable and necessary rider is *guaranteed insurability;* here, the insured protects his right to buy more insurance when he most needs it—*regardless of the state of his health at that time.* (Term policies lacking a *renewability* clause should be avoided.)

While a couple may not really need life insurance when first married, the husband might have taken his straight life policy then. He would have gained a more favorable premium rate at the earlier age, and that rate would continue all his life. Also, if he had a participating policy earning dividends, he would be that much better off.

When buying insurance, you should note that the agent receives less commission on term insurance than on the more expensive cash value policies. But if you think your needs could best be served by term insurance, *plus your own savings and investment program,* you should not allow yourself to be persuaded into taking other policies.

HOW MUCH INSURANCE DO YOU NEED?

You don't know the true answer, because the actual date of death is unknown and even the fatally ill have been known to outwit the prognosticators. It is well to sit down with paper and pencil to do some very hard, cold figuring. You can assess your needs only by asking *just where would the family stand if I died NOW?*

A realistic appraisal calls for drawing up two columns, for liabilities and assets. To begin with liabilities, your family would first face the high cost of death; ask yourself how you stand on medical/hospital-ization insurance in case of prolonged illness or injury prior to death (Chapter 13). Would the house be sold? Would your wife earn? How long would your children be dependent? Note in your calculations that your wife would lose the advantage of filing joint income tax returns.

Check Chapter 16, from which you will get some guidance on es-tate matters, and also on your will.

Consider the funeral arrangements. Do you have a cemetery lot? Would the family have to purchase one or have you stated a prefer-ence for cremation? Common sense, not morbidity, dictates that you investigate and make decisions on final arrangements. Note, on the plus side, that Social Security pays toward the funeral costs of an in-sured worker. (On the subject of funeral cost, the Better Business Bureau of Metropolitan New York, 220 Church Street, New York, New York 10013, will send, free, *"A Guide to Help You Arrange Funerals and Interments."* Supply a stamped, self-addressed envelope.)

Now, your death being paid for, where does your family stand financially? In your estimates, you can only use current figures. The net worth tabulation you worked out (Chapter 2) will help you here. You can write down the state of your assets, including any company or organization benefits payable at death, and also the family indebtedness.

From your budgeting experience (Chapter 1), you know basically what it would cost your dependents to live month by month. (For convenience, use a monthly basis in your calculations.) In so many years, some members of your family are likely to be self-supporting, but you may also have to reckon that others, because of incapacity or declining years, may not be. Write down as close an estimate as possible of your financial commitment. For example, a son, already a capable teenager, might be able to earn through his college years and only need your support for another five years. But the contribution you make toward the support of an incapacitated brother might go on for twenty-five years.

Tabulate the benefits available for your wife and family from So-cial Security (Chapter 14). You have to cover the difference, either through your own assets or through insurance. Essentially, your calculations should take into account these areas exposed by your death:

Last expenses. Cash should be easily available in a joint savings account.

After-death period. If you can keep about half a year's income in savings you can provide adequately for the readjustment your family would be making.

The home. If you are repaying a mortgage, use insurance to cover it. (Page 129.)

Income for living expenses. In general, this is the main area to be covered by life insurance policies by the breadwinner who does not have other very substantial assets.

Education of children. You will use insurance, but the family will have to fend for itself, too.

Your wife. To cover your wife's lifetime income needs *through insurance* would be exceedingly expensive. A wife's best insurance is her ability to earn for herself in case of necessity. Where this would not be possible, try to build up other assets such as investments.

Following, we give a rundown on some of the many types of life insurance available. Your agent will explain the combinations his company offers; you will, at that time, bear in mind the needs of your family you have just defined.

TERM INSURANCE

Term insurance offers coverage for a specific span of time, covering either a certain span of years or up to a certain age. Usually, term policies do not carry beyond age 70.

Because term insurance carries no cash value buildup it costs less than whole (straight) life. It has been argued that a breadwinner is better off with term insurance than with whole life *if* he puts the difference between the two premiums into a savings bank where it will earn interest (less taxes). A man who can establish this rigid program may well prefer never to convert to straight life. The nonsaver will combine insurance and savings in the more expensive cash value policy.

As mentioned earlier, *renewable* term insurance is the type to take, because renewal rates will be stated and guaranteed, even though rates may rise in the meantime, and because the insured person does not have to produce evidence of *insurability*. If health has failed and he would now be judged a poor insurance risk, he can still renew his policy.

If your preference is for straight life, but you cannot presently afford it, make sure that your term policy is *convertible*. This means that, still without giving evidence of insurability, you may convert to a straight life or endowment policy. However, you may have to inform the company that you intend to convert, and the policy may have a deadline for doing so. Be sure to check on this point. If you have ten-year term insurance, for instance, you may have to announce an intention to convert before the first seven years have elapsed.

Term insurance is often used in addition to whole life insurance by people who have extra risks to cover at certain periods of time. Perhaps a man has covered his family's needs with straight life insurance, then, unexpectedly, he is burdened by helping a brother straighten out his debts or becomes responsible for an aged relative. He finds extra protection for his income in one-year or five-year term insurance.

When the insured breadwinner is handling a heavy debt, such as a mortgage, a decreasing term policy or rider is an extra safeguard. The death benefit decreases during the term of the insurance, but so, too, does the amount of the debt and the consequent financial responsibility.

A combination plan of gradually decreasing term insurance and straight life is often suggested by an insurance company's agent as the best means of protecting family income.

WHOLE LIFE INSURANCE

With whole life insurance (also referred to as straight or ordinary life), you pay a certain premium; you receive life coverage and other stated benefits. *The age at which you buy your policy decides the premium rate at which you will continue to pay.* Your policy acquires a "cash value" because the company invests part of the premiums. This cash value is an asset, useful in raising loans (Chapter 6), and can help you to cover your insurance if, at some time or other, you are unable to pay premiums.

If you eventually wish to discontinue premium payments altogether, several possibilities are open to you: You can receive less insurance protection throughout your life (based on the cash value); you can set an ending date to the full protection; you can obtain a cash settlement for your canceled policy; instead of life insurance, you elect to receive income for a certain period.

Note that your policy will automatically put some provision into effect if you fail to pay premiums. Check to find out what it is because, if you cannot pay, you may wish a different provision to be made and you will have to so notify the company.

Straight life carries with it the virtue of being an enforced savings program besides imparting protection to the breadwinner. The cash value accumulated amounts to around 60 percent of the face value. Note that cash value is not an additional sum payable to your beneficiary; it is payable only if the policy is discontinued.

The cost of substantial coverage by permanent insurance may pose a financing problem for a father with young children. Over the next 10 years, his family responsibilities will be greatest. There is still a sizable mortgage debt on the family residence. The cost of children's college education must also be met. After 10 years, though, his need to protect his family against his premature death will gradually lessen. Even so, over the succeeding 15 years, he will still want comparatively substantial insurance coverage. Such coverage under a permanent policy will carry a high premium. Nevertheless, he desires permanent insurance to provide his wife with income-tax-free recovery regardless of when he dies. In effect, he wants (1) highest coverage over the next 10 years, (2) somewhat reduced coverage gradually decreasing in amount over the succeeding 15 years, and (3) permanent insurance continuing thereafter, without any further reduction in amount, for the protection of his wife.

He can purchase a straight life policy with a rider that offers extra coverage against premature death. Under this rider, extra coverage continues in undiminished amount for an initial 10-year period.

Thereafter, over the succeeding 15 years, extra insurance recovery in the event of the insured's death gradually decreases to zero. After 25 years, only the face amount of a straight life policy is payable to the insured's beneficiary. The insured here ties insurance protection to his actual insurance needs under a straight life policy with term rider. Moreover, he benefits from a reduction in premium expense because the extra insurance under the rider is lower-cost term. It is level term insurance for an initial 10-year period and then decreasing term over the succeeding 15 years.

LIMITED PAYMENT LIFE

This policy is actually straight life, but it is paid for within a stated time, say 20 or 30 years, or by a certain age, such as 65, instead of being payable annually over a whole lifetime. Because of the higher premiums, it has the advantage of building up cash value faster, but the cost might prove a burden to the young man who will not reach his highest earning capacity until middle life. For the person whose early years mark the high earning point (an athlete or actor, for example), a limited payment policy may prove useful. Note, however, that early death after completion of premium payments would make this a very expensive policy.

ENDOWMENT

In essence, an endowment policy is a combination insurance and savings program. If the holder of an endowment policy dies, the beneficiary named collects the stated amount; if the policyholder lives, he himself collects on the matured policy. But if before that time he fails to keep up the premiums, he is subject to a penalty and can only recover part of his investment, plus dividends.

Say a person decides against a 20-year endowment policy. Instead, he takes out term insurance for the same period. At the same time, he opens a savings account into which he regularly pays the *difference* between the term insurance and the endowment policy, which is one of the costlier forms of insurance. If he dies, the term insurance would be paid to his beneficiaries; they would also fall heir to the savings account. If the insured person lives more than 20 years, his term insurance will, of course, lapse, but his savings account plus dividends, less income tax, will amount to much more than the paid-up endowment policy. Had he taken the policy, he would still have to pay income tax on the difference between the lump sum received and his original premiums.

Since a combination of term insurance and savings produces better results, why do people buy endowment policies? Some undoubtedly because they would never save otherwise. The penalty feature forces them to mail their premiums on time; no such spur sends them to the savings bank. Some take endowments because the waiver of premium rider can be added to it. In the event of disability, the company would pay the premiums and still fulfill the terms of the contract, i.e., to pay out either a death benefit or a lump sum.

Endowment policies also carry the main features of straight life insurance, such as availability for loans and surrender value.

BASIC LIFE CONTRACTS NOW ARE COMBINED

On the purchase of life insurance, an individual's choice in the past might have been limited to three basic policies: (1) term insurance, (2) whole life insurance, either a straight life or a limited payment contract, and (3) the endowment. However, an individual who intends to purchase life insurance now no longer is limited to a choice of one of these basic policies. Combination insurance contracts are available. For instance, varying straight life-term insurance combinations are available which permit an individual to buy the coverage that most closely meets his insurance needs. Recently, one of the leading life companies announced that it was using computers for presentation so that an insured could better judge values, benefits, and protection offered him by a particular policy. The announcement in itself was not startling. However, this computerized program will cover not one or two but twenty-three policies.

Combined insurance coverage under different policies available usually joins straight life with various forms of term coverage. The variety of coverage is extensive. Some of these policies are directed at younger insureds; others, at the more mature individual.

One new policy combines 50 percent straight life insurance with 50 percent term coverage in reducing premium cost for higher amount of insurance protection. It has appeal for the father with a growing family. He gets high coverage when his insurance needs are greatest. Term coverage can be converted to permanent insurance up to age 62, but such coverage is not required. Continued high coverage decreases at age 65 by 5 percent a year until age 75. However, permanent protection thereafter does not drop further.

In the case of a young husband, another policy available combines straight life insurance with maximum amount of convertible term. A 25-year-old individual could purchase $100,000 coverage at initial cost of about $33 a month. Initially, this insured gets 10 percent straight life coverage with 90 percent term insurance which decreases at age 31, 34, 37, 40, 43 and 46. At any of these ages, however, an insured can convert portion of lapsing term insurance into permanent coverage. True, on such conversion, premium costs would be increased, but increases in an initial low premium are geared to increases in insured's earnings.

A graded-premium policy is also available. It is permanent insurance which gears lower initial premiums to anticipated increase in insured's earnings and future ability to pay. There is a low initial premium which increases over a period (e.g., over first 5 years), but thereafter remains unchanged. For instance, an individual who currently finds it difficult to finance the permanent insurance coverage he wants at regular rates anticipates that his income will increase over the next 5 years. By purchase of graded-premium policy, he can fit his ability to pay premiums to actual premium cost.

One form of graded-premium uses decreasing term insurance with straight life after the first year until at the sixth year the policy becomes a full straight life contract. Under this contract, the low initial premium increases each year for the first five years, but thereafter remains unchanged. In total premium cost, this policy does not promise any premium savings. However, it allows an individual to start a permanent insurance program by matching premium outlay with increasing income.

A modified life policy offers somewhat similar advantages in offering a low initial premium. Under a typical modified life policy, insured would pay an unchanging premium lower than regular rate for the first five years of coverage. Then in the sixth year, premium would be increased. However, increased premium is level thereafter without any further increase.

Double life insurance protection until 65 is available under combined coverage in a single policy. A father takes out a policy which will pay his family $60,000 if he dies before 65. However, coverage is halved after 65. Thus, if he dies after 65, his beneficiary gets $30,-000. Presumably at age 65, his children will be self-supporting adults with the result that insurance needs will have lessened. The policy combines $30,000 permanent insurance with $30,000 term coverage. True, he might buy similar coverage by purchasing a separate $30,000 straight life contract and a $30,000 term policy, terminating at 65. However, under this double protection policy, an insured combines both permanent and term coverage in a single insurance contract. As a result, he benefits from a reduced premium.

FAMILY INCOME

With a separate policy or rider you may obtain term insurance running for a certain period (but not beyond a maximum age limit). During the period of coverage, your beneficiary receives a monthly income from date of your death. If you survive the stated period, the policy pays nothing.

There are three ways in which your beneficiary can benefit, depending on your company. She might receive your basic policy's benefits immediately with the above mentioned monthly income till the end of the period. She could reserve payment of the main benefit till after the monthly payments had run out. She could split the main benefit, having part paid when the monthly payments start, the rest when they end.

Note that if you take out this type of policy, say for 10 years, and you live for 9 of them, your beneficiary would receive one year's monthly income. This may be suitable if you are, say, protecting a child who will be able to earn for himself by the time the term expires.

Examine the settlement options of your basic policy and consider if family income protection is more suitable than supplemental term insurance.

The appeal of family income policy is greatest for a husband concerned that, on his premature death, he would be survived by a comparatively young widow with minor children. Policy combines permanent insurance with *decreasing term* coverage. It can provide an extra in the form of monthly income which starts on the death of the insured and continues for a specified period, e.g., 10, 15 or 20 years from the date the policy was originally purchased. Monthly income might be 1 percent per $1000 permanent insurance (e.g., $10 per $1000), 2 percent or 3 percent (e.g., $20 or $30 monthly income per $1000 permanent insurance). At the end of the monthly income period, face amount of permanent insurance is paid to beneficiary. Note that monthly income is paid only if the insured dies prematurely within the specified period. For instance, assume a man buys $10,000 twenty-year family income policy, paying $100 monthly income (i.e., 1 percent of $10,000 face). If he dies one year after purchase, his beneficiary would get $100 a month for 19 years and then $10,000 face. On the other hand, if he lived for 21 years after policy purchase, his beneficiary would not get any monthly income but would receive immediate payment of $10,000 face.

FAMILY MAINTENANCE

This policy is a combination of permanent insurance and level term insurance. Unlike the family income policy, the period over which monthly income payments will be made to the beneficiary starts at time of insured's death, if he dies within specified period. For instance, a husband is 30 years old. He buys 20-year, 1 percent family maintenance policy, $10,000 face. If he dies prior to age 50, his widow-beneficiary will receive $100-a-month for 20 years and then payment of $10,000 face. However, if he dies after 50, there will be no monthly income payments but $10,000 face amount will be paid immediately to the widow.

A portion of each monthly income payment will reflect interest return on permanent insurance part of policy left on deposit. This interest is taxable income to the beneficiary. Remaining portion of each monthly payment will reflect installment settlement of term coverage, constituting a principal (tax-free) and interest return. The interest portion, though, can be freed from tax—up to $1000 a year —where surviving spouse is beneficiary. Lump-sum payment when monthly income ceases is income tax free.

FAMILY PLAN

There are a number of combination plans offered by various insurance companies, and one is the family policy under which the husband may have $5000 whole life, the wife and children $1000 of term insurance, or a variation of this type of family policy. Some consider this as funeral expense coverage since it would fail to cover the real loss if the wife died and someone had to be employed to care for young children.

Insurance on wife and children is offered by some companies as a rider to the husband's insurance.

Check what your company issues in this type of life insurance and consider if it is for your family. Variations of the family plan are favorites with the insurance agents who sell them, but, in general, do not offer worthwhile protection.

MAIL ORDER INSURANCE

You may be attracted by a newspaper advertisement in which an insurance company in a distant state offers life (or other) insurance. Answering such an advertisement may bring a salesman to your doorstep. Because of the distance, you will have little or no chance of checking on the reliability of the company. Maybe it is sound; maybe the salesman can give good advice, but your best move is to do business nearer home and on a direct basis. Too, you run the danger that the distant company is not licensed to sell in your state. You lose out on the protection your state law may provide, and perhaps open the door to legal complications at your death.

SAVINGS BANK INSURANCE

If you live or work in a state where savings bank life insurance is sold, you have an excellent opportunity. These banks offer advantageous rates. While state law limits the total amount of savings bank insurance an individual may buy (in New York, $30,000), a broad range of straight life, term, endowments, and many variations can be obtained. All savings bank plans pay dividends, which further reduce the overall cost.

No salesman will call to urge savings bank life insurance upon you; a substantial reason for the low cost is the fact that you must take the initiative, applying for your policy by mail or in person at the bank.

At this writing, New York, Connecticut, and Massachusetts are the only states where the law permits savings bank life insurance.

GROUP LIFE

As a member of a union or a professional association, or simply as an employee, you may be able to participate in group life insurance coverage. You may have to contribute to the premium (some employers pay total cost), but your group *term* insurance will not cost as much as you would pay as an individual. Moreover, there will be no medical examination.

Usually, upon retirement or on leaving a group, the member can convert to individual whole life or endowment, but it will cost usual rates, and at 65, say, these would be extremely high. *Group Paid Up* is a plan which helps to overcome such objections. Your contributions go toward paid up whole life insurance; your employer's go toward term, which covers your life. Upon retirement or leaving the group, you have your paid up whole life insurance which you can use in one of several ways. It can remain in force, or be surrendered for cash or life income. You may also be able to buy additional whole life insurance which will make up for what your employer formerly paid in term coverage.

In few cases will group insurance provide all the protection a family needs, but it can prove a useful addition to other policies and lower the overall cost of life insurance.

BENEFICIARIES

You intend the money you are spending annually on life insurance to benefit those financially dependent on you, in most cases, wife and children; sometimes parents. A widowed or divorced career woman may have as much responsibility in this area as a husband or father.

The question is: Have you named your beneficiaries correctly? If not, the people you plan to protect may not derive the benefits you intended. The situation may become particularly involved where divorce is concerned. Perhaps, after a financial settlement has been reached, a former wife and children of the marriage should not benefit from a policy already in force. A change would have to be made in the beneficiaries named.

A point to note here is that *when you first take out the policy you should reserve the right to change the beneficiaries.* If you do not make this proviso, you must have consent in writing from the person formerly named before the company will make the change.

Your insurance company has a legal staff and if your personal situation is complicated, you should have the agent refer the case to these lawyers. He himself should be able to advise you when no unusual difficulties are involved.

If you are consulting an attorney about your will and estate planning, discuss the question of insurance with him. As the years bring changes, you will undoubtedly find that you must alter the names or order of your life insurance beneficiaries.

GI INSURANCE

Veterans frequently fail to change the beneficiary's name in their National Service Life Insurance policy. Originally, the insurance may have been intended to benefit parents. Then the serviceman marries, but he neglects to rename his beneficiaries, leaving his widow to find out that she cannot receive the proceeds of the insurance. Renaming beneficiaries of GI insurance is not complicated; consult your local Veterans' Service Agency.

If you are a veteran who has let his policy lapse, inquire if you are eligible to reinstate it. The maximum available is $10,000. Optional coverage for disability is also available.

PAYING YOUR INSURANCE PREMIUMS

In Chapter 1, we mentioned the importance of saving for heavy commitments. It will certainly pay you to put money aside regularly to meet your life insurance premiums on an annual basis. If you pay every month, quarter, or half year, you will be liable for the carrying charges leveled for payments on the installment plan.

THE DECISION IS YOURS

As we have said, the insurance needs in your family will differ widely from another's. So, too, will your attitude. If you have the resolve to save regularly and to put aside the difference between renewable term and ordinary life, you may well find term insurance which covers the years of your greatest financial responsibility to your family to be the answer. In your later years, the need to protect others may have diminished, if not vanished, and you can avoid carrying high-priced coverage. A prudent investment or a savings program can roll up dividends on money that might have gone into cash value insurance.

On the other hand, you may prefer full insurance coverage until you are 65 and, at the same time, you feel safer with the prospect of the return you will get on the cash value of your policy than with a savings and investment program. Your personal temperament and circumstances will guide your decision.

A valuable and objective analysis of *Life Insurance,* which can assist you in your preliminary investigations, is available to you for $1.50 from Consumers Union, Mount Vernon, New York.

THE LANGUAGE OF LIFE INSURANCE

Since the terms used in life insurance are not familiar to all, we give definitions of some below:

Annuitant. A person during whose life an annuity is payable; the recipient of the annuity income.

Annuity. A contract which provides a guaranteed income for a certain number of years or for life.

Beneficiary. The person named in the policy to receive the insurance money upon death of the insured.

Cash value. The money a policyholder will get back if he gives up that policy.

Convertible term insurance. Term insurance giving the insured the right to exchange the policy for permanent insurance without evidence of insurability.

Disability benefit. A rider which provides for waiver of premium, sometimes monthly income also, when the insured is proven totally and permanently disabled.

Dividend. Amount returned to participating policyholders as a refund of overpaid premium. It is not taxable; but, being dependent on company operations, it is not guaranteed.

Double indemnity. A policy rider which provides for double the face amount of the policy if death should occur through accident.

Endowment insurance. Payment of a definite sum to a policyholder, or his beneficiary, after a stated number of years.

Face amount. The sum stated on the face of the policy to be paid on death of the insured or at maturity.

Grace period. The time allowed after the premium due date for payment during which period the policy does not lapse.

Insured. The person on whose life an insurance policy is issued.

Lapsed policy. A policy ended by nonpayment of premiums.

Limited payment life insurance. Whole life insurance paid for in a specified number of years.

Maturity. When the policy's face value is payable.

Nonparticipating policy. One that pays no dividends.

Ordinary life insurance, also called straight life, is payable by premiums until death.

Paid up insurance. All premiums have been paid.

Participating policy. Dividends are payable.

Policy. The terms of the insurance contract are set forth on this document which is issued to the insured.

Policy loan. A loan made by the insurance company to a policy-holder and secured by the cash value of that policy.

Premium. The regular periodic payment made for the insurance.

Settlement options. Alternative ways in which the insured or beneficiary may have policy benefits paid.

Rider. An endorsement which changes the terms of an existing policy.

Term insurance. A policy payable at death if that event occurs during the term of the insurance.

Waiver of premium. A provision whereby an insurance company will keep a policy in force without payment of premiums. Usually operates as a disability benefit.

Whole life insurance. Includes ordinary or straight life insurance on which premiums are payable until death and limited payment life insurance on which premiums are paid for a certain number of years only.

ANNUITIES

An annuity is an investment that generally guarantees a fixed income for the remainder of a person's lifetime. Where life insurance assures funds to your dependents in case of untimely death, annuities assure you against outliving your financial resources. Life insurance covers the risk of dying too soon, while annuities assume the hazard of living too long.

The principle of annuities is simple, although policy combinations may tend to confuse you. In return for payment of premium, you are promised a guaranteed annual income beginning at a designated age and continuing for the rest of your life, no matter how long or short a time that might be. The amount of annuity income you will receive depends on the amount you invest in premiums, your age at the date of the contract and at the time payments are scheduled to begin.

Although annuity income is often referred to in annual terms, installments may be paid monthly, quarterly, semiannually, or annually, depending upon the arrangement you make with the company.

The price of an annuity can be figured in either of these ways: You can find the amount it would cost to buy an annuity paying a stipulated annual income of, say, $2400. If you had a specific sum to invest, perhaps the cash value of life insurance policies or proceeds of a policy or from the sale of a home, you could find how much income you would receive by investing the sum in an annuity contract.

Annuities may be purchased either on an individual or a group basis. They are available on a group basis under tax-protected plans set up by employers. Some employers pay the full cost of the annuity in behalf of their covered employees. Under other plans, both employer and employee share the cost of the annuity; the employee's contribution may be deducted from his pay check.

TYPES OF ANNUITIES

There are several kinds of annuity contracts to choose from. All provide guaranteed payments for the life of the annuitant. Some annuities contain additional guarantees and coverage; these are more expensive and pay a lower income in relation to the premium paid.

A straight life annuity is a "pure" annuity paying regular installments of income to the purchaser for his entire life. At his death, all payments cease. An annuitant may receive only one installment, or he may receive hundreds, depending on how long he lives. He will, however, under the straight life annuity receive the largest amount of income for his investment. A straight life contract is the most economical annuity you can purchase, but it has this drawback: the possibility always exists that a person may not live long enough to recoup his investment. He may only just start receiving annuity installments when he dies. No further payments would be forthcoming to his heirs under a straight life annuity; the company would have completely fulfilled its obligation. This is a gamble many are reluctant to take. Other, more expensive, types of annuity contracts are available offering more liberal terms.

Life annuity with installments certain. This type of annuity specifies that if the annuitant dies within a certain time, such as five, ten, or twenty years, a beneficiary would continue to receive the installments of income for the remainder of the guarantee period. If the annuitant survives the specified period, no payments would be made after his death. The longer the period of guarantee, the lower the annuity income would be.

Refund annuities promise that the amount invested in the contract will be returned to the annuitant or his beneficiary. If the annuitant recovers his investment during his lifetime, no further payments will be made.

Installment refund annuity. If the annuitant dies before collecting what he paid in, his beneficiary will continue to receive the installments from the company until the annuitant's investment has been refunded.

Cash refund annuity. Instead of installments after annuitant's death, the beneficiary will receive the balance of annuitant's investment in a lump-sum payment.

Refund annuities should not be considered a means of leaving an estate to one's heirs. If you, as the annuitant, live long enough to recover your investment, there will be nothing left for your beneficiary. Under an annuity contract promising payments for at least a certain number of years, once the annuitant survives the guarantee period, the heir has no expectancy.

Remember, these clauses in the annuity contract are not purchased cheaply. Per cash investment, annuities with guarantees give less income than a straight life annuity.

Joint and survivor annuity. An annuity contract may provide income for more than one person's lifetime. It may be based on the lives of two or more persons, usually a husband and wife. Where more than one life is covered under an annuity contract, it is a joint and survivor annuity.

Under a joint and survivor annuity, the income would be paid as long as one of the persons remained alive. Payments would cease after the death of the surviving annuitant. The contract may provide for a constant amount of income during the lives of the annuitants covered, or it may call for a reduction in the amount of the payments after the death of one.

Per cost investment, the joint and survivor annuity provides less income than a straight life annuity, particularly if there is a great disparity in the annuitants' ages.

BUYING ANNUITIES

Annuities may be bought with a single lump-sum payment or on the installment plan. An annuity can be purchased to start paying income immediately, or the contract may provide for installments to begin sometime in the future.

An immediate annuity provides for income to begin shortly after the contract date. Income payments may start one month from the date, if payments are to be made on a monthly basis, or one year from the purchase date, if payments are annual. Widows and persons who are retired or who are planning soon to retire are most likely to purchase immediate annuities.

Under a *deferred annuity* contract, payments begin at a future date. A deferred annuity may be purchased by a single premium. It is more likely to be bought over a period of years in annual or more frequent installments. Should the purchaser of a deferred annuity die before payments start, the amount invested or the cash value, whichever is higher, can be recovered by his beneficiary.

Many retirement plans that are referred to as deferred annuities actually are savings plans. Some include insurance coverage but contain no annuity element during the deferred period. Under these plans, a fund is accumulated which may be used to buy an immediate annuity at the end of the deferred period.

PROBLEM OF INFLATION CAN BE MET WITH VARIABLE ANNUITIES

The standard annuity is supported by fixed-dollar investments, such as bonds and mortgages, and pays a fixed-dollar income; the variable annuity holder's payments are invested primarily in common stocks. Ultimately, the income payments he will receive will depend on the value of his accumulated investment at the time he retires and the performance of the stocks in the company's investment fund.

Variable annuities are designed to overcome a principal drawback of the conventional annuity, the erosion in the value of its fixed payments due to inflation. The shrinkage in the purchasing power of the dollar is strongly felt by persons living on fixed annuity income. They are prime victims of an inflationary economy.

The variable annuity, like the standard annuity, guarantees an income for life. Unlike the conventional annuity, the amount of the payment is not fixed. If you buy a variable annuity, you are actually purchasing an interest in an investment portfolio comprised of stocks. You are credited with "accumulation units" representing your proportionate interest in the fund. If you pay $100 into a fund worth $50,000,000, with 500,000 accumulation units outstanding, you receive one accumulation unit. If the value of the fund is $60,000,000, a $100 payment entitles you to ⅚ths of an accumulation unit; if the fund is worth $40,000,000, $100 buys 1¼ accumulation units. Reinvestment by the fund over the years of its dividends and capital gains entitles participants to additional accumulation units.

In connection with the operation of the fund, there are commission and administrative costs; these charges range from about 8–15 percent.

You generally buy accumulation units until the time your annuity income is slated to begin. You would then receive a fixed number of "annuity units." This is the number of units you would receive each payment date and which number would not thereafter change. However, the value of each annuity unit, representing a proportionate interest in the fund itself, would fluctuate in value, reflecting the changing values of the investment fund. You would be paid each payment date an amount equal to what your annuity units were then worth.

At present, variable annuities are not widely available; few companies write these contracts. Many states prohibit the selling of variable annuities to individuals; others impose many restrictions and/or limitations. Up to now, these contracts have been sold mainly to groups, such as the Teachers Insurance and Annuity Association. Their plan, CREF (College Retirement Equities Fund) combines the variable annuity with the fixed-dollar annuity. An annuitant, under this plan, must put at least part of his contribution into a fixed annuity. He may put only 75 percent of his contribution into the variable annuity. The combination of the variable annuity with the standard annuity is for the protection of the participant in case of a protracted depression. He would have the assurance of receiving at least a guaranteed amount from the fixed-dollar segment of the plan.

SHOULD YOU BUY AN ANNUITY?

Annuities are a conservative method of financing retirement. The chief advantage of the annuity is the assurance that you can never outlive your capital. You can depend on the annuity as a source of income during your entire lifetime and have complete freedom from investment management.

On the other hand, the type of financial security offered by the conventional annuity has the drawback of being vulnerable to inflation. Whereas the fixed dollar payments are guaranteed, their purchasing power is not. As an investment, annuities earn a low rate of interest. Once payments begin, the annuity has no cash or loan value and cannot be used as a source of funds in an emergency.

Annuities should not be purchased if you seek a return on your investment, rather than a secure lifetime income. Finally, you should not consider refund annuities as a way of leaving an estate.

Chapter 11

INVESTING IN SECURITIES

How Much Cash Reserve Do You Need Before
    Investing in Stock?   178
What Are Securities?   179
Risks of Investment on the Stock Market   182
When to Buy Stocks   183
Fixing Your Investment Objectives   185

Opportunities for increase in capital and for a greater annual income are obvious objectives of investing in the stock market. But the present inflationary forces in our economy provide what is probably the most urgent reason for considering stock investments.

If you could be assured that the value of the dollar would remain the same in purchasing power for the next fifty years, you would probably not be concerned with anything more than putting aside enough money in a bank, bonds, or insurance to enable you to meet your future needs at a standard of living you could foresee. There is no such assurance. No one knows how long the inflationary forces will continue. Many economists predict that inflation will certainly continue and the dollar will continue to lose purchasing power.

To meet this trend, you have to place part of your savings in investments that change in value and yield in relation to the purchasing power of the dollar. This simply means that instead of placing, say, $1000 in a bank, you would buy $1000 worth of investments with the expectation that when you sell the investment in the future, you will receive an amount that will have the same purchasing power as the $1000 originally invested 10, 20, or 40 years earlier.

Investments in stock, especially common stock, can give you a hedge against inflation. General Motors, to cite a name known to every investor, provides an excellent example. With only minor variations, the price of the shares and the amount of the dividend have more than offset the rise in the cost of living. Another example is the record of the 30 leading industrial companies in the famous Dow-Jones industrial index. Over a period of years, the value of stocks and the income they yield maintain a relationship to the price of bread, meat, shoes, and houses. On the other hand, both principal and yield have gone down when living costs have declined. Thus, while stock investment bears risks (there is no guarantee against an actual loss in the case of a particular investment), common stocks have at least tended to "keep in step" with current living costs.

HOW MUCH CASH RESERVE DO YOU NEED BEFORE INVESTING IN STOCK?

Before you start planning an investment program, you must decide how much of a cash reserve you will need to fall back on for emergencies and current obligations. For maximum protection, you should have a readily available cash reserve to carry you along for a definite period of incapacity. One suggestion: This reserve might approximate the total of your living costs for one year, overhead costs, and any other known obligations, plus an extra 10 percent, *less* insurance benefits and other supplemental income. Such a reserve would be in savings accounts, or in easily converted investments such as government bonds.

Of course, this yardstick may not cover your particular requirements. Just as you had to evolve your own budget to meet your individual circumstances, you will have to take into consideration your needs and concerns before you can decide how much you can afford to invest. Your answers to the following questions will guide you.

1. Have you income from other sources or will your investments be a major source of your funds for day-to-day living?

2. What is your need for the cash you are investing? Can you afford to keep it invested indefinitely? You may need the money at a fixed

time in which case you must restrict yourself to safe and marketable securities, which can generally be converted to cash at any time.

If you plan to buy a house or furniture or an automobile on the installment plan, you have specified debts that must be met by specified date. You must keep funds free to meet these obligations as they arise. You should not put these funds into securities.

WHAT ARE SECURITIES?

Before going into the specifics of investing, read the following section if you do not know the difference between common stock and preferred stock and the difference between stocks and bonds.

When you buy stock of a corporation, you are investing money in the venture and in a sense, you become part owner of it. In return for your investments, the corporation generally pays you dividends out of its earnings and profits. If the corporation is very successful, you will generally receive dividends and the value of your shares of stock may also increase. Any increase in value of your shares is not taxable until you sell them. On the other hand, if the corporation does poorly, you may receive little or no dividends and your shares of stock will decline in value.

There are two classes of stock, common and preferred. (For investment purposes, stock may also be graded according to the reputation and record of the corporation in its business success or failure and the payment or nonpayment of dividends.) Holders of common stock participate in the concern's profits and most of its losses. Preferred stock is the senior stock of a corporation and its dividend is usually set at a fixed amount. The claim of preferred stockholders on company earnings is second only to that of the company bondholders and takes precedence over that of common stockholders. High-grade preferred stock usually provides a steadier dividend income than common stock, but common stock offers greater chances for appreciation.

Convertible securities are issued in preferred stock or bond form. They are called convertibles because the preferred stock or bonds can be converted into common stock of the issuing company at the election of the investor. Generally, the convertible privilege is included in the provision written into the bonds or preferred stock itself. There are a few issues, however, which are convertible as the result of a detachable warrant issued with the security, usually a bond.

You will find conversion privileges and terms vary with the particular security. The convertible preferred of one company might be convertible into one share of its common stock, while that of another company might be convertible into three shares of its common stock. Also, the conversion privilege might be drawn to continue indefinitely or be limited to a period of time ending on a specific date.

You might want to invest in convertible securities for capital gains and a hedge against market decline. As a convertible security is either a bond or preferred stock, it has a senior position in the company's capitalization before common stockholders are paid off. So if the stock market drops, these securities are less vulnerable to the decline. Thus, danger of a large capital loss with tax limitations is minimized. Since the convertible can be converted into the common stock, its value moves up as the value of the common rises. In fact, once parity point is reached, its capital gain potential is enhanced over that of the common stock.

A convertible preferred that can be exchanged for three shares of the common stock will jump three points on every one-point rise in the common once the parity point is reached.

A convertible generally will command a premium over and above its intrinsic worth. You must pay something for the conversion privilege. Also, you will have to be satisfied with a lower current return than that offered by the underlying common stock. Often these disadvantages are quite slight and sometimes they do not exist.

When you buy a bond, you are lending money to the issuer of the bonds. You do not become an owner; you are a creditor. The borrower pledges to pay you a specified amount of interest on specified dates and to repay the principal on the date of maturity stated on the bond.

Some bonds mature in a few months or years. These are short-term issues. Others mature after many years and are called long-term issues. Bonds often have two rates of interest; a stated rate and an effective rate. The stated rate is printed on the bond, the effective rate is the actual amount received by you and depends upon the price you paid for the bond.

If the stated interest rate is 4 percent and you pay the full value of the bond, or par, the amount of interest you receive will be 4 percent of the amount paid. On the other hand, if you purchase the bond below par, it will return more than 4 percent of your investment because interest is figured on the par value of the bond.

The tax status of the bond is another important feature. Income from corporate bonds is taxable. But income from state and municipal government bonds is tax exempt. Persons in the higher income tax brackets naturally prefer the tax-exempt income. Depending on your tax bracket, the return from a tax-exempt bond can be as high or higher than the net return, after taxes, from other investments.

Most bonds are publicly rated by well-known financial and advisory services, such as Moody's or Standard & Poor's. You may get these ratings at your bank or library. Consider all the facts and get any necessary advice before investing in bonds. They are a safer investment than stocks, but the return may be less and they do not generally increase in value.

Marketability or liquidity (the ease with which you can convert your bonds into cash) is also important. If your bonds are bought and sold frequently, it is likely that you can get a fair price if you should have to sell in a hurry. Registered bonds, however, are safer, in case the bonds are lost or stolen, since payment of principal and interest will be made only to the registered owner.

What bonds should you buy? If the objective is a high degree of liquidity—meaning you may need your cash at a sudden notice—you should invest in top-grade, short-term bonds. If the objective is a steady income plus relative price stability, you may invest in high-to-medium-grade bonds with longer maturities.

Bonds with the highest yield may not be the safest investment. Higher yield generally means greater risk. For example, government bonds find willing buyers even though they carry relatively low interest rates. Bonds of new or unstable corporations are more speculative and the corporations must pay a high return to attract investors.

You should always be interested in the maturity date of your bonds (that is, the year when the borrower has promised to repay the money borrowed). Long-term bonds generally have higher yields than short-term bonds. There are two main reasons: (1) A distant maturity date makes it difficult to predict the financial strength of the borrower at the time the bonds will fall due. This uncertainty makes it necessary to offer some bonds at a higher yield. (2) Informed investors may expect interest rates to rise and thus they may be unwilling to buy long-term bonds with a low yield. To attract investors, issuers of long-term bonds must pay higher rates, corresponding to the expected rise in the interest rate.

RISKS OF INVESTMENT ON THE STOCK MARKET

The value of stock traded in the stock market will generally approximately reflect current values. But you do not invest in the stock market as such. You invest in particular companies. There is no guarantee that the companies in which you invest will meet your investment objectives. Unfortunately, there is no way to eliminate investment risk; no reliable means have been found to predict future economic trends. You can only minimize risk by a constant supervision of your investments. If you decide to invest in stocks, get the best advice you can. If you have a broker who has satisfied you in the past, rely on his judgment. If you have had no experience in security investment, read the literature published by the large investment houses and choose a broker you feel will best serve your purposes.

Because there is an element of risk in any investment transaction, you must be prepared to see the value of your stock decline as well as rise. To reduce the element of risk, familiarize yourself with services available to the investor. Here are sources of important data on investing.

1. The financial sections of newspapers and the publications of concerns specializing in financial developments. Several long-

established, respected financial services operate throughout the country; they summarize basic news. These are available to any subscriber in any town or city. Many libraries have in their reference rooms copies of *The Wall Street Journal, The New York Times, Forbes,* and other periodicals giving financial news.

2. The companies themselves. If you write to a company whose stock you may be interested in buying, you can obtain an annual report and prospectus which will give you information about the company.

3. The officers of a bank in your locality. Banks generally employ security experts to help invest their own deposits and guide their customers in investments. If you go to an officer in your bank and tell him your investment needs and objectives, you can usually get his counsel and advice.

4. Stockbrokers. Many brokerage firms maintain large research departments and many have branches throughout the country. They can provide a valuable source of information.

5. The investment advisory services. They charge fairly substantial fees for their week-to-week and month-to-month reports, however.

6. The investment counsel firms. These charge fixed fees for their advice and may completely manage the investment portfolio of a client. The larger investment counsel firms usually do not accept clients with small accounts and annual fees for personal supervisory service by an investment counselor may run from $500 up.

WHEN TO BUY STOCKS

A review of the stock market's history indicates that there is a cyclical character to prices. The trouble, however, is that the low and high markets stand out clearly only in retrospect on charts already drawn, charts showing "where the market has been," not necessarily where it is going. True, the expert studies the current market to determine whether it is advisable to buy or sell at current market prices and to predict the future moves of a particular stock. But for the average investor, market analysts suggest, "Give up any idea of 'beating the market,'" and develop a program of paying current securities prices with current earnings.

The advice is based on the assumption that securities will tend, in market value as well as yield, to keep step with current living costs. Since the long-term trend of prices has been upward, it follows that a safe rule of thumb would be to buy quality securities on a regular basis and to trust that the long-term uptrend will continue in the next twenty to forty years, just as it has over the last hundred and fifty. Let the day-to-day, month-to-month, and perhaps even the year-to-year price swings average themselves out.

The stock buying system proved best by both actual experience and theoretical computations is that of "dollar averaging." You purchase stock at stated intervals of equal dollar amounts of whatever securities satisfy your particular program. You acquire more shares for your money when prices are low and fewer shares when prices are high. Thus, you are never in the position of trying to guess whether the market is going up or down, but instead are constantly taking advantage of price fluctuations to get your stock at a price which will be below the straight mathematical average for the period of time covered.

The monthly investment plan. A monthly investment plan offered by the New York Stock Exchange provides a method of investing as little as $40 a quarter or as much as $1000 a month in any of the stocks listed on the New York Stock Exchange. The plan takes advantage of the dollar cost averaging principle and lets you invest on a pay-as-you-go basis. You pay the regular commission charged by members of the Exchange, plus the regular odd-lot differential.

The monthly investment plan is noncontractual. You can start and stop whenever you wish and there is no penalty if you skip a payment. Your stock is purchased for you whenever your periodic payment is received, and your account is credited with full shares plus any fractional interest in a share, figured to the fourth decimal point. Under the monthly investment plan, your dividends can be credited to your account and automatically applied to the purchase of additional shares of stock. This automatic reinvestment of dividends enables you to increase your holdings more rapidly than you might by buying stocks without benefit of the plan, an effect similar to the effect that compounding interest has on a savings account.

FIXING YOUR INVESTMENT OBJECTIVES

We have emphasized inflation as an important fact in influencing investments in stock. But in selecting the securities you buy, you must also decide what you want and need from your investments. Do you want stock that will return dividends every few months and that will be relatively stable in price and high quality? Do you want a high income security in the hope that the income may cover part of your living expenses? Is your objective the sale of the stock at a substantially higher price than what you paid for it? Are you mainly concerned with liquidity and marketability, because you will need cash suddenly for some business or personal purpose and you want to be sure you can turn in the issue at a price approximating your cost whenever the need arises?

If your objective is "trading" profits, you will generally have to deal in stocks that are fairly risky and which fluctuate widely in price. If liquidity is your aim, you will have to buy stocks of the highest grade that fluctuate only slightly in price. High income, high profits, high stability, and high liquidity do not come in one package.

Decide on your objective or objectives. As a guide, here are some suggestions to consider.

1. For investment, choose sound, essential industries. Food and transportation are basic industries and can more readily hold their values during economic declines than nonessential industries that provide services and luxuries. Of course, all essential industries must be watched. What is an essential today may not be one year from now. For example, the production of steam locomotives was an essential industry. Today, there is no such production.

2. Invest in companies that are recognized leaders in their industries. True, some analysts do not agree with this advice and hold that the only substantial profits are made in new, unknown companies. The answer to this is that you are investing and not

trying to "get rich quick." Some smaller companies may turn out to be more profitable than well-known firms, but your chance of choosing such a company is often a matter of luck. The advantages in selecting the recognized companies is that they have proven their ability, their management is experienced, they will have resources for research, and can finance their needs more easily than smaller companies.

3. Invest in several different companies, each in a different industry. Over a period of time you will make a bad investment. If you invest in only one company, an error may be costly; if you have, say, six different stocks, your good judgment on four of them may more than offset a bad decision on one or two. Of course, such hedging can also be gotten by investment in mutual funds (see next chapter).

4. Invest about the same amount in the shares of each company you select. Do not make a favorite of any one stock. There are many sound industries.

5. Invest in shares listed on a major securities exchange, preferably the New York Stock Exchange. Before its stock may be listed on a major exchange, a company must file information with both the private financial authorities and the Federal government. Specific standards must be met; regular reports must be published; transactions are under the constant check of the exchange, the Federal government, and expert investors and bankers. Furthermore, a listing on the exchange makes it easier to buy or sell stock. Listing, of course, is no guarantee of merit, but it is a fairly substantial guarantee that the company will operate according to current business standards.

6. Invest in shares that can show an unbroken earnings or a dividend record or both for the last ten years. Such a record indicates that an enterprise is sound.

7. Buy shares that over the past ten years have earned at least five dollars for every four paid out in dividends. A company should not pay out all it earns, but should build up a reserve to handle emergencies or to insure its ability to take advantage of future opportunities. A company that earns considerably more than its dividend is preferred to one that just about earns it.

8. During period of a year or two, sell at least one stock, choosing the weakest on your list without considering its original cost. Invest the proceeds in a more profitable security.

9. Choose an established brokerage firm. When you place an order to buy or sell, do not set a fixed price; buy or sell "at the market." Buying or selling at the market means your order will be filled at about the price of the next transaction in your stock on the exchange. This is a better approach than giving your broker a fixed price. You are a long-term investor, and even an expert cannot fix the value of a stock to within fractions of a point. Since you are investing for the long term, it will be completely unimportant over that period whether you paid $20 or $21 for a specific share of stock.

10. Do not buy on margin. Stocks can decline and you can lose your investment if it is financed by margin loans. Buying stock on margin is not advisable for the investor. Buying on margin is primarily for the trader who is shooting for short-term profits.

Chapter 12

INVESTING IN MUTUAL FUNDS—
LETTING THE EXPERTS MANAGE
YOUR INVESTMENTS

WHAT IS A MUTUAL FUND?	190
INVESTMENT PROGRAMS OF MUTUAL FUNDS	191
GETTING INFORMATION ON MUTUAL FUNDS	193
COST OF BUYING INTO INVESTMENT COMPANIES	193
MEETING THE MUTUAL FUND SALESMAN	196
CONTRACTUAL OR VOLUNTARY PLAN TO BUY MUTUALS	196
CHOOSING INVESTMENT GOALS	198
MUTUAL FUNDS TO PROVIDE RETIREMENT INCOME	199

In the last chapter, we talked about investments in the stock market. The emphasis there was on your decision to plan and execute your own investment program. Perhaps you've come to the conclusion that you do not have the time, ability, or temperament for such a program. If so, you do not have to give up the idea of investing in securities. You can achieve approximately the same investment objectives by investing in mutual funds and, at the same time, turn over the duties of investment management to the fund itself. Even if you do your own investing, you may want to set aside some of your capital in mutual funds.

Although you will invest in mutual funds to relieve yourself of the major burden of investment decisions, you must not and cannot avoid the responsibility of choosing a fund that meets your investment needs. As will be explained in the following pages, first, no two mutual funds are the same; second, you must periodically review the performance of the fund in comparison to the general market conditions and to the performance of other funds.

WHAT IS A MUTUAL FUND?

The mutual fund is based on a practical plan of allowing many individuals to combine their savings so that they obtain the same advantages that larger investors enjoy: They have the services of professional investment managers, diversified investments, and the current supervision of investments.

Types of mutual funds. Mutual funds vary in size, ranging from a few million dollars in assets to well over two billion. They are divided according to their method of operation into the older (but far fewer) "closed-end" investment companies and the far larger group of "open-end" mutual funds which today control nearly forty billion dollars of investments for both small and large individual investors, pension funds, corporate groups, and institutions.

Whether they are large or small, open-end or closed-end, the basic appeals of all investment companies lie first in professional management and second in diversification—a spreading of risk among one hundred or more securities.

Closed-end companies. A closed-end company is simply a corporation that invests in the securities of other companies. You buy shares in the company as you would buy shares of U.S. Steel or General Motors. Among the closed-end companies are: Abacus Fund, Adams Express, Allegheny Corporation, American European, American International, American Research and Development, Argus, Carriers & General, Central Securities, Consolidated Investment, Dominick Fund, Ebasco, Equity Corporation, Eurofund, General American, General Public Service, M. A. Hanna, International Holdings, Japan Fund, Lehman Corporation, Madison Fund, National Aviation, Niagara Shares, Petroleum Corporation, Standard Shares, Tri-Continental, United Corporation, U.S. & Foreign.

Open-end companies. An open-end company is called "open-end" because its capitalization is open. They create and sell shares whenever you want them, buy them back and retire the shares whenever you want to cash in your chips. In other words, you join by turning over your funds to the company and getting newly created shares which represent your pro rata share of the entire fund.

INVESTMENT PROGRAMS OF MUTUAL FUNDS

Mutual funds fall into three broad categories:

1. *Growth funds.* Their objective is to achieve a growth in the value of shares, which eventually leads to growth in income. Growth fund assets are usually invested in common stocks up to about 90 percent. Growth funds appeal generally to younger persons.

2. *Balanced funds.* The fund invests in common stock, preferred stock, and bonds. The idea is that these three kinds of investment provide defensive strength in a declining market. Investments are divided approximately into common stocks, 60 percent; bonds and preferred stocks together, 40 percent. In a rising market, balanced funds generally do not show the increase in value of a growth fund. Balanced funds appeal generally to older persons.

3. *Income funds.* Investments here are primarily in high-yield securities. There are differences even within this category, as some income funds will take slight risks in order to give shareholders a higher yield. Investments are in preferred stocks, bonds, and common stocks with a high yield.

In addition to the three basic types of mutual funds, there are funds which attempt to combine two or more of these basic objectives and others which may be described as specialty funds. Some of these funds are:

1. *Bond funds.* Securities purchased in this kind of fund generally provide a fixed income and do not increase substantially in growth.

2. *Industry funds.* Investments are concentrated in a single industry, including subsidiaries. On occasion, sponsors of industry funds offer funds from several industries. You may switch from one industry fund to another in the sponsor's portfolio at a small sales charge.

3. *Real estate investment funds.* These are designed to encourage small investors to participate in diversified real estate ventures. As

an investor in the real estate fund, you may enjoy a slight tax advantage as you will have nontaxable distributions from depreciation reserves.

Most mutual funds pay quarterly dividends each year. These will, of course, vary in amount from time to time depending on fund earnings. The fund receives many dividend and interest checks from the investments made for its members and each member receives a proportionate share after management fees and operating expenses are deducted. In addition, you may receive capital gains distributions resulting from profitable security sales by the fund. If you invest in several of these funds with different dividend payment dates, it would be possible for you to receive a dividend check each month.

Among the larger funds dedicated to growth of capital are: Chemical Fund, Delaware Fund, Dreyfus, Investors Variable, Keystone K-2, Massachusetts Investors Growth Stock, National Investors, National Securities Growth, T. Rowe Price Growth, Putnam Growth, Television-Electronics, United Science.

Among the larger funds aiming at a combination of capital growth and income are Eaton & Howard Stock Fund, Fidelity, Financial Industrial, Fundamental Investors, Hamilton Series H-DA, Investment Co. of America, Investors Stock Fund, Massachusetts Investors Trust, Mutual Investing-MIF, One William Street, Putnam Investors Fund, State Street Investment, United Accumulative, United Income, Affiliated, American Mutual, Broad Street Investing, Dividend Shares, Group Securities Common, National Securities Stock.

Then there is a group of "balanced" mutual funds which invests in both stocks and bonds with the aim of providing income and stability of capital. Among the largest are the Axe-Houghton Fund B, Boston Fund, Eaton & Howard Balanced, Investors Mutual, George Putnam, Wellington.

Large special purpose funds—generally aimed at maximum capital growth—include Channing Growth, Fidelity Capital, Fidelity Fund, Manhattan Fund, Keystone S-4.

Several large insurance companies have started to sell mutual funds.

GETTING INFORMATION ON MUTUAL FUNDS

Mutual fund data is readily available.

The records of the closed-end companies are found in all the standard manuals. Most of them are traded on the stock exchanges and their day-to-day price fluctuations are easily followed.

The open-end mutual funds are reported on by several special agencies. These are: "Investment Companies," the Arthur Wiesenberger & Co., of 61 Broadway, New York, New York; the *Mutual Fund Directory,* published by the *Investment Dealers' Digest,* 150 Broadway, New York, New York; the Kalb-Voorhis summary, Johnson's Investment Co. *Charts, Trusts and Funds from the Investor's Point of View* published by American Institute for Economic Research at Great Barrington, Massachusetts, as well as others. You can look them over at your bank or broker's office or in the public library.

Quotations are carried daily in many newspapers.

Public information center for the industry is The Investment Company Institute at 61 Broadway, New York, New York 10006.

In checking the records of funds, do not be awed by the past record of a particular fund. With practically no exceptions, the past record of the funds has been good. The next ten years may be a far different matter. Here, the company's objectives and, above all, its management are of the utmost importance.

COST OF BUYING INTO INVESTMENT COMPANIES

The shares of the most closed-end investment companies are traded on the stock exchanges. Some are traded "over-the-counter." In either case, you will pay a commission computed in exactly the same way that your commission would be figured in buying shares of any industrial corporation. These range from 6 percent of total amount of money involved down to around 1 percent on larger purchases.

You buy most open-end mutual funds through brokerage offices or through selling organizations set up to handle a series of funds or one fund. Commission costs will vary, starting as high as 8½ to 9 percent of the total cost of the shares for small investments to half that amount or even less for sums running into the tens of thousands of dollars. Each fund has its own schedule of fees.

You can tell at a glance what the maximum fee is by checking the price of the fund in the special list of mutual fund quotations carried by many newspapers and financial publications. The fund will be listed thus:

	Bid	Asked
XYZ Fund	$11.34	$12.26

The fund's asset value per share (its total assets divided by the number of shares outstanding) stood at $11.34 per share on this day. The asked price is the price you would pay per share. The 92-cent difference represents the commission cost per share which, in this case, comes to 8.1 percent. Another fund might be listed $13.12 bid, $14.00 asked, the 88-cent difference here representing a commission of about 6.7 percent.

Some funds have a compulsory front-load system which consumes 50 percent of the first thirteen monthly payments to prepay commissions for the entire life of the plan. It thus heavily penalizes people who embark on a ten-year investment program if they drop out before completion.

Mutual fund charges have been criticized as being excessive by the Securities Exchange Commission. Legislation in Congress has been proposed to reduce these charges.

The no-load funds. There are over fifty funds which charge no sales commission. That is because they have no salesmen or sales organization. Most of these funds grew out of investment advisory services which originally managed the investment of large sums for individuals, but were prevailed upon by smaller investors to open their services to them, also.

If you want to buy into a no-load fund, you must take the initiative. While these funds also do some of the modest, low-pressure advertising allowed the mutual fund industry, any inquiry on your part will not be followed up by a salesman.

You can always identify a no-load (no commission) fund merely by running your finger down the mutual funds list in any financial publication: the "bid" and "asked" price will be identical. For example:

	Bid	Asked
ABC Fund	$16.94	$16.94

Since no-load funds are likely to be far less advertised than the usual, commission-charging funds and since they do not employ salesmen who will come out and present the story of the fund to you, it may be helpful if we list the names and addresses of some of the better known no-load funds so that you may do your own investigating.

The listing of a company in no way should be regarded as a recommendation.

American Investors Fund, Greenwich, Connecticut 06830

DeVegh, 20 Exchange Place, New York, New York 10005

Dodge & Cox Fund, 1711 Mills Tower, San Francisco, California 94104

Energy Fund, 2 Broadway, New York, New York 10004

Guardian Mutual Fund, 120 Broadway, New York, New York 10005

Johnston Mutual Fund, 230 Park Avenue, New York, New York 10017

Loomis-Sayles Mutual Fund, 140 Federal Street, Boston, Massachusetts 02110

Mutual Shares Corp., 200 East 42 Street, New York, New York 10017

Mutual Trust, 4722 Broadway, Kansas City, Missouri 64112

The Nassau Fund, 37 Wall Street, New York, New York 10005

Northeast Investors Trust, 50 Congress Street, Boston, Massachusetts 02109

One William Street, 1 William Street, New York, New York 10004

Penn Square Mutual Fund, 451 Penn Square, Reading, Pennsylvania

T. Rowe Price Fund, 1 Charles Center, Baltimore, Maryland 21201

Prudential Fund of Boston, 50 Congress Street, Boston, Massachusetts 02109

Rittenhouse Fund, 2 Penn Center Plaza, Philadelphia, Pennsylvania 19102

Scudder, Stevens & Clark, 10 Post Office Square, Boston, Massachusetts 02109

State Street Investment, 140 Federal Street, Boston, Massachusetts 02110

Stein Roe & Farnham, 135 South LaSalle Street, Chicago, Illinois 60603

MEETING THE MUTUAL FUND SALESMAN

Many funds are sold through salesmen who may work for a distributing organization handling one or more funds, or who may represent a brokerage firm. In any event, the business of the salesman is to sell—often using high pressure techniques.

This means that you must be on your guard. When you go to your brokerage firm to discuss investment in a listed stock, the broker can afford to be impartial about the matter. There is no reason for him to favor one or the other except one or the other may best suit your investment aims. Commission rates are the same for buying either. But if you express interest in a mutual fund, you must expect a salesman to try to sell you the fund, or one of the funds, handled by his brokerage firm.

Do not be rushed into buying. Mutual fund shares cannot double overnight so you will suffer no great financial harm if you take time to decide.

CONTRACTUAL OR VOLUNTARY PLAN
TO BUY MUTUALS

You can buy a mutual fund by making a large single investment or you can invest fixed amounts over a set period of time. You can make the periodic investments under either a contractual or a voluntary plan.

Under a voluntary plan, you are not bound by contract to a monthly payment. A voluntary mutual fund plan charges commission at a level rate on each monthly purchase, as you make it. You do not prepay commissions as in a contractual plan (see below). The voluntary plan commission is generally a flat eight percent on each purchase and for reinvestment of divided income over the years. Capital gains are reinvested at no charge. Life insurance is not available with the voluntary plan. You do not have the privilege of replacing withdrawn funds without paying another commission.

Under a contractual plan, you agree to invest a fixed monthly amount. It can be as small as $25 a month. A fixed contractual plan allows you to dollar-average your investments over the years, taking advantage of market changes. The plan can be tied to a declining balance term insurance. Then, if you die during the investment period, the insurance will pay the remaining balance due under your plan. There are these disadvantages to the contractual plan: You must be certain that you can meet the payments. If you drop out early in the program, a disproportionate part of your investment will be lost in prepaid commissions. A contractual plan requires the prepayment of a substantial part of the commissions in the first year of the plan.

For example, a fund would deduct one-half of the first month's investment to prepay commissions. Afterwards, the commission rate would drop. Over the years, you would be paying commissions of 8.63 percent. If you drop the plan before the commissions were averaged out, you would dissipate your investment unduly in the commission expense. However, the contractual plan does allow you to reinvest both dividend income and capital gains over the years without paying any additional commission. (There may be a small custodian charge for reinvesting dividend income.)

If you need funds in an emergency, the contractual plan allows you to withdraw up to 90 percent of your funds and reinvest them later without payment of commissions.

It is difficult to calculate whether a voluntary or contractual plan is less expensive if both are completed over a fixed period of time. The contractual's commission charges may be offset by the reinvestment of dividends and gains at no charge. The lower commission of a voluntary plan may be offset by emergency withdrawal privileges and the fee for reinvestment of dividend income.

In making your decision, consider your ability to make regular payments and your other resources to meet emergencies. Above all, do not commit yourself to a plan unless you know the privileges and charges involved.

CHOOSING INVESTMENT GOALS

If you are young and want capital gain, select a growth-type fund —one invested in growth-type securities such as aviation, electronics, chemicals, life insurance, and synthetics.

If you are approaching retirement and will soon need income, consider only funds which are aimed at providing maximum income —funds which concentrate their investments in coppers, rails, utilities, and cyclical manufacturing concerns.

Do not let a salesman talk you into a growth-type fund with the argument that his fund has been successful in accumulating large annual capital gains, so dividend income is not important. Capital gains are welcome, but dividend income is steadier.

If you are only a few years from retirement, there is no advantage in initiating a ten-year monthly payment program, especially if 50 percent of your first twelve or thirteen payments will be used to prepay part of the commissions for the entire ten-year period. Unless you have money to spare in retirement you may not be able to continue the investment—and those prepaid commissions will be wasted.

Do not be overly impressed by the spectacular success of any particular fund in the past year or in the past five or ten years. You must invest on future prospects.

Insurance with mutual fund investments. Many funds provide life insurance with their monthly contractual plans at low rates. Do not confuse this protection with lifetime insurance. It is in the form of declining balance term insurance and assures the completion of your investment program should you die before the entire plan is paid up. Therefore do not let a salesman talk you into canceling your life insurance policy and substituting this form of mutual fund coverage. In a ten-year $50-a-month program, the protection in mutual fund insurance is $5950 during the first month, but only $50 in the last month of the tenth year, thereafter, zero.

MUTUAL FUNDS TO PROVIDE RETIREMENT INCOME

Assume you complete a ten-year contractual program. You may adopt one of several courses:

1. You may make no further payments, but allow dividends and capital gains to be reinvested in acquiring further shares;

2. You may take your dividends and capital gains in cash;

3. You may set up a level withdrawal plan which will give you so many dollars a month to live on, or

4. You may redeem, cash in your shares.

The level withdrawal plan (3) works this way: most funds in which you have $10,000 invested (one or two set the level at $5000) will allow you to make a regular monthly withdrawal from the fund, measured in dollars or shares.

The widely accepted rule of thumb for this level withdrawal program—which can be helpful in financing retirement—is that $50 a month can be withdrawn from a $10,000 investment, beginning around retirement age, with little danger that the investor will run out of money in his lifetime. To make this payment, the fund will redeem enough of your shares every month to provide a payment of $50. Then, when it declares its dividends and capital gains, it will repurchase shares.

A well-run, income-type fund will generate enough dividends and capital gains to at least keep your investment stake fairly level—offsetting your withdrawals with quarterly and annual reinvestments of the dividends and capital gains. Some funds, in fact, can boast that over various periods of time they have actually been able to increase the $10,000 investment, all the while paying out $50 a month to the investor. In some cases, and at other times the $50 monthly withdrawal will cut into assets a bit. In any event, this plan *is not a guaranteed annuity.* You are drawing $50 a month from an equity investment. Equities may go up or down.

Instead of fixing withdrawals at a dollar figure, the withdrawals can be expressed in terms of shares. If, let us assume, your mutual fund asset value now stands at $10 a share, you might ask the fund to sell five shares a month and send the proceeds to you. If the price goes to $11, you will receive $55; if it falls to $9, you will get only $45. If you need exactly $50 a month, this type of withdrawal is not for you. But if your budget can stand some slight variation from month to month, then the share plan works out slightly better over the years since you will not find yourself having to sell more shares when the price is low and fewer when the price is up—the reverse of the dollar averaging plan which is often so advantageous in buying mutual funds.

Chapter 13

YOUR HEALTH INSURANCE

TYPES OF HEALTH INSURANCE	202
YOUR SOURCES OF PRIVATE INSURANCE PROTECTION	203
YOUR EMERGENCY RESERVE	204
CHOOSING THE RIGHT POLICY	205
MEETING MEDICAL EXPENSES AFTER MEDICAL CARE	
INSURANCE IS USED UP	208
DENTAL INSURANCE	208

Today, the anxiety over sickness or injury is not confined to the thoughts of pain and disability that may result. The fear of financial bankruptcy is almost equally oppressing. One hears of a lifetime of savings wiped out by sudden illness or accident. Widespread concern for this problem is slowly leading to forms of government-financed health plans. Whether you favor or oppose this development, government-financed medical protection is a fact for many. Federal medical insurance already covers the major medical costs of senior citizens sixty-five or over and medical programs cover the medical expenses of many families in the lower income brackets. One need not be a prophet to predict that, in time, almost all medical costs will be covered by governmental programs. However, at the present time if your needs are not covered under the senior citizens' program and you are not in a low income bracket, you personally will have the burden of protecting your family's security through some form of medical insurance. Future government medical insurance is not going to pay the medical bills of today or tomorrow, although you may be entitled for a time to some form of disability payments from your employer, a state government, or Federal Social Security.

You cannot predict how and when an illness or an injury will be suffered. Nor can you estimate, if misfortune does occur, what the financial cost will be. You must assume that you and your family will be prone to the usual illnesses.

Facing the possibility that the worst can occur, you have to develop an insurance program around these possibilities, modified by what you can afford in insurance protection.

If illness or injury struck, you must ask yourself what expenses you would incur and what income you would stop receiving. Directly flowing from the illness or injury would be doctor's and surgeon's fees, hospital care costs of various types, costs of treatments, appliances, drugs. In addition, if you are the breadwinner of the family, your enforced absence from employment would lead to loss of income.

TYPES OF HEALTH INSURANCE

The following types of insurance protection are available to offset these expenses and losses:

Hospitalization insurance. A hospital cost or hospitalization insurance policy pays the cost of a hospital room and board for a number of days and, generally, expenses such as drugs, operating room charges, and laboratory fees.

Surgical expense insurance. Here, the policy pays up to a specified amount for each type of operation, such as hysterectomy, hernia, removal of tonsils, and removal of gallbladder, etc. X-ray examinations and therapy may also be covered. The cost of physician's visits in the hospital may be covered, but at an extra premium charge. Surgical insurance is often combined with a hospital cost policy.

Major or catastrophic medical insurance. This type of policy is generally taken out after you have coverage under a basic hospitalization-surgical policy. A major medical policy is tailored to protect you against severe rather than ordinary illness. As such, a major medical policy will have large deductibles, generally ranging from $250 to $1000. Benefits are not paid until you or your basic hospital-surgical insurance pay medical costs up to the deductible amount. Above the deductible, the policy pays 75 percent or 80 percent of the costs up to a maximum amount, generally $5000 to $25,000.

If you do not have basic medical insurance, you can get a comprehensive major medical policy, but this type is more expensive than a supplemental major policy where you have basic medical policy.

Disability insurance. Here, the policy compensates you for loss of income, not for medical expenses. Payments are set at a monthly rate for a period, during which you are totally disabled or partially disabled. The policy may cover disability arising from an accident or illness or both. Payments do not generally begin until after you have been disabled for a specified length of time.

You may already be protected by some form of disability insurance under an employer's plan, under the laws of your state, or under Social Security. Therefore, before buying a private policy, check the extent of your protection under such insurance programs.

Accidental death and dismemberment. The policy pays an amount for death or injury caused by an accident. For example, the policy may pay $25,000 for accidental death, the loss of both hands, or both feet, or the sight of both eyes or the loss of a hand and foot.

YOUR SOURCES OF PRIVATE INSURANCE PROTECTION

Three sources of private medical and health insurance are: (1) Insurance companies. (2) Blue Cross and Blue Shield insurance. (3) Independent group practice, generally organized and operated by communities, medical groups, or unions.

Generally, it is advisable to seek insurance coverage from an organization that has purchased a group policy, because it can offer medical benefits at lower premium rates. Do not confuse a group policy with a group-practice plan. A group-practice plan usually offers the services of specific physicians and specialists. A group insurance plan provides insurance protection. Your employer may, of course, cover you in a group plan. If he does not have one or you are not employed, you may be able to join a plan offered by your professional society, a fraternal society, or even alumni association. If a group policy is not available, then of course, you must choose an individual plan that meets your needs and pocketbook.

YOUR OWN EMERGENCY RESERVE

One hundred percent insurance protection against all forms of sickness and accident is an impossibility. Moreover, insuring organizations and companies prefer that you carry part of the burden yourself. Almost all policies use "deductible" formulas and limits in paying medical expenses. Therefore, you must employ your own budgeting methods to help you to co-insure. By putting money aside to handle predictable expenses yourself, you will do better than by trying to buy expensive health insurance coverage against all eventualities.

How much health protection reserve money do you need in the bank? Individuals' and families' needs will vary with the size of the family and with basic health, since whatever is said about averages, some people go through life with far less need for medical care than others. Through budgeting, you should be able to work out the average annual sum necessary for your family, taking into consideration your usual type of bills. Above that amount, you will need to cover any deductible stated on your policy or policies, the premiums (unless handled through payroll deduction), and the unpredictable amount you would have to pay in excess of your insurance protection.

While it is impossible to predict exactly how much you might be called upon to pay out of your own pocket for hospitalization resulting from any given sickness or accident, you can bear in mind the following considerations: If you have a paid-in-full type of service contract, such as a 21-day full benefit plan, you have to face 50 percent of charges after that time for a given period. Thereafter, you are wholly responsible for the costs. Unless your income is below a stated level, the fee that would be paid for surgical care under your service-type surgical-medical plan will not cover all a surgeon may charge you; you carry the remainder of the cost. If you have an indemnity type of policy, you may have, in addition to the deductible amount, a limitation on room and board payments. For example, the company might pay only about $45, you pay the excess. The medical, surgical, and other charges are met by 80 percent from the company; you pay 20 percent. This type of policy may also call for your making all immediate payment of bills; reimbursement for the company's portion comes to you direct.

Against this difficult-to-forecast area of financial responsibility, you have the comfort of knowing that the average period of hospitalization is seven or eight days, but you may well fear that your family might be one of those involved in sudden catastrophe, perhaps even long-term or permanent disability of the breadwinner.

For most families, the solution to this worry lies in major medical protection, as offered in policies available from reliable, well-known insurance companies. With most types of sickness and accident covered by your regular group or private health insurance, you would draw upon a major medical policy in case of disaster.

As mentioned earlier, major medical policies usually carry a deductible, the size of which depends on your policy. The higher the deductible, the less expensive the policy, so if you have regular coverage through other insurance, protection through a policy with a deductible of $500 or even $750 may be sufficient for you. Once you (or your other health plan) have paid the deductible, the company pays a substantial portion (usually 75–80 percent) of the costs up to a stated limit. Some pay as much as $25,000.

CHOOSING THE RIGHT POLICY

When you are faced with the actual task of selecting a policy among the many offered by competing services, you will have the task of screening the many details of each policy to see how they will or will not meet your objectives.

1. Do not be overimpressed by higher maximum benefits offered by a medical care policy. Check to see that it covers a larger proportion of usual expenses of common ailments. The chance of a catastrophic bill occurring is not as great as the chance of incurring usual hospital expenses ranging from $300 to $3500.

Check the hospital rates for room and other services in your locality. If a policy does not cover a good proportion of these costs, it is not for you.

Remember that there are no bargain insurance rates, except for the lower rates of policies offered by group plans. If you are buying an individual policy, a lower premium is probably giving you less protection.

Study the method of payment also. A benefit may be paid in terms of services or indemnity. In a service-type policy, the insurance company pays for the service. For example, if the policy states that it will pay the cost of a semiprivate room, the type of payment is a service type. An indemnity policy will state that the company will pay, say, $29 a day for the cost of a hospital room. Therefore, in company policies, you have to be aware of the actual cost of a particular service. If you needed a semiprivate room that costs $42 a day, an indemnity policy paying $29 a day would be inadequate, whereas a service-type policy that pays for a semiprivate room would meet your requirement. For a higher premium, of course, you can obtain an indemnity policy better matching hospital rates in your area.

2. When you take out additional health insurance to back up your present coverage which is, say, group insurance at your place of employment, you will have to check carefully on the regulations governing the payment of benefits. Health associations and insurance companies are combining to ensure that there is no overpayment of benefits. Consequently, if your second, personal policy duplicates the benefits payable under your group policy, you may be paying premiums for benefits you cannot collect. The insuring agencies will settle the matter between themselves. Take care that you supplement, not duplicate, benefits.

3. Check what the policy will not cover. Exclusions are designed to avoid coverage of medical conditions you had before you became insured. Usual policy exclusions are: Diseases or physical impairments contracted before the policy was taken out. Medical expense of care provided by a Veterans Administration hospital, state workmen's compensation plan, or other Federal or state program. Injuries received in a military action. Pregnancies that began before the effective date of the policy. Long-term care in a mental institution.

4. Do not buy mail order insurance unless you are sure of the

company's reputation, that it will pay any benefits that meet your needs, and that it is licensed by the insurance department of your state. Mail order policies providing inexpensive premium come-ons, such as a first month premium of $1, offer little protection. Some of these companies carry names that are designed to be confused with the names of reputable firms.

5. Review the policy terms for renewability. They vary from policy to policy. A policy can be renewed only if the company accepts your election. This type of policy is usually called an optionally renewable or commercial policy. In addition, the company can change the premium rate on renewal. A guaranteed renewable policy is renewed at your election. The premium rate changes only if the company revises the rates for those in your classification. A noncancelable or noncan policy is a noncancelable, guaranteed policy that you can renew with no change in premium. For this privilege you are charged a higher premium. Paying the extra charge may be advisable if you are concerned about getting insurance protection in case you become seriously ill and thus become a "poor risk."

Blue Cross and Blue Shield insurance protection is generally renewable as long as you continue to pay premiums.

6. In choosing a policy providing disability income benefits, you must find out from your insurance agent exactly what you are buying. Ask these questions and get satisfactory answers before you buy a health, accident, or disability policy: (1) Are there any benefits for accidental death, and, if so, how much will your beneficiary receive? (2) What will you receive and when if you are disabled? (3) How does the policy define accident and sickness disability? (4) Does this policy provide benefits only for total disability or will it pay for partial disability too? Does disability on the policy mean incapacity to engage in your usual work or incapacity to do work for which you are suited by education and training or incapacity to perform *any* work at all? Must you be confined to your home to receive benefits? (5) How long will you receive any benefits if you are disabled? (6) Is there provision for waiver of premium in the event of long total disability? (7) Are there any other benefits outside of payment for loss of time, such as payment of hospital bills, medical fees, nursing expenses, etc.?

Remember in buying disability insurance, to consider any disability income to which you may be entitled from your employer, the state law, and Social Security. Also check your life insurance policies, which may contain disability income provisions.

MEETING MEDICAL EXPENSES AFTER MEDICAL CARE INSURANCE IS USED UP

Expenses can be reduced by following these economies:

Use semiprivate or even ward facilities instead of a private room unless there are medical reasons for a private room.

A private nurse at home may cost less than the cost of care at a hospital. Perhaps even the services of a visiting nurse might be adequate.

If recuperation will take time, a nursing home may offer adequate facilities at a cost considerably less than that of a hospital.

Diagnostic services or therapy may be obtained at a lower cost on an outpatient basis.

DENTAL INSURANCE

Dental costs are a constant and costly expense in most families. Unfortunately, dental cost insurance is not generally available, except in certain group plans of unions, employers, and communities.

Chapter 14

WHAT YOU SHOULD KNOW ABOUT
SOCIAL SECURITY

ARE YOU WITHIN THE SOCIAL SECURITY SYSTEM?   209
SOCIAL SECURITY AND YOUR PLANNING   211
THE AMOUNT OF YOUR SOCIAL SECURITY BENEFITS   212
KEEP A RECORD OF YOUR CREDITS   213
YOU MUST ACT TO COLLECT YOUR SOCIAL SECURITY   213

Social Security is much more than a governmental system of providing senior citizens with retirement benefits. It provides insurance protection for the growing family if the breadwinner dies, disability benefits for the seriously ill, the injured or disabled, and, of course, pension benefits and medical care at retirement as well as death benefits.

ARE YOU WITHIN THE SOCIAL SECURITY SYSTEM?

You probably are. At one time coming within the Social Security system was a problem to many workers and their dependents. But current laws extend coverage to almost all citizens and resident aliens.

What is your Social Security status? You must work for a required period of time in covered employment to obtain an insured status. The required time depends on your age or the date of your retirement, death, or disability. If you have worked for at least ten years in covered employment, you are fully insured, regardless of your age. If you have not, you may still qualify under one of several tests which give insured status even if you have less than ten years in covered employment. There are two types of coverage, currently insured status and fully insured status.

Currently insured status protection is designed for the benefit of the families of those who die without having enough coverage to qualify for retirement benefits. Currently insured status is achieved when you have at least six quarters of coverage, generally during a period of over three years and one quarter before death.

If you have currently insured status, your children and the mother who cares for them receive the following insurance benefits on your death:

1. Children's benefits. On your death, Social Security pays survivor benefits to:

Your unmarried children under 18

Your unmarried children who are full-time students under 22

Your unmarried children 18 or over who are totally disabled because of a physical or mental impairment suffered before they became 18.

2. Mother's benefits. Your widow receives benefits if she cares for your child (except generally students over the age of 18 entitled to benefits on their own).

3. Lump-sum death benefits. Paid to your widow.

If you have fully insured status, you and your family may receive retirement and disability benefits, and your family also receives protection in case of your death. Here, briefly, are the benefits available to fully insured workers and their families.

1. Your retirement benefit when you retire or reach the age of 62 or over.

2. Your wife's retirement benefit when she reaches 62. If she is under 62 when you retire, she can receive benefits only if she cares for your child who is under 18 or who was totally disabled before 18. But you must be 62 or over and receiving benefits in order for her to receive retirement benefits on your account.

3. Child's retirement benefits to any child of yours who is under 18 or who is a full-time student under 22, or who was totally disabled before 18.

4. If you die, benefits are paid to your widow when she reaches 60, or at age 50 if she is disabled.

5. Parent's survivor benefits at 62.

Disability protection. If you are unable to earn a living because of illness or injury after you are fully insured, you and your family receive the following benefits:

Disability benefits for you.

Wife's benefits to your wife if she is aged 62 or over or

Mother's benefits to your wife (of any age) if she is caring for your child under age 18 or for a disabled child of any age.

Child's benefits to your unmarried children who are under 18, and to those between 18 and 22 who continue in school or college, and to disabled children of any age while they remain disabled.

SOCIAL SECURITY AND YOUR PLANNING

For many, Social Security is a necessary mainstay of their income in their retirement years. But if you have been accustomed to more than the minimum needs in housing, food, recreation, and clothing, the benefits of Social Security cannot be the sole financial basis in your planning for retirement. They will be inadequate to meet a large part of your basic needs. True, Social Security benefits have periodically been increased. (In 1968, an across-the-board increase of 13 percent was given.) However, the increase does not fully restore the loss of purchasing power of the dollar because of inflation.

You will have to provide savings and investments to cover your requirements. The way the present Social Security law is set up, you cannot rely on making ends meet by supplementing your income by working after retirement. You can lose all or part of your Social Security benefits because of your earnings after retirement. Under a law effective in 1968, a retired person under Social Security can earn up to $1680 a year without loss of benefits. Regardless of how much he earns in a year, he does not lose benefits for any month in which he earns not more than $140 in wages or does not engage in substantial self-employment. However, 50 percent of the first $1200 over $1680 of annual earnings is deducted from benefits and $1 is deducted for each $1 of earnings over $2880.

No reduction in benefits is made for earnings of those 72 or over. However, in the year a person becomes 72, he may lose benefits for excess earnings in the months in which he was under 72. The earning limits periodically change, but whatever their amount, they limit and tend to penalize the person who earns more than a minimum amount of wages or self-employment income. The loss of benefits is not permanent; as soon as earned income drops below the limits, all or part of benefit payments are reinstated.

THE AMOUNT OF YOUR SOCIAL SECURITY BENEFITS

Benefits are calculated by averaging the amount of your earnings subject to Social Security taxes during a certain period. To get maximum benefits, you have to consistently earn the maximum amount subject to Social Security tax during the period for which wages are averaged. In this book, it is not practical to explain the somewhat complicated method of averaging benefits, which over the years has been subject to change. Below is a table of sample benefits payable under the amendments effective in 1968. If you are interested in finding the amount of your benefits, we suggest you contact your local Social Security office for advice, and for the excellent pamphlets available that explain the Social Security system and its operation.

Do not overlook the importance of Social Security in planning your insurance program if you have young children. Consider the fact that Social Security will provide benefits to your children if they are minors, disabled, or are attending school up to the age of 22. In addition, your wife will receive benefits as long as the children are under her care. Here, if you have been earning an amount equal to or exceeding the maximum amount subject to Social Security taxes, your family may be entitled to over $300 a month in benefits. Depending on your family's needs, you should plan to supplement the income with funds coming from insurance, savings, and other investments. Also consider the "blackout period" placed on a widow between the time her youngest child reaches the age limit when benefits for the child and herself cease and the time she reaches 60 years of age.

Average Yearly Earnings	$4200	$4800	$5400	$6000	$6600	$7800
Retirement Benefits at 65 or Disability Benefits	$140.40	$153.60	$165.00	$177.50	$189.90	$218.00
Retirement Benefit at:						
Age 64	131.10	143.40	154.00	165.70	177.30	203.50
Age 63	121.70	133.20	143.10	153.90	164.60	189.00
Age 62	112.40	122.90	132.00	142.00	152.00	174.40
Wife's Retirement Benefit at 65, or with child in her care:	70.20	76.80	82.50	88.80	95.00	105.00
Wife's Retirement Benefit at:						
Age 64	64.40	70.50	75.70	81.50	87.10	100.00
Age 63	58.50	64.00	68.80	74.00	79.20	90.90
Age 62	52.70	57.60	61.90	66.60	71.30	81.80
Each child of Deceased Worker	105.30	115.20	123.80	133.20	142.50	163.50
Widow, Widower, or Parent at 62	115.90	126.80	136.20	146.50	156.70	179.90
Widow at 61	108.20	118.40	127.20	136.80	146.30	168.00
Widow at 60	100.50	109.90	118.10	127.00	135.90	156.00
Widow under 62 (Mother's Benefit) and 2 children	280.80	322.50	354.60	375.00	395.70	434.40
Family Maximum	280.80	322.40	354.40	374.80	395.60	434.40
Lump-Sum Death Payment	255.00	255.00	255.00	255.00	255.00	255.00

KEEP A RECORD OF YOUR CREDITS

At least once every four years, you should mail Form OAR-7004 to the Social Security Administration, Baltimore, Maryland, requesting a statement of the wages credited to you. You may secure this form at the local Social Security Agency (for address, look in your telephone book), or you may write a request for the form to headquarters in Baltimore.

YOU MUST ACT TO COLLECT YOUR SOCIAL SECURITY

You cannot collect Social Security without applying for it. The Government is not obligated to remind you of your rights to benefits.

All you have to do is write to, telephone, or go to your local Social Security office for information. Social Security personnel will try to help you. Their objective is to give you your full benefits under the law.

Chapter 15

TAX PLANNING AIDS TO INCREASE YOUR AFTER-TAX INCOME

KEEP RECORDS	216
BASIC PRINCIPLES	221
TAX RETURNS FOR YOUR CHILDREN	224
TAX SAVINGS FOR MARRIED COUPLES WHO FILE JOINT RETURNS	226
TAX SAVINGS IN FAMILY INCOME PLANNING	226
SETTING UP A TRUST FOR YOUR CHILDREN'S COLLEGE YEARS	229
TAX SAVINGS FOR INVESTORS IN SECURITIES	230
WAYS TO SAVE TAXES	234

Income taxes are inevitable, and for most taxpayers, the largest annual expense. Year after year, they cut deeply into income. Perhaps the regularity of income tax and the fact that its terms are couched in complicated legal language has made you fatalistic about your ability to reduce your tax burden.

"What can I really do?" you ask. "Taxes are withheld from my pay, tax rates are increasing without the prospect of significant reductions. The Government utilizes data processing systems to check my return so that everything I receive is noted and reported. What can I do but prepare my tax return and pay the tax?" But your personal and economic life are not static. Income and family relationships do change. You can change your prospects and sources of income. As these events occur, you may have an opportunity to reduce your tax liability. And even if your income is fixed, your present approach to your tax liability may be inadequate. You may be failing to keep adequate records of tax reducing items and be unaware of tax law benefits you can apply to reduce your tax.

Only you can take the steps necessary to reduce your taxes. The Internal Revenue Service has no obligation to tap you on the shoulder and say, "Mr. Taxpayer, you have been overpaying your taxes because you have not taken advantage of these provisions."

The complexities of the tax law require more than the space of this chapter for explanation; moreover, there are changes year by year. But here you will find basic approaches to income tax savings.

KEEP RECORDS

Record keeping is an essential part of your all-around tax planning. Your detailed records will help you figure your income and deductions at the end of the year. Do not trust to memory. With bills accumulating during a year, you are bound to overlook items. But more important, you will have no record to present to the IRS if they should call you down. Reprinted in this chapter is a sample of the type of record book you can keep to ease your tax-recording chores. It replaces your checkbook stubs and, as you write checks, allows you to list deductible items in addition to other major items that you may want to record.

Make a rule to keep a detailed record of any expense ordinary and necessary to the production of income. Keep bills for investment, legal, or tax counsel, or for rent of a safe deposit box. Legal or accounting fees paid for advice on investments are tax deductible. Also deductible are costs involved in the preparation of a tax return.

When you hold property as an investment, keep statements of expenses pertaining to maintenance, management, or conservation of the property. You may deduct these even if there is no probability that the property ever will be sold at a gain or produce income. Included in such expenses are: (1) Investment counsel fees or commissions. (2) Custodian fees paid to banks or others. (3) Auditors' and accountants' fees. (4) Traveling costs for trips away from home to look after investments, conferring with your attorney, accountant, trustee, or investment counsel about tax or income problems. (5) Maintenance costs of idle property where effort has been made to rent or sell.

Good record keeping applies particularly to rental property. Because there are many deductible expenses involved, record keeping is extremely important. You must have a complete record of the cost of the property, including legal fees, title insurance, the date the property was acquired, the date and cost of each material alteration or addition. The records you must keep during each year include:

1. Amount of rental income received.
2. Bills paid for utilities (heat, light, water, gas, telephone).
3. Bills paid for repairs (painting, cleaning, papering, redecoration).
4. Property taxes.
5. Management expenses.
6. Salaries and wages paid to janitors, elevator men, service men, maintenance men, etc., and Social Security taxes paid on their wages.
7. Legal expense for drawing short-term leases, dispossessing tenants, acquiring rentals.
8. Fire, liability, plate-glass insurance premiums.
9. Interest on mortgage or other indebtedness.

That you rent only one-half of your house, or one room out of eight, doesn't change the need for a record of every item. In renting part of your house, you may deduct a proportionate part of the expense of running the house against the rental income. You do not know what to deduct unless you have a record of all the expenses. On the same statement, you can keep an explanation of the basis of the apportionment you use for the tax return.

Even if you occupy the house you own and do not rent any part of it, you are entitled to certain of the deductions listed above. You should keep a record of taxes, interest, and casualty losses for your tax deduction list.

Canceled checks are adequate proof of contributions you make, which are deductible. But contributions may be in forms other than cash. Keep a record, therefore, of the cost of articles you purchase and give to charitable or religious organizations. This may include such items as donations of food baskets, contributions to bazaars, preparation of food for charitable dinners or picnics. Or if you give

Date	Source of Items Deposited	Amount of Each Deposit Item	Amount of Total Deposit		Amount	Check No.	Date	To Whom Paid	Explanatio
	Opening Balance	//////	$		$				
		$							
1	TOTAL OF OPENING BALANCE PLUS DEPOSITS	$							
2	LESS: TOTAL EXPENDITURES							BANK CHARGES	
3	BALANCE CARRIED FORWARD	$			$			TOTAL MONTHLY EXPENDITURES	

DEDUCTIBLE EXPENSES

Taxes	Interest	Medical & Drugs	Contri- butions	Other: Job Costs Tax Help, etc.	Insurance	Savings & Invest.	Home: Utilities, Repairs, etc.	Personal: Food, Clothing, etc.	Auto & Trans- portation		
	$	$	$	$	$	$	$	$	$	$	$
	$	$	$	$	$	$	$	$	$	$	$

household or miscellaneous articles to recognized charitable, religious, educational, or similar organizations (such as Red Cross or a hospital), establish a fair-market value of the property you give and keep a list of the contributions.

If your work involves travel, you should keep a day-by-day record of expenses.

If you have purchased appliances, an auto, or other goods or services on the installment plan, keep a record of the interest portion of your payments.

For dividend and interest income from stocks and bonds or for trading investments, keep a record of: (1) Name of issuing company. (2) Number of shares or bonds owned and certificate or serial number of each. (3) Date of purchase. (4) Amount paid (including stamp taxes and broker's fees). (5) Date of sale. (6) Amount received (net after stamp taxes and broker's fees). (7) Broker's statements. (8) Each dividend or interest payment received.

You may hold a number of shares of stock of the same company purchased at different times at varying prices. If you wish to sell some of them the question of whether you have a gain or a loss and whether short-term or long-term depends on which particular securities you sell. If you cannot identify each particular lot and its cost, the law will assume that the shares you are selling are those you first acquired. This may be contrary to what you really wish. Consider the case of an investor who didn't bother to keep the certificate numbers of the various shares he bought from time to time. When he sold some of the stock in a declining market, he thought he was selling shares he had bought at a high price and was therefore taking a tax loss, but when an agent of the Internal Revenue Service questioned the deduction, he couldn't prove which shares he had sold; he didn't have any records. The result was that the agent ruled he had sold shares that had been bought cheaply. Instead of taking a tax loss that he needed to offset other income, he realized a taxable gain in a top tax year.

Here are some pointers to help you avoid this trouble:

1. Keep a record of each certificate registered in your name. The date it was acquired, the certificate number, and any other identification should be recorded. How it was acquired should be shown.

Then, when it is sold, you can identify the particular certificate number sold. You need not sell the earliest acquired shares first.

2. If the certificate numbers are unknown, you should inform your broker (and have him confirm) that you wish to sell particular lots. The broker should be told the date of purchase. If possible, the original purchase memorandum should be referred to, giving date and number.

3. If the certificates were received as a stock dividend or in the exercise of rights, the date they were issued should be recorded. The date the option was exercised, the numbers, and other information should be noted. When a sale is ordered, this data should be referred to precisely and the dealer given the facts.

4. When new certificates for old are received in a recapitalization or in a reorganization, each particular certificate should be identified with the old certificate. This is done by taking the lowest numbered certificate of the new and identifying it with the lowest numbered certificate of the old. Then the next higher numbers are correlated. When finished, all the new certificates should be correlated with the old certificate numbers.

5. All brokers' and dealers' purchase and sales memoranda should be kept, together with all notices or slips from the corporation whose securities are held.

Your records should be kept for a minimum of three years after the year to which they are applicable. Some authorities advise keeping them for six years, since in some cases the IRS may go back as far as six years to question a tax return. In cases of suspected tax fraud, there is no time limitation at all.

BASIC PRINCIPLES

You should know the answers to these basic questions about income tax: What income is taxable? What is not taxable? What expenses or other items are deductible from your taxable income? What are the effects of graduated income tax rates? What is capital gain income?

Income. Your common-sense idea of what constitutes income probably approximates the tax law definition of income. Income is the payment made for labor (wages, salaries, commissions), for capital investments (dividends, interest), and for business or partnership profits. Income also includes the gain on the sale of property. Most of what you receive for your work or from investments is taxed. But the following type of receipts are generally not taxed: Gifts and inheritances, Social Security benefits, employee death benefits up to $5000, scholarships, accident and health benefits, certain employee fringe benefits, sick pay up to certain limits, most life insurance proceeds, and interest from state and local government obligations and bonds.

Everyone is allowed to reduce this income total by exemptions for his dependents and for himself. Each exemption is equivalent to a $600 deduction. A deduction is an item that reduces income subject to tax.

Deductions may be divided into two types: (1) Money spent in order to earn your income. (2) Money which is spent for personal reasons (not connected with earning income), but which the law allows as deductions.

The first class of expenses are such costs as business travel and entertainment, management fees, depreciation of equipment used to produce income, etc.

The second class includes a mixed group of items: Charitable contributions up to a certain amount, medical expenses and alimony paid, interest, taxes, losses of personal possessions by casualty or theft.

Credits are somewhat like deductions, but they are more advantageous. A credit is deducted from your tax, dollar for dollar, whereas a deduction reduces income subject to tax. Credits are available for certain retirement income, income taxes paid to foreign countries, and purchases of assets used in business.

Income tax rates. Income tax rates are based on a graduated scale. As your income increases, your tax increases. Tax planning attempts to avoid the effect of graduated rates in several ways: (1) A taxpayer may try to split his income among family members instead of having to report all of his income on his own return and thus having it subject to higher rates. He may give a family member some of his investments so that the income from the investments is reported in a lower tax rate bracket of the family member. Income splitting requires the complete transfer of the investment property. You cannot split income by just assigning your wage, interest, or dividend income. For example, if you wanted to split dividend income with your son, you would have to give him the stock on which the dividend income is earned or place the stock in trust for a number of years.

(2) A taxpayer may try to postpone income to a time when his income from other sources decreases or he may want to accelerate certain income in a year when income from other sources may drop. For example, you may be due a large bonus in a year when your income is high. It would be tax-wise to defer the payment of the bonus to a year when your income is lower. Such deferment requires careful planning.

(3) A taxpayer may try to increase his deductions in a year his income is high. Conversely, if his income is low in a particular year, he may try to postpone deductions to another year when his income will be higher.

Capital gains. Profits from sales of property (securities, real estate, land, etc.) held for more than six months is taxed at one-half of regular tax rates (before the surcharge) of up to 50 percent, but never more than 25 percent of your full gain. When surcharge rates are applicable, the effective capital gain tax is proportionately higher. For capital gain treatment, you generally have to show:

1. You have a capital asset or the kind of asset the gain on which qualifies as capital gain. For example, securities which you hold for investment are capital assets.

2. You sold or exchanged the property or the transaction was the kind that is treated as a sale or exchange. This presents no problem when you sell your property, for example, securities, real estate, etc. However, other kinds of dispositions that may not be sales may also qualify for capital gain treatment. For example, receipt of a lump-sum payment from a qualified pension or profit-sharing plan is usually a capital gain.

3. You have held the asset for longer than six months. Capital gains and losses are either short-term or long-term. This is an important distinction. Short-term capital gains do not qualify for capital gain treatment. Only long-term capital gains do. A short-term gain results from the sale or exchange of property held for six months or less; long-term gain after a holding period of more than six months. The line between long-term and short-term gain may be a matter of a day. One day past the six-month holding period gives long-term gain. Do not make a mistake and sell a day too early.

TAX RETURNS FOR YOUR CHILDREN

Your minor child is a separate taxpayer. His income is not included in your tax return. If his gross income (from all sources—earnings, interest, dividends, capital gains, trust income, etc.) is $600 or more, he must file his own return. He files a return like any other individual. He has the same exemptions and deductions, including the 10 percent or minimum standard deduction. If his gross income is less than $600, he must file a return to get his refund of the taxes withheld. If the child's gross income is $600 or over and his withholdings are not equal to his tax, he is required to pay the difference. If his withholdings are in excess of his tax, he gets the refund.

Although he is required to file a return, a minor can earn up to $900 in wages and still owe no tax. He gets a $600 exemption and a minimum standard deduction of $300.

If a minor files a return, he is entitled to the benefit of a $600 exemption. This is true even if he actually receives more than half of his support from his parent or other close relative who claims him as an exemption.

In figuring whether a minor has $600 of gross income, long-term capital gains are included in full—at 100 percent. For example, if the minor has no other income except a long-term capital gain of $601, he must file a return. But he would owe no tax. Here are some important points to consider:

You can claim an exemption for a child earning $600 or more if he is under 19—or a student of any age—and you furnish more than half of his support. In addition, the child gets an exemption for himself on his own return, if he has to file one.

Pay for personal services of a child is included on his separate return—not that of his parent or guardian. This is so even though the parent makes the contract of employment and gets the wage, and regardless of the local state law governing the earnings of a minor.

You may employ your minor child in your business or income-producing activity and pay him a reasonable salary for services actually rendered. That gives you a deduction for the fair pay you give him, plus the exemption you get for supporting him if he is under 19 or a student of any age. On top of that, he gets a $600 exemption and is taxed in a very low bracket. If you pay your child less than $600, and he has no other income, he is not required to file a return. But he may want to file a return to get a refund of any taxes withheld on his pay.

Keep records of the payments to your children who work for you. Informal family relations is no excuse for not keeping records. A lack of records may jeopardize the wage deduction.

If your child pays you for board and lodging, the payments probably are not income to you. The amount contributed by the child is usually less than the cost of his board. If the child works for you, you cannot take a deduction for board and lodging you provide—unless the child has been freed from your parental control.

A child may be self-employed (a newsboy over 18, for example) and have income between $400 and $600. Ordinarily, he does not have to file a return. But he must pay self-employment Social Security tax. For that purpose only he must file Forms 1040 and Schedule C. You can still claim him as a dependent if he earns less than $600, or more than $600 and is under 19 or a student attending school full time.

When a child owes income tax but is unable to file a required return, the law makes his parent or guardian responsible. If necessary, he may sign the return for the child. Furthermore, a parent is liable for tax due on pay earned by the child for services, but not on investment income.

TAX SAVINGS FOR MARRIED COUPLES
WHO FILE JOINT RETURNS

A married couple filing a joint return pays less tax than a single person who reports the same amount of income. Joint return tax rates are based on the assumption that a married couple shares equally the income reported on the joint return. However, you do not have to give your wife any income to file a joint return. You merely prepare one tax return reporting the income and deductions belonging to both of you. If your wife has no income or deductible expenses, you report your income and deductions. You then figure your tax using the joint return rates and both you and your wife sign the return.

However, note that joint returns do not always reduce taxes. This may happen when you and your wife each have net capital losses in excess of $1000. You can deduct only $1000 of the aggregate losses from your combined joint income. But on separate returns, each of you can deduct $1000 against your separate incomes.

Separate returns may also be advisable when both of you have separate and comparatively equal incomes and one of you incurs and pays medical expenses. By filing separate returns, you can deduct a larger amount of the medical expenses.

TAX SAVINGS IN FAMILY INCOME PLANNING

Family income can be increased by the tax technique known as income splitting. You split income by spreading income now taxed in your top tax bracket among the lower tax brackets of your children or other relatives.

Assignment of income alone does not shift tax liability. You must give away the property that produced the income, such as stocks, United States bonds, mutual fund shares, and rental property. For example, an owner of a service station made a gift to his parents of the right to collect rent from the station and notified the tenant to pay the rent directly to them. But he retained title to the property, paid the property taxes, and deducted depreciation. He did not report the rent income on his tax return, claiming the income belonged to his parents. But a court held he had to pay tax on the income since he did not transfer the property.

How to give securities to a child. Purchase of securities through custodian accounts provides a practical method for making a gift of securities to a child, eliminating the need for a trust. Gifts of securities to children under 21 can be made through a custodian account. The mechanics of opening a custodian account are simple. A parent can open a stock account for his child in a few minutes at a broker's office. He registers the securities in the name of a custodian for the benefit of the child. The custodian may be a parent, a child's guardian, grandparent, brother, sister, uncle, or aunt. In some states, the custodian may be any adult individual or a bank or trust company. The custodian has the right to sell securities in the account for the child, collect sale proceeds and investment income, and to use them for the child's benefit or reinvestment.

There are some minor limitations placed on the custodian. He cannot take proceeds from the sale or investments or income from investments to buy additional securities on margin. While he should prudently seek reasonable income and capital preservation, he generally is not liable for losses unless they result from bad faith, intentional wrongdoing, or gross negligence.

When the minor reaches 21 and property in the custodian account is turned over to him, no formal accounting is required. The child, now an adult, can sign a simple release freeing the custodian from any liability. But on reaching majority, the child can acquire a formal accounting if he has any doubts as to the propriety of the custodian's actions while acting as custodian. Because a formal accounting can be required by the child and also for tax record keeping purposes, a separate bank account should be opened in which proceeds from sale of investment and investment income are deposited pending reinvestment on behalf of the child. Such an account will furnish a convenient record showing receipt of sales proceeds, investment income and reinvestment of the same.

Although custodian accounts can be opened anywhere in the United States, the legal rules governing the account may vary from state to state depending on which law is in force: Model Act or Uniform Act. They differ in that: (1) Under the Model Act, the donor can only appoint himself, a member of the minor's family, or any other competent adult person as custodian. Under the Uniform Act, the donor may appoint any bank, trust company, or any adult as custodian. The donor can also deposit cash to the account, as well as securities. (2) Under the Uniform Act (but not under the Model Act) the minor, when he reaches 14, can ask the court to have the custodian use the account's funds for his support. The Model Act is limited to Alaska and Georgia. However, Georgia allows gifts of cash.

The differences between the two Acts do not affect the tax treatment of a custodian account. The income tax treatment is the same for both.

As long as income from the custodian account is not used to support the child, income realized through the custodian account is taxed to the child, if taxed at all. Actually, no tax will be due on income up to $1000 where at least $100 of that income comes from dividends.

There is still an added income tax advantage. Even though the custodian accumulates a substantial amount of income for the ultimate benefit of the minor child, the child remains a dependent of the parent for tax purposes. On his Federal income tax return, the parent is still allowed a $600 tax exemption for the child. That is so even if the giver of the securities is both the custodian and the parent of the child.

When setting up a custodian account you may have to pay a gift tax. The Treasury says a transfer of securities to a custodian account is a completed gift. But you are not subject to a gift tax if you properly plan the purchase of securities for your children's accounts. Each year, you can make gifts up to $3000 to one person and be free of any gift tax. This $3000 is called your *annual exclusion* and it is applied each year to as many people as you make gifts to. If your wife consents to join with you in the gift, you can give taxfree up to $6000 to one person. All you need do is add her annual exclusion to yours. And even if your gift to one person is over the $3000 or $6000 limit, you may still avoid a gift tax. You can do this by applying part or all of your lifetime exemption of $30,000 against the excess of the gift over the annual exclusion. Here again, if your wife consents to the gift, you can apply a $60,000 lifetime exemption by adding her lifetime exemption to yours. By combining the annual exclusion and lifetime exemption, this year you can give up to $66,-000 taxfree to one person, as long as you have made no prior gifts which have been applied against you and your wife's lifetime exemption.

If the custodian account is set up at the end of a calendar year, for example in December, another taxfree transfer of $6000 can be made in the first days of January of the following year. In this way, a total of $72,000 is shifted within the period of one month. From this brief discussion, you can see that you have room in which to make gifts without running afoul of the gift tax.

As for the estate tax, the value of a custodian account will be taxed to your estate if you die while acting as custodian of an account before your child reaches 21. But remember, no estate tax is incurred if an estate is under $60,000 because of the $60,000 exemption. And if an estate is between $60,000 and $120,000 and the maximum advantage of the marital deduction is taken, the estate tax liability is eliminated. Furthermore, if there's a chance the custodian account will be taxed to your estate, you may avoid the problem by not naming yourself custodian but by naming someone else, for example, your wife.

SETTING UP A TRUST FOR YOUR CHILDREN'S COLLEGE YEARS

A trust can be set up to provide funds for your child's college education. In setting up the trust for your child, make sure that you will not be taxed on income used by the trust to pay for educational expenses. Under the tax law, where your legal obligation to support your minor child is discharged by a trust which you set up, you are taxed on income so applied by the trust to your child's support.

Whether you are legally obligated to send your child to college is determined by the law of the state in which you live. The current trend of law recognizes that a father who is financially able to provide a college education for his children has an obligation to do so. This, however, does not mean that the law in your state has reached this conclusion. You will have to review this point with your attorney.

The issue of whether you are obligated to send your child to college might be avoided by setting up the trust when your child is young, say seven or under. You transfer property to a trust which is to continue until the child reaches college age—a period of at least ten years. You also set up a bank account in the child's name to which trust income is paid, or invest the income in government bonds in the child's name. Before the child reaches college age, the trust ends and you receive back the trust property. When your child starts college, he begins to withdraw funds from the bank account or to cash in the bonds to pay his college expenses. Under this approach, the trust has not been used to pay the college costs directly, as it no longer exists. In setting up the trust, see that the trust deed does not state that income is for educational purposes if there is a danger that you may be held legally obligated to provide a college education.

TAX SAVINGS FOR INVESTORS IN SECURITIES

As an investor, you have a major tax advantage. Appreciation on investments you hold for more than six months is subject to low capital gains rates when you finally liquidate your holdings. This advantage alone would be sufficient to encourage investments. But certain types of investments bring additional advantages. Investments in tax-exempt bonds, for example, permit you to receive income without a tax cost. Tax on dividend income from domestic companies is reduced by the dividend exclusion, and is even taxfree from some companies under certain conditions.

Planning year-end tax saving strategy. First find your gain and loss position for the year. Then study how to minimize your tax liability or improve your investment position.

Any substantial change in the market during December may require fast action on your part to get the best tax break.

In organizing your survey, review the records of earlier years to find any capital loss to be carried over against this year's gains or ordinary income. Include nonbusiness bad debts as short-term capital losses. After you know the gains and losses already realized during this year from completed securities transactions, go over your paper gains and losses. What transactions might now be completed to:

Offset actual gains?
Utilize potential losses?
Step up the tax cost of your securities?
Improve your tax position for future years?

The following check lists provide suggestions for deciding which securities to sell. The suggestions are based on these points: It is preferable to realize long-term capital gains when they will not be offset by short-term or long-term losses. Both types of losses should preferably be realized to offset short-term gains and ordinary income.

If your completed security transactions show:

Long-term gains. You might avoid taking any losses this year and pay low capital gains tax on these gains. But if you want to realize losses, first sell securities giving long-term losses.

Short-term gains. You might realize losses to offset these gains which otherwise would be taxed at ordinary income tax rates. Realize long-term losses first.

Long-term and short-term gains. You might realize short-term losses. These will first offset short-term gains, which are fully taxable, rather than the tax-favored long-term gains.

Long-term losses, short-term losses, or both. You might first realize offsetting short-term capital gains. Avoid realizing long-term gains. By realizing long-term gains, you are offsetting income that otherwise would be taxed at low capital gain rates.

If you have realized neither gains nor losses this year (that is, if you have only paper profits or losses), check these guides to determine your year-end sales, if any. Remember, paper profits or losses have no tax consequences unless you actually sell your securities.

You have unrealized short-term gains. Hold the securities until your holding period is more than six months. The gain then becomes long-term.

You have unrealized long-term gains. You may want to realize a substantial amount of your gains now, especially if your income is low this year. Conversely, if this was a high income year and next year offers a smaller income return or lower tax rates, you may want to postpone your sales until next year. But if during the last few weeks of the year you fear that the price of your stock may decline by the time you make the sale next year, you can freeze your profit by ordering a short sale of the stock this year. You transact a short sale by selling shares borrowed from your broker. In January of next year, you deliver your shares to the broker as a replacement of the borrowed shares you sold last year. By delivering the stock in January, the gain on the short sale is fixed as next year's. For tax purposes, a short sale is not completed until the covering stock is delivered.

You have unrealized long-term gains and long-term or short-term losses or both. You may want to realize your gains in one year and your losses in another year. Avoid realizing both gains and losses in the same year. The losses will be offset against your gains and only the excess gain is taxed at low capital gain rates.

Which should you take first, gains or losses? If your losses are under $1000, you may want to take your losses this year. This has a double effect. It reduces the tax due this year, postpones tax on gains taken in January until the succeeding year. But where your losses are substantial so that you will have a carryover, it may be better to take your long-term gains first, even though that increases your tax. Otherwise, your loss carryover will be offset against your later gains.

You have unrealized long-term or short-term losses. You may want to realize losses up to $1000 to offset your other income. Take long-term losses in preference to short-term losses. Then, if early next year you have substantial long-term and short-term gains, you can realize your short-term losses to reduce your short-term gains first. In other words, you will not have retained loss securities that reduce long-term gains.

You have unrealized long-term and short-term gains and also long-term or short-term losses. You can offset losses in full against gains and then use any excess of loss against other income up to $1000. The remainder of the loss can be used as a carryover loss in later years.

Remember, these guides consider only the tax consequences of your security planning. You must weigh also the investment value of your stock and general market and economic conditions. A large volume of tax-selling at the end of the year can depress stock values below their usual levels. Therefore, it might be advisable to avoid selling during the wave of tax-selling by other investors in December. If you are interested in a security because of its long-term potential, you might hold off buying until late in December, or perhaps until January of the following year for possible lower price purchase at the later date.

In planning year-end sales, watch the deadline for recording sales. The deadline depends upon whether you have a gain or loss and are on the cash or accrual basis. When you buy and sell securities through a registered stock exchange, the holding period starts on the day after the "trade date" although you do not pay for and receive the securities until the "settlement date" several days later.

The reason for the intervening days is that stock exchanges do not require delivery and payment to be made until the third or fourth full business day after the day on which a sale or purchase is ordered. Often the period may be longer because of intervening holidays.

Although this stock exchange practice does not affect the tax consequences of security transactions made during the year, it can seriously alter the timing of gain taken at the end of the year. Because of the holiday season, the settlement date of a sale ordered a week before the end of the year may occur in the next year with this result: A gain which you wanted to report this year is taxable next year. The reason: As a cash basis taxpayer you do not realize gain until you actually or constructively receive payment, that is, on the settlement date. Generally, stock exchanges give advance notice of the last trading date on which profit-seeking sales can be made for the year. In December, look for the date so that you can properly time your profitable sale orders. As for losses, you need not be concerned with this particular timing problem. You can sell until the last business day of the year and realize your losses regardless of the settlement dates.

WAYS TO SAVE TAXES

1. Claim all your exemptions. The more exemptions you have, the less tax you pay as each exemption reduces your taxable income by $600. Exemptions are not divided or prorated, so even if you got married on the last day of the year, you claim your wife as a full exemption. There is no limit on the number of dependents you can have on your tax return as long as they meet these tests: (a) Your dependent is a close relative such as a child or parent, or a person who has made your home his principal residence for the entire year as a member of your household. (b) You contribute more than one-half of the dependent's support. (c) Your dependent's gross income for the year is less than $600. However, if the dependent is your child under 19 years of age, or a full-time student, then the amount of his income doesn't matter. You claim him as an exemption even if his income is over $600.

2. If you receive payments from an employer of a deceased parent, relative, or friend who made you his beneficiary, these sums are taxfree up to $5000 if they were paid because of the deceased's death and he did not have a nonforfeitable right to the payment while he was alive. Check these two points with the company paying you the benefit.

3. Claim the dividend exclusion on dividend income you received. You get a dividend exclusion by reducing the dividend income by $100. If your wife also earns dividend income, she has her own $100 exclusion, so on a joint return your exclusion can be as high as $200.

4. Distinguish between the different types of dividend payments you get from your mutual fund investments. Mutual funds generally pay their shareholders three kinds of dividends: (a) Ordinary dividends which are fully taxed but entitled to the dividend exclusion. (b) Capital gain dividends which are taxed at low capital gain rates.

(c) Return of capital proceeds which are not taxable. Check your mutual funds annual statement; it will tell you what percentage of your receipts fits into each of these three categories.

5. Do not report as taxed income stock dividends or stock rights which you received on your stock investments. You pay no tax on this kind of dividend unless you had a choice of taking either cash or the stock, or the dividend was a payment of certain arrearages on preferred stock.

6. If you own stock in a utility, check the company's statement. Some utilities pay taxfree dividends because of the way they report profits. The company's statement will tell you whether the dividend is taxed or taxfree.

7. You have a tax saving election with United States savings bonds. You can report the annual interest by merely including it on your tax return each year, or you can wait to report the interest in the year you finally redeem the bonds. The latter method can help you build up the value of E bonds during your lifetime without tax.

8. Apportion home expenses if you use part of your residence as an office. Then deduct the household expenses apportioned to your business. Any reasonable plan of apportionment will be approved, allowing you to deduct a portion of the heat, light, telephone, insurance and depreciation fairly apportioned to the office. Your apportionment might be based on the ratio of the number of rooms devoted to your office to the total number of rooms in the house.

9. Installment reporting of a sale of property can cut the immediate tax due on the profit made on the sale. It can also help you spread the tax payment over future years. You can use the installment sale method whenever you sell personal property for a price of more than $1000 or real estate for any price. You do not have to receive payments in the year of sale. But if you do, they must be 30 percent or less of the sale price.

10. Make sure you deduct debts due you in the year they become worthless. Unless you deduct them in that year, you lose the deduction. In fixing the year a debt became worthless, you must show that the debt had no value because, for example, the debtor went bankrupt or disappeared in that year.

11. If you have an endowment policy that is going to mature in the near future, you have a tax-saving election. If you take an annuity option before the policy matures or within sixty days after maturity, you pay no tax on the insured policy. You pay tax only during the years you receive annuity payments. If you wait more than sixty days after maturity to make the election, you pay tax on the matured policy.

12. You do not report gifts or bequests you have received. Gifts, bequests, and inheritances are taxfree. However, income you receive from such property after you own it is taxable.

13. You do not report as income any insurance proceeds you receive as beneficiary of a deceased relative or friend. However, if you receive the proceeds as installment payments, you may have to pay tax on the interest that is paid on the principal. However, if you are a surviving spouse you get a special tax-free annual exemption for interest up to $1000.

14. You can deduct donations to religious, charitable, and educational institutions. A contribution need not be in cash. A donation entitles you to a contribution deduction. You can deduct generally up to 30 percent of your adjusted gross income depending on the type of charity you give to. Giving a charity property that has appreciated in value permits you to get a deduction for its full market value while avoiding tax on unrealized profit (the difference between the cost basis for the property and its market value).

If you do voluntary work for a charitable organization without pay, you can deduct as charitable contributions your unreimbursed commutation expenses to and from the charity's place of operation. As a measure of your auto costs, you can use a rate of 5 cents a mile. However, you cannot deduct the value of your services.

15. If you receive a large amount of income in one year, check to see if you can reduce your tax by averaging your income. You may even be entitled to average if your income has steadily increased over the last five years or if your wife has gone back to work thereby raising your joint income. More specifically, you may average if your taxable income in a current year exceeds by more than $3000 an amount that is ⅓ greater than the average of your taxable income in the four preceding years.

Averaging can apply to almost all types of income such as salary, dividends, interest, short-term capital gains, rental income, and business or professional income. It does not apply to long-term capital gains, gambling winnings, and income of over $3000 received on property you received as a gift or inheritance during the past four years and current year.

16. Deduct all interest you pay on your borrowings including all business, personal, and family debts. Interest on money borrowed to defray personal expenses, or money borrowed to purchase property is deductible. The debt need not be evidenced by a note or mortgage.

17. Deduct interest paid on installment purchases. When you buy on the installment plan, you also pay interest. But the interest charge is not always clearly stated. When it is, you have no problem. You deduct the interest when you pay it. If the interest is not separately stated, then you deduct as interest 6 percent of the average balance which you owe during the year.

18. In figuring your medical expenses, be sure to include the medical bills which you have paid for your wife, children, and other dependents. You can deduct medical expenses of your children and other dependents even though they are not exemptions on your tax return. All you have to show is that you paid the expense and contributed to more than one-half of their support.

19. You can deduct as medical costs the expense of a trip prescribed to relieve a specific chronic ailment; for example, to remedy arthritis; or the cost of a trip to visit a specialist in another city. However, the costs of board and lodging incurred on an out-of-town trip are not deductible. The deduction is limited to the actual cost of transportation.

20. You might deduct some home improvements as medical expenses. An ailment may require you to construct special facilities or equipment in your home such as an air conditioner, or a type of stair elevator to carry a heart patient upstairs. To get this deduction you must show that the equipment alleviates the illness and does not increase the value of your home.

21. Deduct as medical expense the cost of sending a mentally or physically handicapped person to a special school or institution that is designed to overcome or alleviate such a handicap. Such costs can

cover teaching in Braille or lip-reading and the training and care of a mentally retarded person, including the cost of meals and lodging.

22. Deduct one-half of the insurance premiums paid for a medical care policy covering yourself, your wife, or your dependents. The maximum deduction cannot exceed $150. Premium costs exceeding $150 are deductible as a medical expense subject to the 3 percent of adjusted gross income limit.

Premiums are deductible if the insurance contract covers the payment of deductible medical care expenses. If it pays for other than medical care (such as for loss of income, or for loss of life, limb or sight), premiums are not deductible unless (1) the contract or a separate statement from the insurance company specifies what part of the premium is allocated to medical care, and (2) the premium allocated to medical care is reasonable in relation to the total premium.

23. Deduct the cost of courses you take to maintain your job skills. Include in this deduction not only the cost of courses you take but also travel expenses to and from a school which is away from your home city. Living expenses such as food and lodging while at school away from home can also be deducted. Regular courses of study leading to a degree may be deductible if it does not prepare you for a different occupation or profession.

24. Deduct expenses incurred to produce or collect income. For example, you have investments in securities. You can deduct investment counsel fees, the rental fees of a safe deposit box to hold your securities, or the salary of an accountant you employ to keep track of your investment income.

25. Deduct the costs for preparing your Federal, state or local tax returns. This deduction covers not only the expenses of preparing your income tax return but also the expenses of defending your return in a Treasury examination.

26. You can recoup losses suffered from storms, fire, accident, or other casualties by claiming casualty loss deductions on your return. Your loss is generally the difference between the value of the property before and after the casualty. However, if you received any insurance, you must reduce your loss by any insurance received and also a $100 limitation for each casualty.

27. Deduct losses of property that has been stolen from you. To insure the deduction you should get statements from witnesses who saw the theft, or police reports of persons breaking into your house or your car. When you suspect a theft, make sure you make a report to the police. Even though your report doesn't prove that a theft was committed, your failure to report is evidence that you are not sure that your property was stolen.

28. Use the correct tax rate schedule in figuring your tax. If you are married and file a joint return, use the joint return rates which give you the advantage of splitting income between yourself and your wife. If you are unmarried and support dependents in your home, see if you are able to take advantage of the head of household rates. These rates give you about half the advantage that a married couple gets on a joint return. If your wife has died within the last two years, you may still be able to use joint return rates as a surviving spouse if you have dependent children.

29. If you earned income from foreign investments, don't forget to take a tax credit for any foreign taxes that have been paid on your income. Generally, you will save money by claiming a credit rather than a deduction. A deduction is only partially offset against your United States tax, whereas a credit is deducted in full from your tax.

30. If you have sold your residence for a profit, you do not have to pay tax if you buy or build another house (or acquire a cooperative apartment) at a cost at least equal to the sales price of the old house. However, make sure you buy and use your house within one year before or after you sell your old house. Or, if you build a new house, build and use the house within one year before or 18 months after you sell your old house.

31. If you are 65 or older and you sell your house at a gain, you may elect to avoid tax on gain attributed to the first $20,000 of the sales price of your house. To get the tax break, you must have used the house as a residence (and owned it) five out of the eight years preceding the sale.

32. Losses on the sale of a personal residence are not deductible. However, one way you might get a deduction is by renting the house before you sell it. Rental usually converts the house to business

property on which there is a deduction available if you have to sell at a loss.

33. Convert dividend income into capital gain by selling the stock when the dividend is declared but not yet paid. The selling price reflects the dividend which becomes part of your profit. Be sure you make this sale before the record date of the dividend. If you still hold the stock on the record date of the dividend, you will not get tax savings when you sell the securities.

34. You can sometimes control the year of real estate income. Generally, the tax is due in the year that title to the property sold passes to the buyer. However, often you can control the year the title passes. For example, you intend to sell property this year but you figure that by reporting the profit next year it will cost you less in tax because you expect lower income next year. Plan to have title pass next year. But make sure you do not give the buyer possession this year. If you do, you will be taxed this year even though title doesn't pass until next year.

35. Don't lose a loss deduction on the sale of property to a relative such as a child or parent. The law disallows losses on sales to close relatives even though the sale is in good faith or occurs through a public stock exchange and a family member buys equivalent property on the exchange.

36. If any property you own has been condemned by a government authority to make way for a highway or for public works, you can avoid tax on profit realized on the condemnation. Do this by investing the condemnation award in other real estate. Be sure you make your investment within one year after the end of the year in which you realized the profit. If you cannot buy a replacement within the required time, ask your local District Director for an extension of time.

37. If you pay a maid or sitter to watch children or other dependents so you can go to work, you may be able to deduct all or part of these payments. Child care costs cannot exceed $600 for the care of one dependent, or $900 if there are two or more dependents. The costs are limited to the wages of a maid or sitter for looking after children under the age of thirteen and dependents of

any age who are physically or mentally defective. You must hire the maid or sitter to enable you to work at or seek employment. Costs of a nursery, boarding or day school that cares for your children while you work also qualify. If you are married, you must file a joint return and reduce deductible care costs by the amount by which adjusted gross income on your joint return exceeds $6000. In other words, if you have one dependent under care, you cannot deduct care costs if your joint adjusted gross income is $6600 or more. If you have two or more dependents under care, you lose the deduction if your adjusted gross income is $6900 or more. The joint income reduction does not apply to expenses incurred by a wife during a period when her husband is incapable of self-support because of a mental or physical disability, or expenses incurred by a husband during a period his wife is in a hospital or similar institution for at least 90 consecutive days or a lesser period ending in her death. You can claim the deduction if you are a woman, whether you are single, married, separated, divorced, or deserted. If you are a man, you must be a widower, divorced or legally separated, or have a wife who is incapacitated for at least 90 consecutive days.

38. Deduct expenses of moving to a new job location if you meet these tests: (1) Your new job location is at least 20 miles farther than the distance between the location of your old job and your former home. (2) You remain in the new locality as a full-time employee for at least 39 weeks during the 12 months immediately following your arrival. The 39-week and 12-month periods are measured from the date you arrive at the new location to begin work on a regular basis. The 39-week test does not apply to any moving expense item to the extent that it is reimbursed by your employer. But if your moving expenses exceed the reimbursement, you must meet both tests in order to deduct your excess costs.

You may take the deduction whether you are starting a new position, being transferred by your present employer, or beginning your first job.

39. Costs for work clothes may be deductible, and the cost of cleaning and repairing them if: (1) They are specially required for your job and (2) they cannot be worn as ordinary streetwear. Tools

and equipment you use on the job are also deductible. If the items last only one year, you can deduct their full cost in the year you buy them. Otherwise, you must depreciate them over their useful lives.

Chapter 16

DECIDE THE FUTURE OF YOUR ESTATE NOW

JOINT OWNERSHIP OF PROPERTY—ADVANTAGES AND
   DISADVANTAGES | 244
MAKING A WILL | 246
  Who Are Your Beneficiaries? What Do You Have to
    Leave? | 246
  The Executor of Your Estate | 248
  Guardians for Your Children | 249
  Reviewing Your Will | 249
YOUR ESTATE AND FEDERAL TAXES | 250
  Finding the Value of Your Estate | 251
  State Death Taxes | 252
  You Are Now Ready to Estimate the Federal Estate
    Tax | 253
    Rates for Estimating the Estate Tax | 254
  Reducing or Eliminating a Potential Tax | 255
GIFT PLANNING | 255
THE MARITAL DEDUCTION | 257
LIFE INSURANCE PROCEEDS | 258
PROVIDING LIQUID FUNDS FOR PAYMENT OF ESTATE
  TAXES | 259
A FINAL WORD | 259

We have been discussing money management and the current expenses of living. The eventuality of death and its effect on the finances of your family have been considered in the chapter on life insurance. Now we come to plans for the distribution of your estate. Many people tend to push this question aside—as if death itself can so be avoided; their failure to face the problem squarely often causes pain and expense to members of the family who should have been protected.

In this chapter, we will discuss your estate and the plans you can make, including the making of a will, followed by guidance on estate taxes. First, we will take up the question of joint property, which is sometimes used indiscriminately as a substitute for a will.

JOINT OWNERSHIP OF PROPERTY— ADVANTAGES AND DISADVANTAGES

There are sound reasons for joint ownership being widely used by married couples and relatives. Joint ownership is easy to arrange and, instead of a provision in a will, it can be used to direct the inheritance of property. Title passes to the surviving joint owner without legal entanglements and delays; he or she has immediate right to possess and control the property.

Because jointly owned property passes outside the will, it is not subject to the costs which affect property that passes either by will or by the laws of intestacy that govern property when no will is left. All wills must be probated, that is, proved to be valid. Executors' or administrators' fees and other expenses of estate administration are usually based on the size of the probate estate.

Some people, trying to avoid the costs of probate, think that they can arrange for joint property ownership and so eliminate the need for a will altogether. But this maneuver may result in most unfortunate results because joint ownership does not adequately meet all the eventualities that take place after a death. The principal objection is that jointly owned property may pass to people who would not have been named as sole heirs.

Here is an example. A childless couple put all their property in joint names; neither made a will. The husband died in an automobile accident that left the wife seriously injured. A few weeks later, she, too, died. Because she was sole owner of the property for those weeks, all of it went to her brothers and sisters. Her husband's parents received nothing. Had the couple made a will they would have been able to distribute the property fairly between both families.

The popular notion that joint ownership frees property from estate tax is incorrect. *Under Federal estate tax law, it is assumed that all property held in joint names belongs to the owner who dies first.*

Say the survivor in fact paid for, inherited, or otherwise acquired the property which was held as joint property. The law assumes that the property belonged to the person who died. The survivor must prove that he was the original owner.

For example, a husband buys property and names his wife as joint owner with him. On his death, the *full property,* not half, will be included in his taxable estate. But say the wife died first. The Federal Government could claim that she was the original owner of the property and consequently it is taxable in her estate. The surviving husband would have to prove that he alone bought the property.

That jointly owned property is liable to *increased* estate tax liability can be seen dramatically in this case: Over a period of years, the wife received over $40,000 from her parents. She turned all the money over to her husband so that he could invest it for her. He bought municipal "bearer" bonds on which the owner's name does not appear and placed them, together with his own securities, in a safe deposit box. This box was rented in the joint names of husband and wife.

The husband died and, as required by state law, a representative of the state tax commission was present when the safe deposit box was opened. The wife was unable to show that she was the true owner of the bonds which were listed among her husband's assets. Because she was the sole beneficiary, she ultimately recovered the bonds, but only after tax in her husband's estate had been paid on them.

We suggest that when husband and wife purchase property or stock in joint names, complete and accurate records should be kept of the contributions made from the personal funds of each one.

Here is another danger which arises because jointly owned property automatically passes to the survivor. The executor or administrator of the estate generally cannot use that property to pay the taxes or debts of the deceased person. To raise needed cash, other estate assets may have to be sold, perhaps at sacrifice prices, to satisfy obligations.

Certain tax alternatives can be used to reduce estate taxes, but joint ownership may prevent their use. For example, a husband wisely sets up trust arrangements for the benefit of his wife and, ultimately, the children or other relatives. Estate tax is avoided on the property so passing. Had the property been jointly owned it might have been subject to tax.

For most individuals, gift tax is not a problem because the tax is not imposed until gifts reach certain limits and, through proper planning, the gift tax can usually be avoided. But, it should be noted, the setting up of joint ownership may make the property involved subject to Federal gift tax.

MAKING A WILL

Through a will you can direct who is to inherit your property and the amounts your heirs are to receive. Without a will, state law will fix the heirs and shares. Thus, people you did not intend to benefit may inherit; others whom you wished to share in the estate might receive a smaller share or none at all.

To prevent such an occurrence—and the ill feeling likely to arise, to say nothing of possible lawsuits—you need your own written will. Here, we have some very direct advice. Do not draw your own will! Have an attorney prepare it. If you do not have a regular attorney, contact a local bar association for recommendations. The fee for drawing a will is not large, and the experienced attorney charges no more than the inexperienced.

The purpose of the following discussion is to help you consider and decide what you want to achieve with your will. Once you have reviewed the extent of your property and your objectives, you can intelligently discuss your will with an attorney.

WHO ARE YOUR BENEFICIARIES?
WHAT DO YOU HAVE TO LEAVE?

Your first step is to *list your beneficiaries*. Write the names of your immediate family, your wife, your children (and their ages), your brothers and sisters, your parents. List other beneficiaries you may wish to remember, such as a trusted friend, employees, your place of worship, your college, a medical, educational, or other philanthropic organization.

Many charitable organizations have similar names. Be careful that the correct titles go into your will. If you misname a charitable beneficiary, its identity may have to be decided by a court and the legal expenses involved will be a charge against your estate. List alternative charities in case those you name cease to function or cannot take your bequest.

Next, *list your assets*. Here, your review of your net worth and your household inventory (Chapter 2) will help you. Be sure that you have not overlooked a bank account or a bond bought many years ago. This is a common occurrence. Each year banks and other financial institutions list names of persons who have forgotten their accounts. You might also forget small jewelry or heirlooms, a valuable collection of stamps or coins laid aside many years ago.

What of the shares of stock you purchased years ago and put away? An investment or property not producing income now may seem of little value but in time it may become valuable. A business that you consider a sideline may become an asset which will put your estate into a high tax bracket. (See page 250 for further comments on listing assets.)

When you list properties, be sure they are really yours to give. Note that title to certain properties passes outside your will. Examples are jointly held property and property held with your wife as tenants by the entirety; insurance payable to a named beneficiary, even though for tax purposes it may be part of your gross estate; United States savings bonds held in your name but payable to another at your death; estates in which you had a life interest, after your death the remainder goes to another.

Do you have two residences, say one up North, the other down South? If so, list your possessions in the two states involved for your attorney. He will draw your will in accordance with the laws of the state in which the will must be probated. Generally, dispositions of personal property are controlled by laws of the state of your principal residence; real property, according to those of the state in which it is located. The laws of one state may be more beneficial for your estate than the other. Ask your attorney now what steps you can take to ensure that the disposition of your estate will be made in accordance with the laws you prefer.

In making a will, your marital status must be considered. Some states, in certain circumstances, allow widows to elect to take the share of a husband's estate under the laws of intestacy in place of the bequest left under a will. In many states, the law protects the rights of adopted children and after-born children not named in a will to share in a parent's estate.

Your state's laws may provide your widow or children with homestead rights or give your widow the right to remain in your home for a certain length of time, with a sustenance allowance from your estate. If the laws of dower or curtesy are in force, they, too, limit your right of disposition over property. In most community property states, each spouse is limited in the portion of property that can be left by will to others.

There should be provision covering the possibility of a simultaneous death of both spouses, for example, in a plane or automobile crash. The laws of most states provide that in case of simultaneous death, it will be presumed that the person writing the will survived his spouse. You may not want this presumption to apply. See page 257 for a discussion of the marital deduction for which you may wish your estate to qualify for Federal estate tax purposes. A provision can be made in your will to rebut the presumption that, in the case of simultaneous deaths, the writer of the will lived longer.

THE EXECUTOR OF YOUR ESTATE

If you leave no will, the court will appoint someone to administer your estate. He may not be acquainted with your family or sympathetic to their interests. With a will, you can select the person or persons you feel qualified to administer your estate. You may appoint your wife, an adult child, or both to serve jointly as executors.

If the administration of your estate requires business or professional training and experience, consider appointing an attorney or a business associate as executor. It is possible that the person you name will become unable to perform his function as an executor. You may provide alternative names.

The executor may serve without bond if you so stipulate. This is usually the case when you name a member of your family as your executor.

Your executor is entitled to commissions for his services, generally computed on a percentage basis of the gross value of all your property and income that passes through his hands. The amount he receives is a deductible expense in computing your taxable estate. Commissions are fixed by local law, but you can provide in your will that your executor shall act without compensation or that he should have a specified allowance in place of statutory commissions. Your attorney will advise you how to handle your executor's commissions.

GUARDIANS FOR YOUR CHILDREN

Will you leave property to a child under 21? If so, name a guardian of his property. If you do not, the court will appoint one. Although a parent is considered the natural guardian of the person of an infant, he is not the guardian of his property unless so named. If you name your widow as guardian of your child's property, provide an alternate in case she should not qualify to act. The duty of a guardian of property is to hold, manage, and conserve the property for the infant until he reaches 21. You can name one guardian, or two or more persons to act jointly in this capacity.

REVIEWING YOUR WILL

Review your will periodically, especially when these events occur: Your family relationships change; you marry, separate, are divorced; your wife dies; a child is born, dies or is adopted; a grandchild is born, dies or is adopted; your estate increases or decreases substantially; you acquire property in another state or abroad; you move to another state; you retire.

Some changes in your will may only require a codicil; others may require a new will entirely. When adding a codicil, remember it must, like your will, be legally drawn and witnessed. Any handwritten or typed changes in your will or codicil will invalidate it. So, if you have a good will, do not spoil it. When you make a new will, follow your attorney's instructions on how to destroy the old one and any codicils to it.

YOUR ESTATE AND FEDERAL TAXES

The estate of every deceased citizen or resident in this country is allowed an exemption of $60,000. If your estate does not amount to more than $60,000, Federal estate taxes will not be due, and no return need be filed. However (unless you live in Nevada and have no property elsewhere), your estate will probably be liable to a state death tax. (See page 252.)

Understand what the word estate means in the Federal estate tax law so that you do not underestimate the value of your taxable estate. The estate includes not only your real estate (foreign and domestic), bank deposits, securities, personal property and other more obvious signs of wealth, but can also include insurance, your interest in trusts, and jointly held property.

The estate tax is a tax on the act of transferring property at death. It is not a tax on the right of a beneficiary to receive the property; the estate and the estate alone pays the tax.

You cannot intelligently estimate what will remain for your family unless you consider estate taxes. To help you make an estimate of what will remain for your heirs, we offer this guide to Federal estate taxation. It will alert you to the cost of the estate tax, if any, and if you find that you have an estate subject to tax, to plans for estate tax savings that you may discuss with your attorney.

The listing of your assets was briefly discussed on page 247 in regard to making your will. If those assets are substantial, you will have to give a considerable amount of thought, time, and work to making the necessary appraisal of your estate.

The first step in estate planning follows a simple business custom of taking inventory. But inventory of what? Of everything you own.

Listing one's belongings takes thought, time, and a surprising amount of work with lists, records of purchases, fire and theft insurance inventories, bank books, brokers' statements, etc. You need to include your cash, real estate (here and abroad), securities, mortgages, rights in property, trust accounts, life insurance payable to your estate or payable to others if you have kept a certain measure of ownership, personal effects, collections and art works. You should also list property you gave away recently. This is necessary since gifts made within three years of a donor's death may be subject to tax in his estate as having been made, under the law, "in contemplation of death."

If you own property jointly with your wife, list the entire value of the property unless you have proof that she invested her own funds in the property. Her investment is not taxable in your estate. (See page 245.)

If you have had appraisals made of unusual or specially treasured items or those of substantial value, file such appraisals with your estate papers and enter the value on your inventory.

There are some assets that you might not ordinarily consider as part of your taxable estate. Nevertheless, include in your inventory any trust arrangements in which you have kept (1) a life estate (the income or other use of property for life); (2) income that is to be used to pay your legal obligations (support of a child, for example); (3) the right to change the beneficiary or his interest (a power of appointment); (4) the right to revoke a trust transfer or gift; or (5) a reversionary interest (possibility that the property can come back to you).

FINDING THE VALUE OF YOUR ESTATE

When you have completed your inventory, assign to each asset what you consider to be its fair market value. This may be difficult to do for some assets. We all tend to overvalue articles which arouse feelings of pride or sentiment, and undervalue some articles of greater intrinsic worth. For purposes of your initial estimate, it is better to err on the side of overvaluation.

If you have a family business, your idea of its value and that of the Treasury may greatly vary. Many well-made estate plans have been upset by the higher value placed on such a business by the Treasury. You can protect your estate by anticipating and solving this problem with your business associates, accountant, and legal counsel.

If your business is owned by a close corporation, and there is no ready or open market in which the stock can be valued, get some factual basis for a figure that will be reported on the estate tax return. One of the ways to do this is by arranging a buy-sell agreement with a potential purchaser. This agreement must fix the value of the stock. Generally, an agreement that binds both the estate and the purchaser and restricts lifetime sales of the stock will effectively fix the value of the stock for estate tax purposes. Another way would be to make a gift of some shares to a family member, and have value established in gift tax proceedings. Unless there is a drastic change, the valuation thus established will have considerable weight in later estate tax proceedings.

You can list ordinary personal effects at nominal value.

Proceeds from insurance policies can provide the necessary liquid funds to meet the estate tax, especially when combined with a trust. You can make a trust the beneficiary of a life insurance policy, direct the trust to purchase the nonliquid assets of your estate and so furnish your estate with the necessary cash to pay the estate tax. The trust holds such assets until they can be sold at a fair price. Insurance funding can be combined with the stock-purchasing agreements mentioned above to provide the necessary money with which the purchasers will buy the stock from your estate.

In addition to the $60,000 exemption, credit is allowed for state death taxes, for gift taxes paid on property includable in the estate, for taxes paid on prior transfers of property includable in the estate, and for foreign death taxes paid.

STATE DEATH TAXES

State death taxes are levied in all states but one, Nevada. Generally, they are levied against the estates of residents and on the property of nonresidents that is located within the state. Federal estate tax laws allow a limited credit for state death taxes paid, and states generally allow credit for taxes paid to other states having reciprocal taxing arrangements.

No state can tax real property or tangible personal property not within its borders. Intangible personal property, such as securities, is generally taxable by the state in which the decedent was domiciled at the time of his death, regardless of where the intangible property is located.

Some states levy an estate tax, similar to the Federal tax, on the entire estate. Others levy a tax on the shares received by the beneficiaries, called an inheritance tax. Still others use both types and may also levy additional taxes on residents; some levy taxes on residents and nonresidents alike.

YOU ARE NOW READY TO ESTIMATE THE FEDERAL ESTATE TAX

Once the value of the estate has been determined, the next step is to compute the itemized allowable deductions against the gross estate. The balance will be your taxable estate. Follow these steps:

Gross estate (put in the value you estimated in your
    inventory) $_____

Less:

    Administration expenses (executor's commissions, attorney's fees, etc. Estimate about
    5% of your estate.) $_____

    Debts, mortgages, liens _____

    Funeral expenses _____

Total deductions from gross estate $_____

Adjusted gross estate $_____

Less:

    Marital deduction (put here property going to your wife. But the deduction cannot be more than 50% of adjusted gross estate.) $_____

    Charitable deduction (gifts to tax-exempt charities.) _____

    Exemption $60,000

Total deductions from adjusted gross estate $_____

Your taxable estate $_____

Your estimated estate tax. (See estimated estate tax rates
    below.) $_____

RATES FOR ESTIMATING THE ESTATE TAX

Taxable Estate Over	But Not Over	Tax*	Plus Following Percentage	Over
$ 0	$ 5,000	$ 0	3.%	$ 0
5,000	10,000	150	7.	5,000
10,000	20,000	500	11.	10,000
20,000	30,000	1,600	14.	20,000
30,000	40,000	3,000	18.	30,000
40,000	50,000	4,800	21.2	40,000
50,000	60,000	6,920	24.2	50,000
60,000	90,000	9,340	27.2	60,000
90,000	100,000	17,500	26.4	90,000
100,000	140,000	20,140	28.4	100,000
140,000	240,000	31,500	27.6	140,000
240,000	250,000	59,100	26.8	240,000
250,000	440,000	61,780	28.8	250,000
440,000	500,000	116,500	28.	440,000
500,000	640,000	133,300	31.	500,000
640,000	750,000	176,700	30.2	640,000
750,000	840,000	209,920	32.2	750,000
840,000	1,000,000	238,900	31.4	840,000
1,000,000	—	289,140	33.4	—

* The tax here is computed on the assumption that the state death or estate tax is equal to or more than the credit allowed by the Federal estate tax law. The net tax rate on estates exceeding $1,000,000 ranges from 33.4 to 61%.

© J. K. Lasser Tax Institute

To give you an idea of how an estate tax is computed, here is a simplified illustration: Assume the gross estate of an unmarried person is $200,000. There are debts, administration, and funeral expenses totaling $10,000, and charitable contributions of $10,000.

Gross Estate		$200,000
Less:		
Funeral and administration expenses, debts, etc.		10,000
Adjusted gross estate		$190,000
Less:		
Charitable deduction	$10,000	
Exemption	60,000	70,000
Taxable estate		$120,000
Estate tax due		$ 25,820

But see the difference in estate taxes when the person is married and leaves half his estate to his wife—all other figures being the same:

Gross Estate		$200,000
Less:		
Funeral and administration expenses, debts, etc.		10,000
Adjusted gross estate		$190,000
Less:		
Marital deduction	$95,000	
Charitable deduction	10,000	
Exemption	60,000	$165,000
Taxable estate		$ 25,000
Estate tax due		$ 2,300

REDUCING OR ELIMINATING A POTENTIAL TAX

Here are general approaches to eliminating or reducing a potential estate tax: You can make direct lifetime gifts to remove property from your estate before it becomes subject to tax. You can make a will in which you leave your property in such a way that will provide maximum tax savings for your estate, such as providing for the marital and charitable deductions.

GIFT PLANNING

If you have a substantial estate that is subject to estate tax, your attorney may suggest you make gifts rather than leave your beneficiaries property for distribution at your death. Gift tax rates are about 25 percent lower than estate tax rates. This cost may be reduced even more through the offsets provided by the lifetime exemption of $30,000 and the yearly exclusion of $3000 for each donee. In fact, giving which coordinates timing and amounts with the special gift-splitting advantages allowed to married couples may avoid the gift tax altogether.

A well-planned gift program produces not only estate tax savings but also income tax savings. Gifts of income producing property that shift income from your higher tax brackets to the lower tax brackets of a donee (whether an individual or a trust) bring about considerable tax advantage.

It may sound like a simple matter to give property away during your lifetime so that it is not included in your estate. But note these problems that arise when a gift planning program is contemplated:

1. You may not want to give up control of your property during your lifetime. You have to equate your reluctance to give up control with an estate tax rule which states that when you make a gift and still keep some control over it, the gift is part of your estate for tax purposes.

2. You have to provide for future needs during your life.

3. The recipients of your gifts may be minors or persons otherwise not competent to manage property. Gifts in trust can usually overcome this problem.

4. The person you plan to benefit may already have large personal resources that will eventually be taxed in his own estate. A gift from you might reduce the tax in your estate but only at the expense of increasing his tax.

Transferring the gift to a trust might avoid this possibility. For example, you could put the property into a trust giving one person the income during his life, with the principal passing to his children at his death. With this arrangement, no Federal estate tax is paid on your death or at the death of the lifetime beneficiary, provided the lifetime beneficiary does not have the right to take any of the principal of the trust, or to revoke it or name other beneficiaries.

After you have resolved these problems, time your gift-planning program with the gift tax law in mind. The gift tax law permits you to make annual taxfree gifts up to $3000 to each individual in any tax year ($6000 when made jointly with your spouse), and in addition grants a lifetime exemption of gifts up to $30,000 ($60,000 jointly). The lifetime exemption may be used in any one year or spread over many years. When more than $3000 is given to one individual in a tax year, a gift tax return must be filed and the gift tax due paid. Since gift tax rates are considerably lower than estate tax rates, it might prove to your advantage to discuss a program of lifetime gifts with your attorney in planning your estate.

THE MARITAL DEDUCTION

If you are married, the tax on your estate can be greatly reduced or even eliminated by the marital deduction. The law allows you to pass to your surviving spouse on your death up to one-half the value of your adjusted gross estate taxfree.

To qualify for the marital deduction, the property must be given to the wife outright or by other legal arrangements that are equivalent to outright ownership in law.

When planning property arrangements for a marital deduction, you should ask yourself the following two questions:

1. How much property does your wife own? The marital deduction gives best tax results when a wife has less property than her husband. When she has an equal or greater amount, the husband's estate tax saving may be at the expense of her estate and the surviving children may be the losers.

2. What kind of property do you intend to leave your wife? To qualify for the marital deduction, property you leave your wife must be left outright or in an equivalent manner. Where you leave a fractional share of your estate to her outright with no restrictions, few problems should arise. However, as a safety measure, your will and marital deduction plans should be periodically reviewed for technical disqualifications of which you are not aware. For example, when you plan to have the proceeds of life insurance qualify as marital deduction property, your wife should not only be the unconditional beneficiary of the proceeds but should also have unrestricted control over any unpaid proceeds. If this control or power of appointment is not given to her, then the proceeds remaining unpaid at her death should be made payable to her estate. Otherwise the insurance proceeds will not qualify for the marital deduction. If your policies are intended to be marital deduction property and they do not by their settlement terms meet these requirements, have them changed now.

What should be done if you believe your wife cannot manage the property you leave her? You will not want to give her complete and personal control. The law permits you to put the property in certain trust arrangements that are considered equivalent to complete ownership. Your attorney can explain how you can protect your wife's interest and qualify the trust property for the marital deduction.

LIFE INSURANCE PROCEEDS

Life insurance is one of your most important aids to estate planning. With care, it can be used to provide an almost taxfree transfer of wealth. Life insurance proceeds are subject to estate tax only if they are payable either to:

1. Your estate, regardless of who owned the policy; or
2. Other beneficiaries, if you owned certain incidents of ownership in the policy.

What are these incidents of ownership that make the policy part of your gross estate? The right to sell the policy or pledge it for a loan. Or the right to change the beneficiary, or to revoke an assignment already made. Your payment of premiums alone will not of itself make the proceeds includable in your estate. Thus, the cue to removing life insurance proceeds from your taxable estate is to give away the ownership rights in policies made payable to beneficiaries other than your estate.

However, if you are married, the retention of a minor incident of ownership in an insurance policy that you have assigned to a charitable organization can increase the marital deduction and reduce your estate tax. Say that when you assigned the policy to the charity you reserved the right to choose the settlement option. The retention of such minor right will make the policy includable in your gross estate. This will, it is true, increase your gross estate. But at the same time it will increase the marital share to go to your wife taxfree. And since the policy is payable to a charity, your estate will have a charitable deduction to offset the amount by which the estate was increased.

PROVIDING LIQUID FUNDS
FOR PAYMENT OF ESTATE TAXES

An estate may have substantial assets but no cash with which to pay estate taxes. This can be a pressing problem for the executor. The assets might be close-corporation stock, art collections, or large personal residences which the family does not want sold to outsiders—or for which there is no ready market. You will want to guard against the necessity of a forced sale of assets to obtain cash for taxes. Careful planning can anticipate the difficulties your estate will have to face in raising the cash necessary for taxes. For example, lifetime gifts of shares of stock to family members can reduce your taxable estate and keep control of the business in the family.

It is not too difficult to estimate the estate tax that may be levied by a state. But inheritance taxes are more difficult to estimate since they are levied against the shares of the beneficiaries and each class may have a different exemption allowance.

From this you can see why it is necessary when planning your estate to tell your attorney where each item of your property is located. All applicable state laws must be considered when your will is drawn.

A FINAL WORD

You are now aware of the costs of transferring an estate and of the amount of tax that may be levied. But no estate plan is ever really final. Economic conditions and inflation steadily change values. For this reason, your plan must be reviewed periodically as changes occur in your family and business; when a birth or death occurs; you receive substantial increase or decrease in income; you enter on a new business venture or resign from an old one; you merge, retire, bring a son or son-in-law into your business. A member of your family may no longer need any part of your estate, while others may need more. Estate or gift tax laws may be revised, or material changes may occur in the health or life expectancy of one of your beneficiaries.

A final word of caution: Estate tax planning is not a do-it-yourself activity. We suggest that you contact experienced counsel to help you.

Chapter 17

PLANNING AHEAD FOR RETIREMENT

WHAT WILL YOUR INCOME BE?   261
REAL ESTATE INVESTMENT   263
YOUR NET WORTH AT RETIREMENT   264
RETIREMENT RESIDENCE   265
MEANINGFUL OCCUPATION OF RETIREMENT TIME   266
YOUR HEALTH IN RETIREMENT   269
CONCLUSION   269

Though retirement may lie many years ahead for you, you would do well to start your retirement planning early so that the after-sixty-five years are free of the cares that beset so many retired people. Your basic considerations are:

What will my (or, more usually, our) income be?

How will my net worth stand?

Where will I live?

How shall I occupy my time?

Will health affect my plans?

We discuss these points below.

WHAT WILL YOUR INCOME BE?

Here are usual sources of retirement income:

Social Security

Pension from employment

Annuity or other insurance payments

Investment

Interest from savings

U. S. Savings Bonds

Rents, royalties, personal business

How many of these sources will you have when you retire? If you are fairly young, you may not have thought beyond the Social Security benefit and a pension from the company that you will collect someday. But with the purchasing power of the dollar declining, you should start early to develop as many of the other sources as possible.

The amount of your Social Security pension will depend on how many years you have paid on a maximum amount of earning (see Chapter 14), and that maximum is rising. If the salary range you are on does not reach the Social Security maximum, your retirement benefits will be correspondingly lower.

Are you with a company or in the type of employment which will provide retirement benefits through pension or profit sharing plans? (If not, should you make a change?) Many people who started young with a company are handed a booklet on the pension plan, then they promptly forget all about it even though they may contribute to the plan through salary deduction. Asked to state the benefit they will enjoy eventually, they do not know if the plan will pay off a percentage of their salary at retirement, a fixed sum, a lump sum, benefits to dependents if they die before retirement, or a widow's pension if the employee dies early in retirement.

Provision for a widow is of particular importance since the average woman starts out with life expectancy seven years greater than the average man. The gap decreases in time, but at 65 it is still over three years. Too, a wife is likely to be younger than her husband. The husband planning for retirement must take into consideration the possibility of his earlier death. Whether or not his widow can benefit from his company's retirement plan is a major factor in his planning. In face of little or no provision for a widow, the husband may wish to plan an annuity (see Chapter 10).

If you are not thoroughly acquainted with your company's retirement benefits, check up on them early so that you can incorporate them in your total planning.

From earlier chapters in this book, you will have noted the retirement income possibilities from life insurance, endowment, annuities, investment, interest from savings; the earlier you can start developing some of these potential sources the better.

REAL ESTATE INVESTMENT

The specialized field of real estate has proven highly profitable to investors who study its cycles and move in at the right time. Too, alert couples have developed a personal business by buying homes, furnishing them tastefully, living in them a time, and then selling, complete to the last picture on the wall. Others, more modestly, derive a useful income from seasonal renting of a second home in a summer or winter resort area. You may be one of those who can profitably invest in real estate. But there are many pitfalls. You may know of senior citizens who have been deceived by glib advertising of swamp or desert areas as "Your retirement home in Paradise" or "Profitable Real Estate Investment." You may not realize that fine property desirably located can result in years of anxiety and financial loss to an older person, as the following example illustrates:

Martha Jay, a well-to-do widow in her seventies now, owns a home in Connecticut. Some ten years ago, she bought two houses in Florida, one for winter living, the other for renting. Early, she found it difficult to secure reliable tenants; some were destructive; some simply did not pay the rent. She put the rental property up for sale. Though excellently situated, the house has not sold. It is constantly the victim of hurricanes and vandals, and its tenants—when it rents. Continually, the owner has to draw upon her resources to support it. She tried to sell the other Florida home. It, too, has stuck on the market.

Gladly, Mrs. Jay would sell *both* Florida properties; she would then rent her own living quarters each winter. She has tried to sell her Connecticut home so she could move into one of the Florida houses permanently. Neither of these possibilities has worked out. All the properties are good, but still the right buyers have not appeared. Mrs. Jay, harassed by worry, continues to spend money where she had hoped to receive income.

Though another person of retirement age might not experience the same misfortunes as Mrs. Jay, the warning is plain: avoid tying up capital in investments that lack liquidity and immediate marketability; avoid investments that require the personal attention which becomes burdensome to older people. (True, an agent will handle real estate problems, but his services will add to the cost of unprofitable ventures.)

On the other hand, you may already have enjoyed success in real estate investment. With knowledge of the field, you can count on income from sales and rentals in your retirement years. Others who, like Mrs. Jay, have no more experience in real estate than home ownership, should be wary in their later years of channeling money into investment property.

If you are interested in real estate for profit, an early start during your high-earning years makes good sense. Though some inexperienced retirees may have struck the jackpot with investment in motel, apartment house, or new development, many more have lost their savings. Begin young with a thorough study of this lucrative field, and you may well derive a handsome income from it in retirement.

YOUR NET WORTH AT RETIREMENT

If you are close to retirement, you can reach a generally accurate estimate of your net worth. A method of doing so is suggested in Chapter 2.

If you are years from retirement, any estimate would be speculative. One cannot foresee how fortune or misfortune will strike. Despite this unknown factor, you should try to project some estimate of your net worth at retirement. You might go about it this way:

Start with your present net worth.

Estimate how much this amount will increase over the years because of investment income and savings. As a rule of thumb, use your present rate of savings and income return.

If you expect gifts or inheritances, you might add a conservative estimate of these amounts.

Reduce your total estimate by major expenses you expect to incur. For example, if you have children who will attend college and you will not be able to finance their tuition through current income, you must expect to reduce your savings by this cost.

It will be difficult to say what the market value of your house and other property will be at retirement unless that time is very close indeed. But you do know whether or not your property will be free and clear of mortgage payments. You can also form a reasonable forecast of your financial responsibility for dependents when retirement time comes. If, for example, you will still have expenses for a child attending college or graduate school at the time your income is reduced, you have time to bolster the reserves so your commitments can be met without drawing upon that reduced income.

RETIREMENT RESIDENCE

A surprising number of people let themselves in for considerable expense, upheaval, and mental anguish because they fail to work out the question of where to live upon retirement. On the basis of a few visits to Florida, say, a couple decide they will retire there. They dispose of the family home, say goodbye to their friends and depart to a small house or an apartment they have quickly located. Before long, even within a year or two, they are back in the friendly old home area looking for somewhere to live.

This kind of unhappy experience and financial loss can certainly be avoided. Some people should never move away from familiar scenes, good friends, relatives, and attachments to a place of worship, volunteer interests, and social life. Others, whose working life neighborhood is unsuited to retirement, will have their eye on distant places, but they should become reasonably well acquainted with them, and perhaps make some friends there, before making the physical move. If business commitments make it impossible to study an area before retirement, take time afterwards to do the research; meanwhile, keep the home intact. Money set aside in advance for this type of vacation is well worthwhile and can save a far greater, vain outlay.

If you have, during working years, purchased a summer home, it, or other housing in the same location, may be ideal for retirement.

You know the area, the opportunities, and the people; you are not taking a leap in the dark in moving there.

Note the tax considerations involved in selling your house after age 65. (Chapter 15. See page 239.) Your forward planning for retirement will include the fulfillment of the residential requirement before selling your family home.

Throughout the country, many communities for retired people are springing up. In some, small houses are available at modest prices; in others, condominiums and apartments are specially geared to the living requirements of old people. Retirement villages, where recreation, entertainment, social life, and medical care are offered, find high favor with those who wish to avoid the inactive, lonely life often associated with retirement. Such surroundings speedily bring new friends, and they offer the retiree a sense of security and belonging instead of being a cast-off from former business and family responsibilities and ties.

In the vast majority of cases, it is a mistake for older people to have their married children set up housekeeping in part of the family home or, as is more often the case, to go live with the younger people when left alone on death of the spouse. The problem of expenses can better be solved by joining forces with a congenial friend in similar circumstances and of the same age. Both sell their original homes and then set up housekeeping together, thus cutting expenses and gaining companionship.

MEANINGFUL OCCUPATION OF RETIREMENT TIME

A fortunate number of people know exactly what they want to do upon retirement, they carry out their plan, and they thrive on what they do. These people have a goal; for them, retirement time is not a vacuum to be filled by whatever turns up, by happy chance or the good offices of another person. They made their own plans in accordance with their own interests and disposition; they did not lean upon others. All enjoy their leisure because they have struck a balance between work and play. Few find all leisure to be completely satisfying; the majority of retired persons need active participation in the workaday world. Many engage themselves in volunteer work for church, hospital, charity, or civic organization; others will seek out full or part-time employment, or will develop a profitable hobby into a personal business.

It is a fact that many people who have avidly looked forward to quitting the job at age sixty-five find themselves at a total loss when they no longer report for a working day. Even with adequate finances the retired person is likely to tire quickly of travel, sports, bridge, friendly gossiping, watching television, or whatever it was he thought would absorb his time and interest—if he had thought the matter through at all, and many don't. Doctors' offices are filled with older people whose aches and pains miraculously vanish at those times when the patient's mind is diverted, whether happily or by an emergency. When called by illness or accident to take over duties in a child's home, or to fill in temporarily at a job, they are suddenly well. Again, they feel wanted and useful.

Useful is the key word. The person whose work in plant, shop, or office, or in the home, made him or her a necessary link in a chain of well-being to others, cannot abide being left on perpetual vacation or occupied by nonpurposeful activities. Since this is a book on money management, we address ourselves to the retired, and soon-to-retire, people who need a supplemental income. The necessity to earn can be a spur to activity to those who might otherwise become bogged down in a lonely routine.

The loss of Social Security benefits when earnings rose above a certain level has deterred many retired persons from working as much as they wished. The level of benefit before loss is now rising, and it is to be hoped that eventually the person who earns after retirement will enjoy the same advantages as the person whose retirement income comes from unearned sources, and who suffers no loss of benefit.

Whether you are prepared to face loss of Social Security benefits (see Chapter 14) or simply wish to earn up to the maximum permitted, you will find there are many opportunities open to the forward-looking retiree. Turn to Chapter 5 for a general discussion of profitable sidelines, personal businesses, and part-time work.

As an older person, you may not want to tax your health and

strength by long hours, high pressure work, or too much physical activity. Also, being retired, you want to enjoy leisure, and not tie yourself down to a fifty-weeks-in-the-year commitment. You will find many small businesses or professional offices will accept the part-timer on his own terms for a busy season, or for regular hours so many days a week. You may not see the particular opportunity you want advertised, but you may well make a niche for yourself by sending a résumé and covering letter to prospective employers, or by having a notice posted on a church or club bulletin board. Note that a number of employment agencies handling temporary office personnel are happy to offer part-time assignments to older men and women.

Part-time Employment for Older People is the title of a government booklet you can obtain for fifteen cents (*stamps not acceptable*) from the address below. (Quote Cat. No. FS 14.11: K41/2 in your request.)

Books on retirement fully discuss the self-employment possibilities open to enterprising men and women over sixty-five. Also, write to the Superintendent of Documents, U. S. Government Printing Office, Washington, D.C. 20402, for a price list of publications on small businesses. In particular, ask for the Domestic Commerce Publications Price List. For a very modest price, you will be able to secure basic information on starting and operating a wide range of enterprises.

In some areas, there are nonprofit, no-fee, personnel placement bureaus which specialize in jobs for older people. In one city suburban area, the local newspaper daily reports job opportunities for senior citizens. Examples of openings are companion, payroll-bookkeeper, hotel desk clerk, alteration tailor. The news item also reports applicants available, such as a secretary, bookkeeper, carpenter, and taxicab dispatcher.

Throughout the country, the interests and needs of the older people are receiving the attention of government and community. If you are retired and find that in your area older people and suitable jobs are not being brought together, you may be able to initiate this valuable service yourself.

YOUR HEALTH IN RETIREMENT

Obviously, good health is a major factor in a happy retirement. Good health not only means having the strength and energy to enjoy life and participate actively, but it means money saved. Though the Medicare program covers a large proportion of expense, it does not cover all. Moreover, some doctors insist on the patient paying the bill when due, which means the patient must have the ready money to put out. In time, he will receive reimbursement for the proportion paid by Medicare.

For good health in retirement, begin early with safeguards; annual physical checkups, regular visits to dentist and oculist. Watch weight and diet. Avoid excessive exertion, such as snow-shoveling. (Useful government publications from the address on page 268 are *Facts About Nutrition,* 15¢, Cat. No. FS 2.22: N95 and *Food Guide for Older Folks,* 10¢, Cat. No. A 1.77: 17/6.) Avoid self-medication. In that connection, another government pamphlet, *Your Money and Your Life,* an FDA Catalog of Fakes and Swindles in the Health Field, is available for 10¢, Cat. No. FS 13.111: 19. While everyone is vulnerable to the health quack, older people seeking lost youth, looks, and energy are ready and willing targets. Knowledge of some of the many frauds will make you cautious, and save you dollars.

CONCLUSION

We hope this book, *Managing Your Family Finances,* has presented to you techniques through which you can program, protect, and increase your income; that it has offered many suggestions for the more effective use of income to enhance the lives and extend the interests of yourself and your family.

The basic ideas in this book will remain current for many years, but, of course, there will be changes in certain areas because of economic and political events. When you read of new developments and of Federal or state legislation that affects this book, you can provide yourself with useful reference material by clipping and filing each news item. If you send for pamphlets suggested in the text, put them into folders with other relevant data. This personal supplement will be of immeasurable help to you in achieving the objectives of this book.

You can manage money successfully! We wish you luck in your personal endeavor.

INDEX

Accidental death and dismemberment insurance, 203

Allowances for children, 38–40; covering routine expenses, 39; handling of, 39–40; charge accounts for teenagers, 40

American College of Life Underwriters, 155

Annuities, 21, 25, 171–76; types of, 172–74; buying of, 174; variable, 175–76; as conservative method of financing retirement, 176

Apartment, renting of, 107–8; what lease should include, 108–9

Automobile bank loans, 93

Bank accounts: keeping record of data on, 29, 142; regular checking, 36, 136; special checking, 36–37; joint checking, 37; Christmas Club, 136, 137; savings accounts, 136; dormant accounts, and laws of escheat, 142–43

Banks, commercial: loans by, 92–93; credit plans of, 94–95; credit cards issued by, 96; saving money at, 136–37

Banks, savings. See Savings banks

Beneficiaries: of life insurance, 168, 169, 170; of will, 246–47

Birth certificate, 28

Blue Cross and Blue Shield insurance, 203, 207

Boat bank loans, 93

Bonds, corporate, 21, 180–82; keeping record of income from, 220

Bonds, U.S. savings. See U.S. savings bonds

Broker, role of, in real estate transactions, 113–14, 118–19

Budget, 5–16, 22, 157; advantages of, 5; and pattern of income, 6–8, 9; programming commitments, 8; making adjustments in, 9–11; record-keeping of present rate of expenditure as key to setting up of, 11–14; categories of everyday expenditure, 11–12; weighing up spending, 13–14; projecting figures on annual basis, 14–15; and credit spending, 15–16; deduction method of keeping track of spending, 16; programming savings, 17–18

Business enterprise, investment in, 22, 27

Business loans by banks, 93

Buying on margin, in stock market, 187

Buying wisely, 50–58; in food and household items, 50–51; practicing smart buyer tactics at supermarket, 51–52; being alert to overpricing, 52–53; avoiding the advertising trap, 53; watching out for gyp artists with fantastic offers, 54–56; being on the alert at sales, 56; thrifty buys, 57; buying at discount stores, 57–58

Capital gains, and income taxes, 223–24

Cash refund annuity, 173

Casualty loss income tax deductions, 238

Central charge account plan, 83

Central credit bureau, 81

Certificates, documenting events of personal life, 28–29; where to obtain certified copies of, 29

Charge accounts at department stores, 81–83; real cost of, 83

Charge accounts for teenagers, 40

Chartered Life Underwriter (C.L.U.), 154–55

Child care expenses: and the working mother, 45–46; and income taxes, 240–41

Children: allowances for, 38–40; financing college education for, 40–44, 229–30; tax returns for, 224–25; giving securities to, 227–29

Christmas Club accounts, 17, 136, 137

City versus suburb, as place of residence, 106–7

Closed-end mutual funds companies, 190; getting information on, 193; cost of buying into, 193

Clothing costs, cutting of, 60–61

College education for children, financing of, 40–44; scholarships and loans, 41–44; the college as source of aid, 42; setting up trust for, 229–30

Comaker or cosigner loans, 90–91

Combination family income life insurance, 156

Commercial banks. *See* Banks, commercial

Common stock, 177, 178, 179

Condominium, buying and selling of, 111

Consumer Bulletin, 53, 63

Consumer interests, government booklets available on, 50, 51

Consumer Reports, 53, 63

Convertible securities, 179–80

Cooperative apartment, buying and selling of, 110–11

Cosmetics industry, overpricing in, 52–53

Cost of living, increase in, 49; steps for beating drop in dollar value, 49–50

Courses for maintaining job skills, cost of, as tax deductible, 238

Credit, 79–103; credit rating, 80, 89–90; charge account credit at department stores, 81–83; central charge account plan, 83; real cost on charge accounts and installment buying, 83; credit cards, 84–85, 96; installment buying, 85–88; and making a loan, 88–98; bank credit plans, 94–95; credit costs and true rate of interest, 98–103

Credit cards, 84–85; loss of, 30, 85;

insurance on, 85; issued by banks, 96

Credit unions, 21, 95–96, 100; saving at, 139–40

Custodian accounts, 227–29; and gift taxes, 228–29; and estate taxes, 229

Custom-built house, 115–16; retaining architect, 116–17; and general contractor, 117–18; prefabricated house, 117–18

Cutting costs, raising cash through, 49–63; buying wisely, 50–58; trade-in values, 58; saving money through rental services, 58–59; watching random spending, 59; paying only what is owed, 59; saving through home economies, 60–62; having fun for free, 62; saving, as a consumer, becomes long-term investment, 62–63

Death certificate, 28

Debt: repayment plan for, 4, 19; handling of problem of, 18–19; and credit rating, 19; worthless debt as tax deductible, 235

Deferred annuity contract, 174

Dental insurance, 208

Disability insurance, 203, 207–8; disability protection under Social Security, 211

Discount stores, buying at, 57–58

Dividends: on participating life insurance policy, 153–54, 170; on savings bank life insurance, 167; on corporate stock, 179, 220–21, 235, 240; of mutual funds, 192, 234–35; keeping records on, for tax purposes, 220; on utility stock, 235

Divorce certificate, 28

Do-it-yourself program for the family, saving money through, 61–62

"Dollar averaging" stock buying system, 184, 197

Double indemnity life insurance, 164, 170

Easy payment plans, 82–83

Education loans. *See* Scholarships and loans

Endowment insurance policy, 161–62, 170; waiver of premium rider, 162; and tax-saving election, 236

Escheat, laws of, and dormant bank accounts, 142–43

Establishing one's own business, 76–78; raising capital, 77–78

Estate planning, 243–60; joint ownership of property, 244–46; making a will, 246–49; Federal estate taxes, 250–55; gift planning, 255–57; marital deduction, 257–58; life insurance proceeds, 258; providing liquid funds for payment of estate taxes, 259; periodic review of estate plan, 259–60

Estate taxes: and custodian accounts, 229; and joint-ownership property, 244–45; levied by state, 253, 259; providing liquid funds for payment of, 259. *See also* Federal estate taxes

Everyday expenses, and financial program, 4

Family cooperation. *See* Financial planning, family cooperation in

Family income, increasing of, 65–78; ideas for a second income, 65–67; vital factors to keep in mind, 67–68; personal attitude and, 68; steps to be taken in putting money-making ideas to work, 69–70; marketing money-making ideas, 71; selling by mail, 72; keeping profit objective always in mind, 72–73; caution against fraudulent business opportunities, 73–74; working for others, 74–75; outside employment, 75–76; establishing one's own business, 76–78

Family income life insurance, 164–65

Family maintenance life insurance, 165–66

Family plan life insurance, 166

Family records, keeping record book on whereabouts of all data, 28–30

"Federal Aids for College Students," 41

Federal Consumer Credit Protection Act, 99

Federal Deposit Insurance Corporation, 140

Federal educational loans, 43–44

Federal estate taxes, 250–55; determining value of estate, 251–52; credit for state death taxes, 252; estimating tax, 253–55; rates for estimating tax, 254; reducing or eliminating potential tax, 255. *See also* Estate taxes

Federal medical insurance, 201

Federal Savings and Loan Insurance Corporation, 140

FHA: mortgages, 113, 130–31; home improvement loans, 131

Financial future, programming of, 1–20; first steps, 2; developing of financial program, 2–20

Financial planning, family cooperation in, 27, 33–48; working partnership in handling money, 27, 34–35; establishing working habits and schedule, 35; manner of paying bills, 35–36; bank accounts, 36–37; personal allowances, 37–40; financing college education for children, 40–44; working wife, and money management, 44–48; importance of cooperation, 48

Financial program, agenda for, 21–31; establishing net worth, 22–24; dealing with inflation, 27–28; family records, 28–30; priorities in, 30–31

Financial program, developing of, 2–3; fixed and everyday expenses, 3–4; defining spending goals, 4, 22; budget, 5–16; programming savings, 17–18; handling a debt problem, 18–19; looking toward expanded living, 19–20

Financial statement (annual) for family, 22–24

Financing home ownership, 121–33; economists' guides on cost of house in relation to income, 121; initial expenses on buying house, 122–24; financing mortgage, 123, 126; obtaining mortgage, 126–27; terms of payment of mortgage, 127–28; open-end mortgage, 128; prepayment of mortgage, 128–29; mortgage-redemption insurance policies, 129; second mortgages, 129; by veterans, 129–30; FHA mortgages, 130–31; FHA home improvement loans, 131; insuring against property losses and claims, 131–33

Fixed expenses: and financial program, 3–4; and the budget, 8, 9, 14

Flexible charge account, 82

Food expenses, and the working wife, 46

Foreign investments, and income taxes, 239

Four-Square Program for Successful Living, 21, 24–27, 31

Freedom shares, U.S. savings notes, 148–49

Funeral costs, providing for, 157, 166

GI Bill lending program, 93

Gift planning, 255–57

Gift taxes, 228–29, 246, 255

GI life insurance, 169

Group health insurance, 203–4, 206; group policy, 203–4; group-practice plan, 203; dental insurance, 208

Group life insurance, 167–68; paid up, 167–68

Guaranteed insurability rider of life insurance policy, 156

"Guide to Help You Arrange Funerals and Interments," 157

Health insurance, 21, 25, 201–8; government-financed health plans, 201; types of, 202–3; sources of private protection, 203–4; emergency reserve, 204–5; choosing right policy, 205–8; method of payment, service or indemnity, 206; meeting medical expenses after insurance is used up, 208; dental insurance, 208; Medicare, 269

Higher Education Act of 1965, loan program available through, 43

Home economies, saving through, 60–62; cutting clothing costs, 60–61; do-it-yourself program for the family, 61–62

Home ownership. *See* Financing home ownership

Hospitalization insurance, 202

House, buying of, 109–10; tax deductions, 109–10; build-up of equity, 110; increase in value, 110; services of lawyer in, 111–13; role of real estate broker in, 113–14; initial expenses on, 122–24; check list on

buying family home, 124–26. *See also* Financing home ownership

House, renting of, 108; what lease should include, 108–9

House, selling of, 118–19; income tax consequences of residence sales, 119, 239–40

Household inventory, 30

Household services, expenses of, and the working wife, 46

Immediate annuity, 174

Income: pattern of, and budget, 6–8, 9; from stocks and bonds dividends and interest, keeping records on, 220; tax law definition of, 222; taxable, 222; non-taxable, 222; income splitting for tax purposes, 222–23, 226–27; income postponing for tax purposes, 223; averaging of, for tax purposes, 236–37; sources of retirement income, 261–62. *See also* Family income, increasing of

Income taxes, 215–42; keeping records, 216–21; basic principles, 221–24; taxable income, 222; non-taxable income, 222; exemptions, 222, 228, 234; deductions, 222, 223; credits, 222; graduated rates, and tax planning, 222–23; capital gains, 223–24; tax returns for children, 224–25; savings for married couples filing joint returns, 226; tax savings in family income planning, 226–29; setting up trust for children's college years, 229–30; savings for investors in securities, 230–34; ways to save on, 234–41

Inflation: dealing with, in agenda for financial program, 27–28; and rising cost of living, 49–50, 62–63; and variable annuities, 175–76; and conventional annuities, 176; investments in stock as hedge against, 177–78, 185

Inheritance taxes, 253, 259

Installment buying, 83, 85–88; installment contract, 86; signing installment contract, 87–88; interest paid on, as income tax deductible, 237

Installment refund annuity, 173

Installment reporting of sale of property, 235

Insurance: as element in Four-Square Program for Successful Living, 21, 24–26; recording information about each policy, 29; on credit cards, 85; loans on, 90, 171; for home owner, 122–23, 129, 131–33. *See also* Health insurance; Life insurance

Insurance companies, selling of mutual funds by, 192

Interest charges: on installment buying, 86, 88; on bank loans, 92–93; on pawnbroker loans, 92; on credit union loans, 95, 100; on savings bank passbook loans, 96; of small loan companies, 97, 100; and the loan shark, 98; credit costs and true rate of interest, 98–103; types of loans and ways of stating interest, 99–102; simple interest, 99–100; unpaid balance, monthly interest, 100–1; on add-on loan, 101, 103; on discount loan, 101–2, 103; formula for determining true annual interest, 102; table of true annual interest, 103; on mortgages, 127, 130; paid on borrowings and on installment purchases, as income tax deductible, 128, 237

Interest rates on savings accounts. *See* Savings accounts, interest rates on

Investing, sources of important data on, 182–83

Investment: as element of Four-Square Program for Successful Living, 21–22, 26; in securities, 177–87; on stock market, risks of, 182–83; points to consider in fixing objectives of, 185–87

Investment advisory services, 183

Investment counsel firms, 183

Investment programs of mutual funds, 191–92; growth-type funds, 191, 192, 198; balanced funds, 191, 192; income-type funds, 191, 192, 198, 199; specialty funds, 191–92

Job skills, courses for maintaining, cost of, as tax deductible, 238

Joint income tax returns, 226

Joint ownership of property, 244–46

Joint and survivor annuity, 173–74

Lawyer, services of: in establishing one's own business, 78; in real estate transactions, 111–13

Life annuity with installments certain, 173

Life insurance: loans on policies, 90, 171; on loans, 91; savings bank, 137–38, 154, 167; for credit union shareholders, 139; major objective, and other uses of, 151–52; as tax protected, 152; first steps in setting up program of, 152–53; mail order, 153, 166–67; types of companies and policies sold, 153–54; insurance agents, 154–55; type of insurance needed, and when, 155–56; amount needed, 156–58; term insurance, 158–59, 171; whole life insurance (straight or ordinary life), 159–61, 171; limited payment life, 161, 171; endowment policy, 161–62, 170; combination contracts, 162–64; graded-premium policy, 163–64; modified life policy, 164; double life insurance protection, 164, 170; family income, 164–65; family maintenance, 165–66; family plan, 166; group, 167–68; beneficiaries, 168, 169, 170; GI insurance, 169; payment of premiums, 169; definitions of terms used in, 170–71; annuities, 171–76; with mutual fund investments, 198–99; and estate planning, 258

Limited payment life insurance, 161, 171

Loans: credit rating and, 89–90; on insurance policies, 90, 171; co-maker or cosigner loans, 90–91; life insurance on, 91; by pawnbrokers, 91–92; by banks, 92–93; using stocks and bonds as collateral, 93–94; by credit unions, 95–96, 100, 139; passbook loans by savings banks, 96–97; by small loan companies, 97, 100; by loan sharks, 97–98; types of, and ways of stating interest, 99–102; FHA home improvement, 131

Loan shark, operations of, 78, 97–98

Lovejoy's Scholarship Guide, 42

Mail order insurance, 153, 166–67, 206–7

Major medical insurance, 202–3, 205

Margin, buying on, in stock market, 187

Marital deduction, and tax on estate, 248, 257–58

Market research, free-lancing in field of, 75

Marriage certificate, 28

Medical expenses, and income taxes, 226, 237–38

Medicare program, 269

Money: as age-old problem of civilization, 1–2; building more satisfying life through wiser use of, 2; fostering realistic attitude toward, through budgeting, 15; value and availability of, 135; how and where to save, 135–50

Moonlighting, 75

Mortgages. *See* Financing home ownership

Moving to new job location, expenses of, and income taxes, 241

Mutual funds: investing in, 21, 189; types of, 190–91; investment programs of, 191–92; getting information on, 193; cost of buying into investment companies, 193–96; meeting the salesman of, 196; contractual or voluntary plan of buying, 196–98; choosing goals in investing in, 198–99; to provide retirement income, 199–200

Mutual life insurance company, 153

Mutual savings banks. *See* Savings banks

National Commission for Cooperative Education, 42

Naturalization certificate, 28

Net worth: establishing of, 22–24, 157; assessment of, 30; at retirement, estimating of, 264–65

New York Stock Exchange, monthly investment plan of, 184–85

No-load mutual funds, 194–96; list of, 195

Nonparticipating life insurance policy, 153, 171

Open-end mutual funds companies, 190–91; cost of buying into, 194

Optional charge account, 82

Ordinary life insurance. *See* Whole life insurance

Paid up insurance, 167–68, 171

Participating life insurance policy, 153, 171

Part-time projects for increasing family income, 66–67

Party plans for selling, 74

Pawnbrokers, loans by, 91–92

Payroll deductions, as liabilities or assets, 3

Pension plans, 21, 25, 262

Personal elements in Four-Square Program for Successful Living, 22, 27

Piggy bank method of saving, 18

Prefabricated house, 117–18

Preferred stock, 179

Professional enterprise, investment in, 22, 27

Profit sharing plans, 21, 25, 262

Property: installment reporting of sale of, 235; joint ownership of, 244–46. *See also* Real estate transactions

Property improvement: bank loans, 93; FHA loans, 131

Real estate transactions: service of lawyer in, 111–13; role of broker in, 113–14, 118–19; getting building expert's opinion, 114; and income taxes, 119, 240; senior citizens, and real estate investment, 263–64. *See also* Residence, renting, buying, selling of

Record book of whereabouts of family personal and financial data, 28–30

Record-keeping of expenditures, 11–14; methods of keeping track, 12–13; for income tax purposes, 216–21; on joint-ownership of property, 245

Refund annuities, 173

"Rehabilitation" loan for handling debt problem, 18

Rental property, keeping records on, 216

Residence, renting, buying, selling of, 104–19; decisions to be made in looking for place to live, 104–6; city vs. suburb, 106–7; apartment, renting of, 107–8; house, renting of,

Residence (*cont'd*)
108; what lease should include,
108–9; house, buying of, 109–10;
cooperative apartment, buying and
selling of, 110–11; condominium,
buying and selling of, 111; services
of lawyer, 111–13; role of real estate broker, 113–14, 118–19; getting
building expert's opinion, 114; old
houses vs. new, 114–15; custom-
built house, 115–18; selling of
home, 118–19; income tax consequences of residence sales, 119,
239–40

Retail installment credit, 82

Retirement: and annuities, 176; mutual funds to provide income for,
198, 199–200; and Social Security,
209, 210, 211–12, 262; earnings
after, 211–12, 267; planning ahead
for, 261–70; sources of retirement
income, 261–62; and real estate investment, 263–64; estimating net
worth at, 264–65; retirement residence, 265–66; meaningful occupation of time, 266–68; and health
care, 269

Revolving charge account, 81, 82

Revolving credit account, 81

Safe deposit box, 30, 216, 238

Sales, buying at, 56

Saving money, the how and where of,
135–50; commercial banks, 136–37;
savings and loan associations, 137;
mutual savings banks, 137–38;
credit unions, 139–40; points to
check before opening savings account, 140–42; U.S. savings bonds,
143–50; ways to save on income
taxes, 234–41

Savings: programming of, 17–18; as
element of Four-Square Program
for Successful Living, 21, 26; safety
of, 140–41

Savings accounts, interest rates on:
commercial banks, 136; savings and
loan associations, 137; mutual savings banks, 137–38; interest on
credit union shares, 139; compounding of interest, 141

Savings banks, 17; interest payments
by, 18, 96–97; passbook loans by,
96–97; saving money in, 137–38;
life insurance, 137–38, 154, 167

Savings and loan associations, saving
at, 21, 137

Scholarships, Fellowships, and Loans
(Feingold), 42

Scholarships and loans: securing information on, 41–42, 43–44; miscellaneous sources of, 42–43; Federal
loans, 43–44; loans from finance
companies, 43; loans from banks, 93

Securities: investing in, 177–87; cash
reserve needed before investing in,
178–79; stocks and bonds of corporation, 179–82; risks of investment on stock market, 182–83;
when to buy stocks, 183–85; fixing
objectives in investing in, 185–87;
giving of, to children, 227–29; tax
savings for investors in, 230–34

Selling: by telephone, 71, 75; by mail,
72; party plans for, 74

Small Business Administration, 71, 72,
76, 77

Small loan companies, loans by, 97,
100

Social Security, 21, 24, 77, 209–14;
listing data on, in record book, 29;
and funeral costs, 157; coverage of,
209; status and benefits available,
209–11; disability protection, 211;
and planning for retirement, 211–
12; amount of benefits, 212–13;
keeping record of credits, 213; collecting of, 213–14

Spending goals, defining of, 4

Spending plan. *See* Budget

State death taxes, 252–53

Stockbrokers, 183

Stock of corporation, 21, 179; when
to buy, 183–85; "dollar averaging"
stock buying system, 184; monthly
investment plan of N.Y. Stock Exchange, 184–85; keeping record on
dividends and interest from, 220–21

Stock life insurance company, 153

Stocks and bonds as collateral for
loans, 93–94

Straight life annuity, 172–73

Straight life insurance. *See* Whole life
insurance

Suburb versus city, as place of residence, 106–7

Surgical expense insurance, 202

Take-home pay, and financial program, 3–4
Taxes. *See* Estate taxes; Federal estate taxes; Gift taxes; Income taxes; Inheritance taxes; State death taxes
Telephone, selling by, 71, 75
Term insurance, 158–59, 171; convertible, 155, 159, 170; renewable, 159; group, 167–68
Thrift shops, buying at, 57
Trust for children's college years, 229–30

U.S. savings bonds: keeping record of, 29; getting replacements of, 29, 144; what should be known about, 143–50; disadvantages of, as form of investment, 144–45; Series E, 145–47, 150, 235; Series H, 147–48, 150; tax aspects of, 149–50, 235; checking of old bonds being held, 150
United Student Aid Funds, 43

Variable annuities, 175–76
Veterans: and financing of home ownership, 110, 113, 129–30; and GI insurance, 169

Waiver of premium rider: on life insurance policy, 156, 171; added to endowment policy, 162
Whole life insurance (straight or ordinary life), 159–61, 171; cash value, 160, 170; with rider for extra coverage against premature death, 160–61; limited payment life, 161, 171
Will, making of, 246–49; beneficiaries, 246–47; listing of assets, 247–49; naming guardians for children, 249; periodic review of will, 249
Women's Exchanges, selling through, 71
Work clothes, cost of, and income taxes, 241–42
Working wife, and money management, 44–48; question of wisdom of wife's working, 44–46; factors to be considered in working husband/wife partnership, 45; part-time or temporary work, 46–47; wife's pay check, 47–48

I